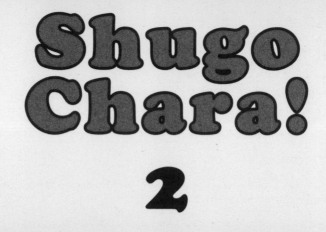

2

PEACH-PIT

Translated by
Satsuki Yamashita

Adapted by
Nunzio DeFilippis and Christina Weir

Lettered by
North Market Street Graphics

BALLANTINE BOOKS · NEW YORK

Shugo Chara! volume 2 is a work of fiction. Names, characters, places, and incidents are the products of the author's imagination or are used fictitiously. Any resemblance to actual events, locales, or persons, living or dead, is entirely coincidental.

A Del Rey Trade Paperback Original

Published in the United States by Del Rey Books, an imprint of The Random House Publishing Group, a division of Random House, Inc., New York.

DEL REY is a registered trademark and the Del Rey colophon is a trademark of Random House, Inc.

Publication rights arranged through Kodansha Ltd.

First published in Japan in 2007 by Kodansha Ltd., Tokyo

ISBN 978-0-345-49927-1

Original cover design by Akiko Omo

Printed in the United States of America

www.delreymanga.com

9 8 7 6 5 4 3 2 1

Translator—Satsuki Yamashita
Adaptors—Nunzio DeFilippis and Christina Weir
Lettering—North Market Street Graphics

Contents

Honorifics Explained

Throughout the Del Rey Manga books, you will find Japanese honorifics left intact in the translations. For those not familiar with how the Japanese use honorifics and, more important, how they differ from American honorifics, we present this brief overview.

Politeness has always been a critical facet of Japanese culture. Ever since the feudal era, when Japan was a highly stratified society, use of honorifics—which can be defined as polite speech that indicates relationship or status—has played an essential role in the Japanese language. When addressing someone in Japanese, an honorific usually takes the form of a suffix attached to one's name (example: "Asuna-san"), is used as a title at the end of one's name, or appears in place of the name itself (example: "Negi-sensei," or simply "Sensei!").

Honorifics can be expressions of respect or endearment. In the context of manga and anime, honorifics give insight into the nature of the relationship between characters. Many English translations leave out these important honorifics and therefore distort the feel of the original Japanese. Because Japanese honorifics contain nuances that English honorifics lack, it is our policy at Del Rey not to translate them. Here, instead, is a guide to some of the honorifics you may encounter in Del Rey Manga.

-san: This is the most common honorific, and is equivalent to Mr., Miss, Ms., or Mrs. It is the all-purpose honorific and can be used in any situation where politeness is required.

-sama: This is one level higher than "-san" and is used to confer great respect.

-dono: This comes from the word "tono," which means "lord." It is an even higher level than "-sama" and confers utmost respect.

-kun: This suffix is used at the end of boys' names to express familiarity or endearment. It is also sometimes used by men among friends, or when addressing someone younger or of a lower station.

-chan: This is used to express endearment, mostly
                  toward girls. It is also used for little boys, pets,
                  and even among lovers. It gives a sense of childish
                  cuteness.

Bozu: This is an informal way to refer to a boy, similar to
                  the English terms "kid" and "squirt."

Sempai/Senpai: This title suggests that the addressee is one's
                  senior in a group or organization. It is most often
                  used in a school setting, where underclassmen
                  refer to their upperclassmen as "sempai." It can
                  also be used in the workplace, such as when a
                  newer employee addresses an employee who has
                  seniority in the company.

Kohai: This is the opposite of "sempai" and is used
                  toward underclassmen in school or newcomers in
                  the workplace. It connotes that the addressee is
                  of a lower station.

Sensei: Literally meaning "one who has come before," this
                  title is used for teachers, doctors, or masters of
                  any profession or art.

-[blank]:   This is usually forgotten in these lists, but it is
                  perhaps the most significant difference between
                  Japanese and English. The lack of honorific means
                  that the speaker has permission to address the
                  person in a very intimate way. Usually, only
                  family, spouses, or very close friends have this
                  kind of permission. Known as *yobisute*, it can
                  be gratifying when someone who has earned the
                  intimacy starts to call one by one's name without
                  an honorific. But when that intimacy hasn't been
                  earned, it can be very insulting.

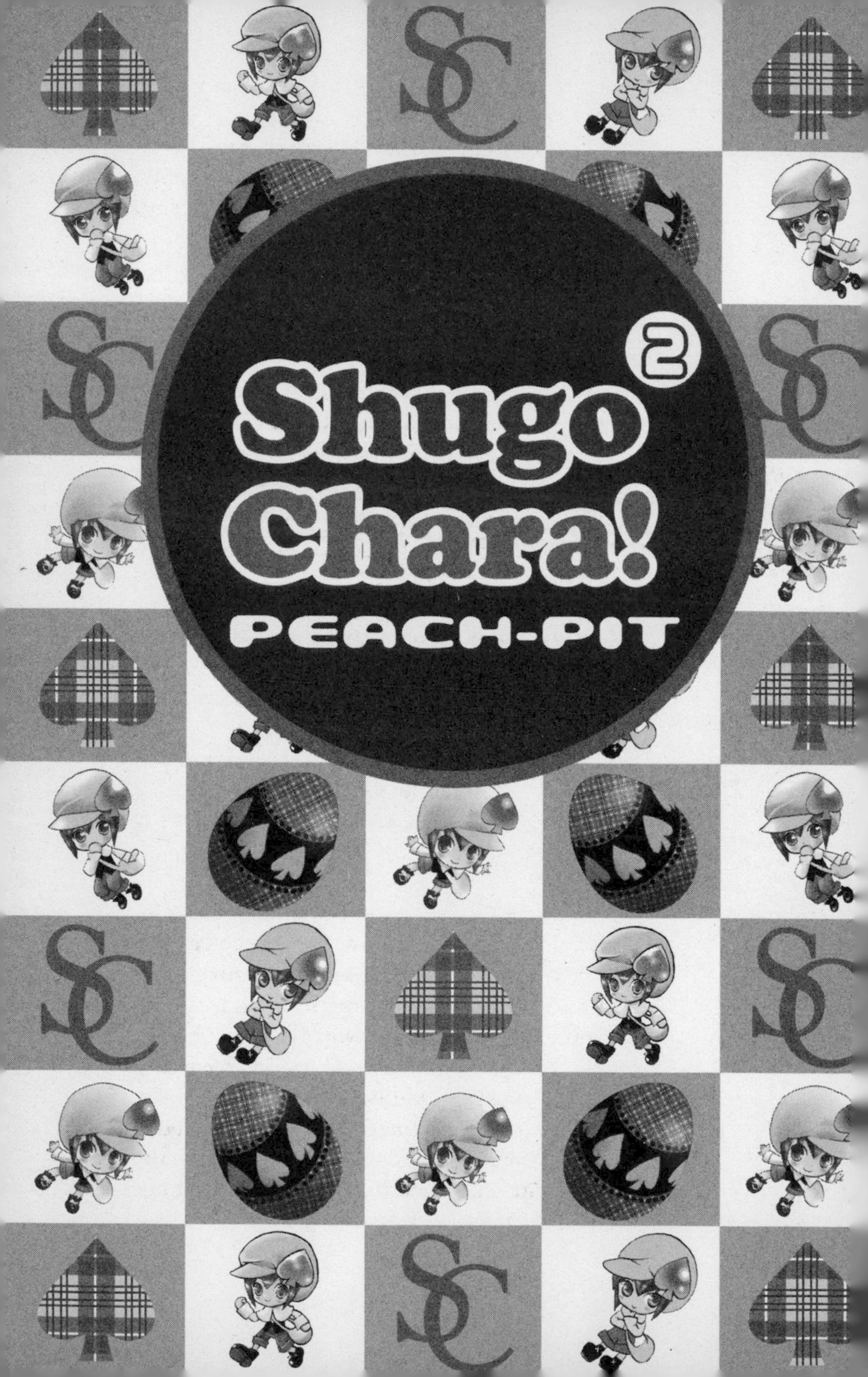
Shugo Chara! 2
PEACH-PIT

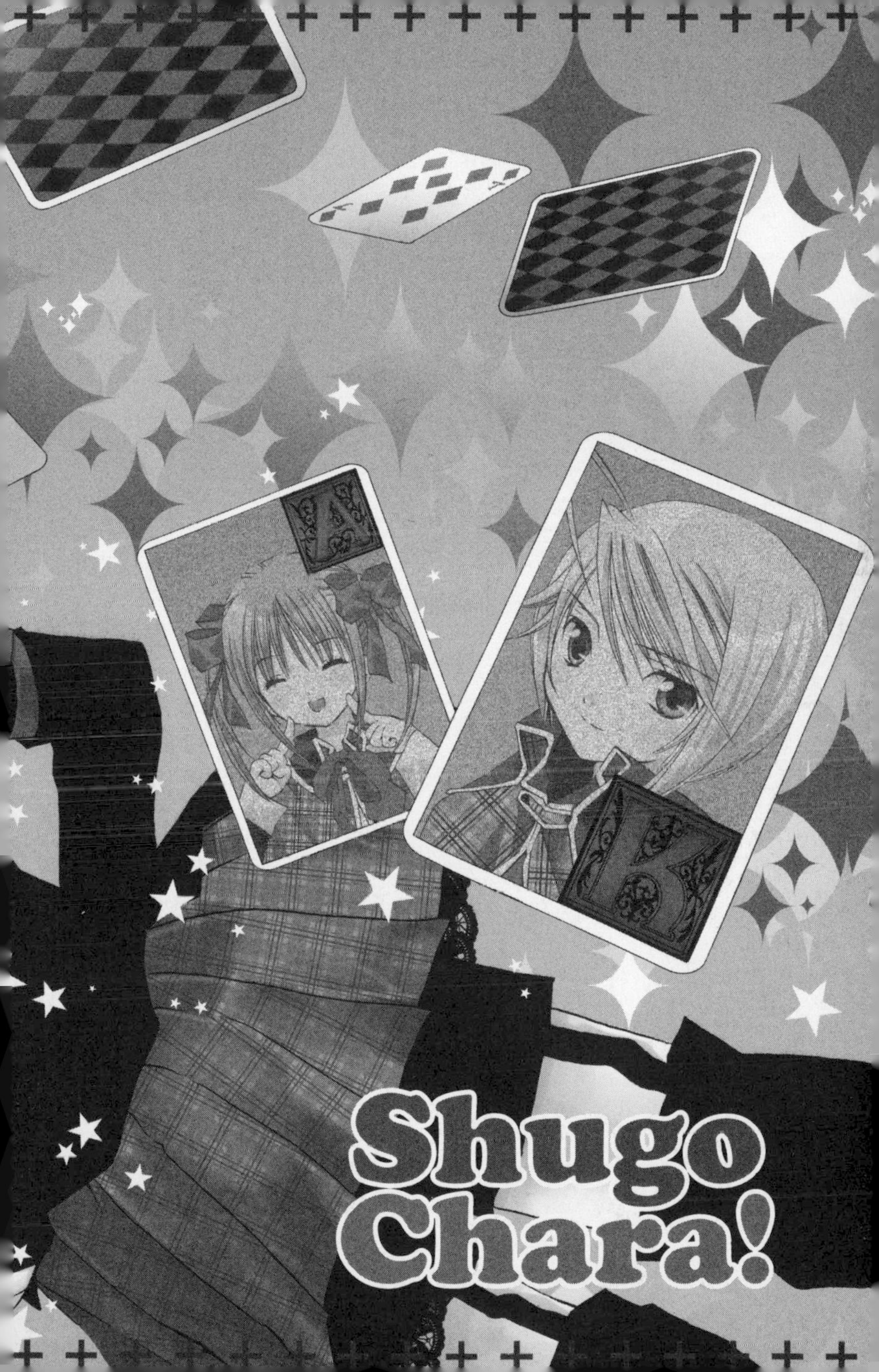
Shugo
Chara!

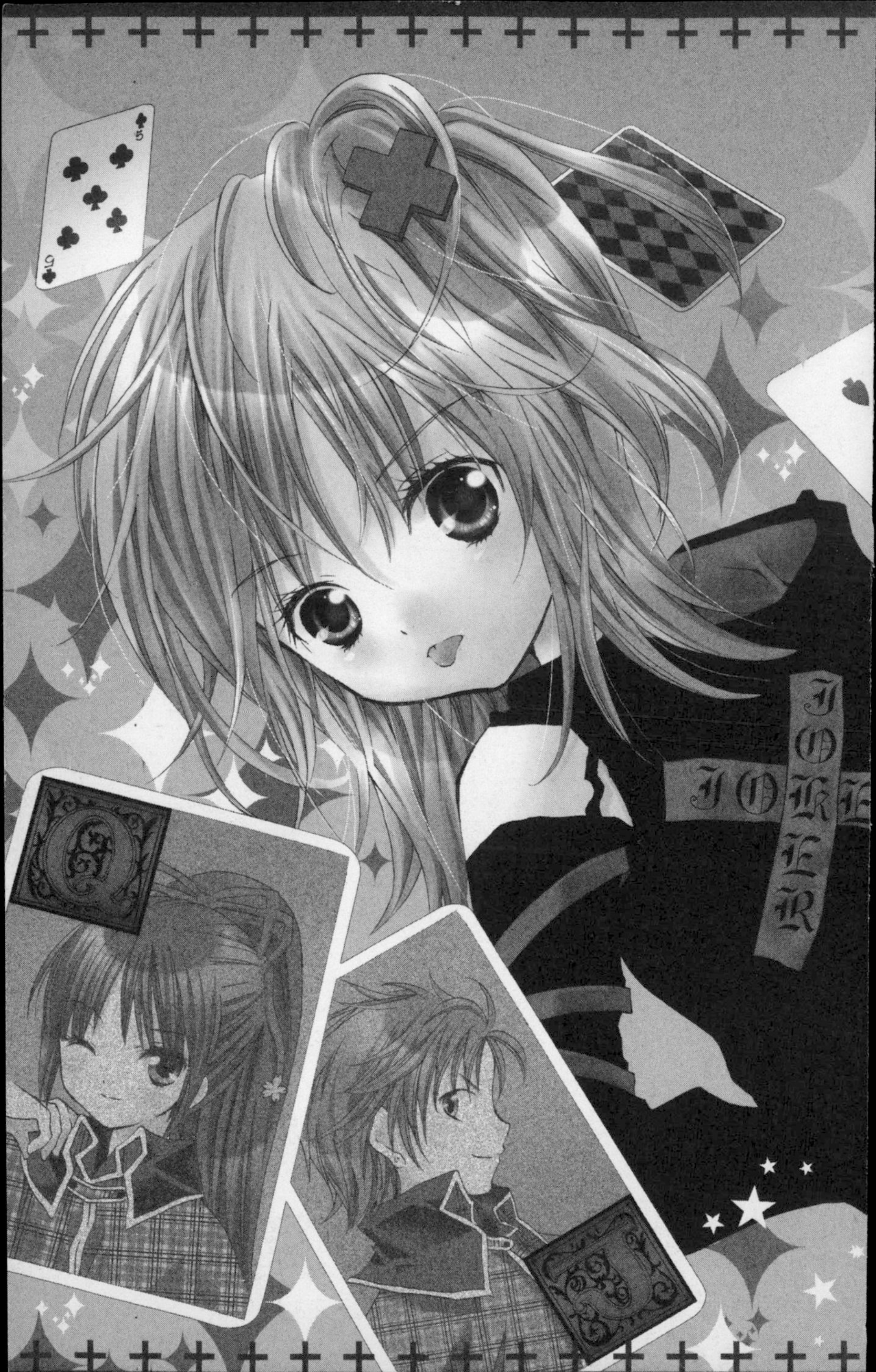
JOKER

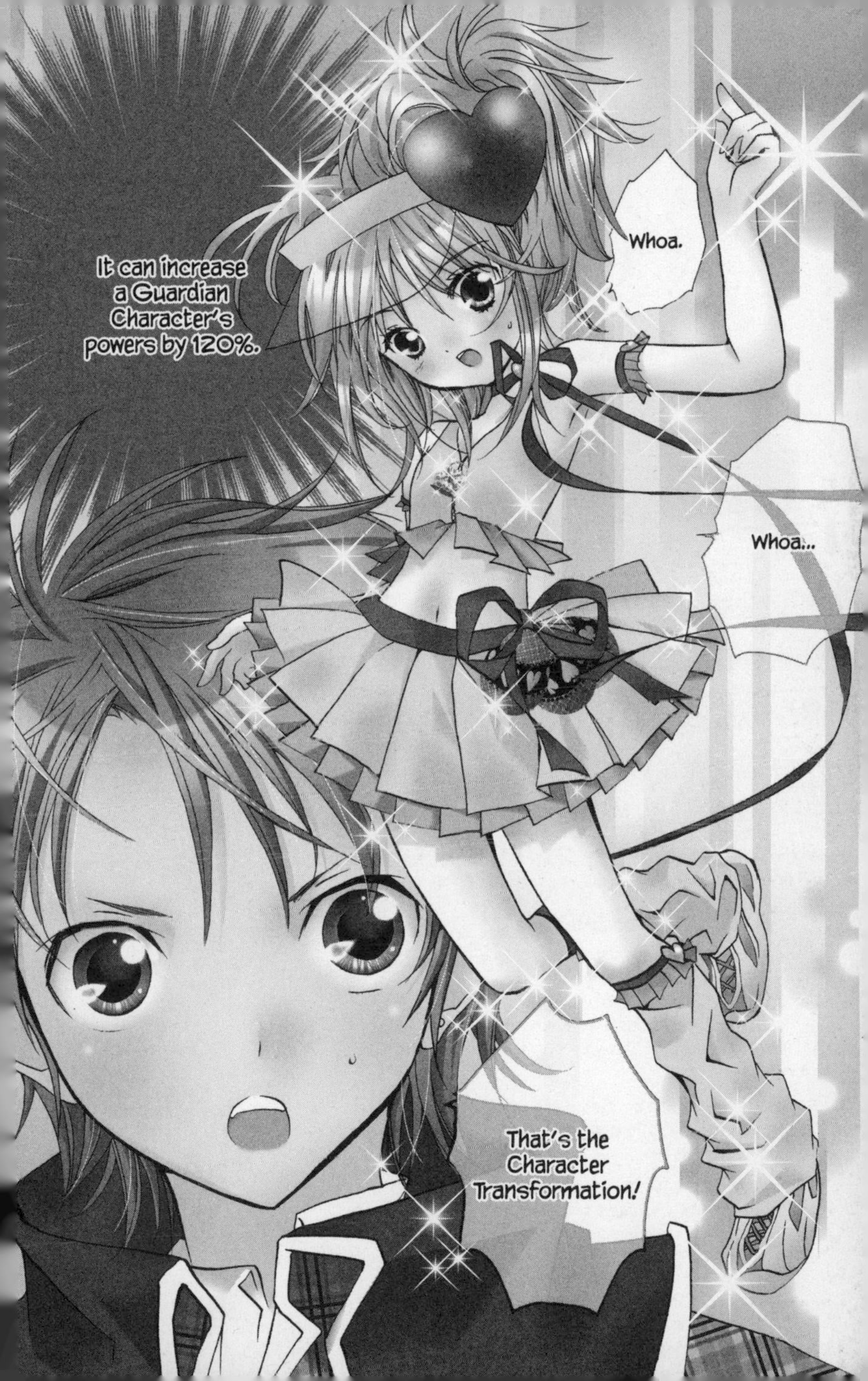
Whoa.
It can increase a Guardian Character's powers by 120%.
Whoa...
That's the Character Transformation!

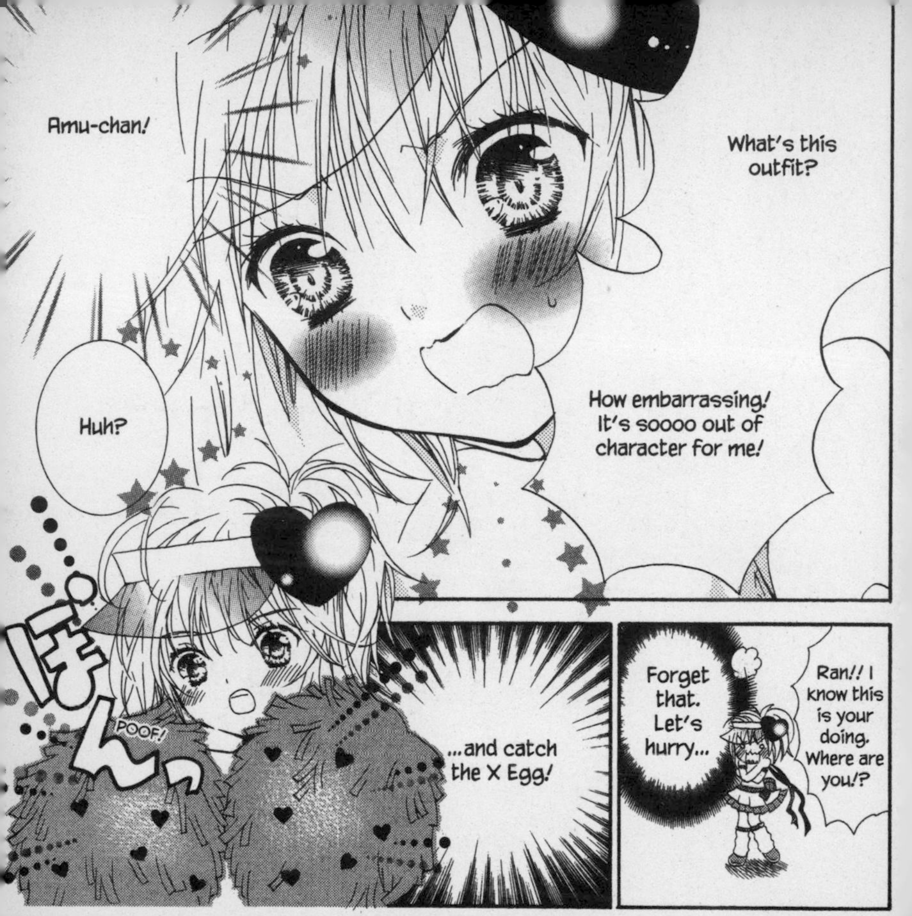
What's this outfit?
Amu-chan!
How embarrassing! It's soooo out of character for me!
Huh?
Ran!! I know this is your doing. Where are you!?
Forget that. Let's hurry...
...and catch the X Egg!
ぽんっ
POOF!

The Story So Far:

• Amu is socially awkward and has a hard time being true to her heart. One day she wished that she could change and become the person she wanted to be. And three Guardian Characters appeared!

• They each claim to be the person she really wants to be. Amu is surprised by the things they can do.

• Amu was asked to join the Guardians of Seiyo Elementary School, a group of students who each have their own Guardian Characters as well. Her first job as a Guardian was to hunt for X Eggs. But during the hunt, she underwent a Character Transformation!!

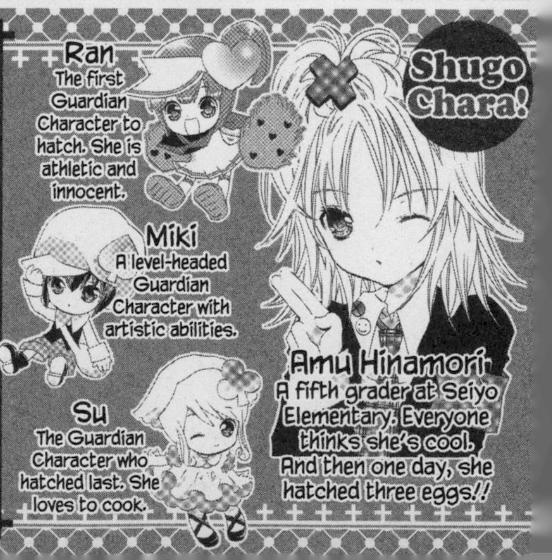
Shugo Chara!
Ran
The first Guardian Character to hatch. She is athletic and innocent.
Miki
A level-headed Guardian Character with artistic abilities.
Su
The Guardian Character who hatched last. She loves to cook.
Amu Hinamori
A fifth grader at Seiyo Elementary. Everyone thinks she's cool. And then one day, she hatched three eggs!!

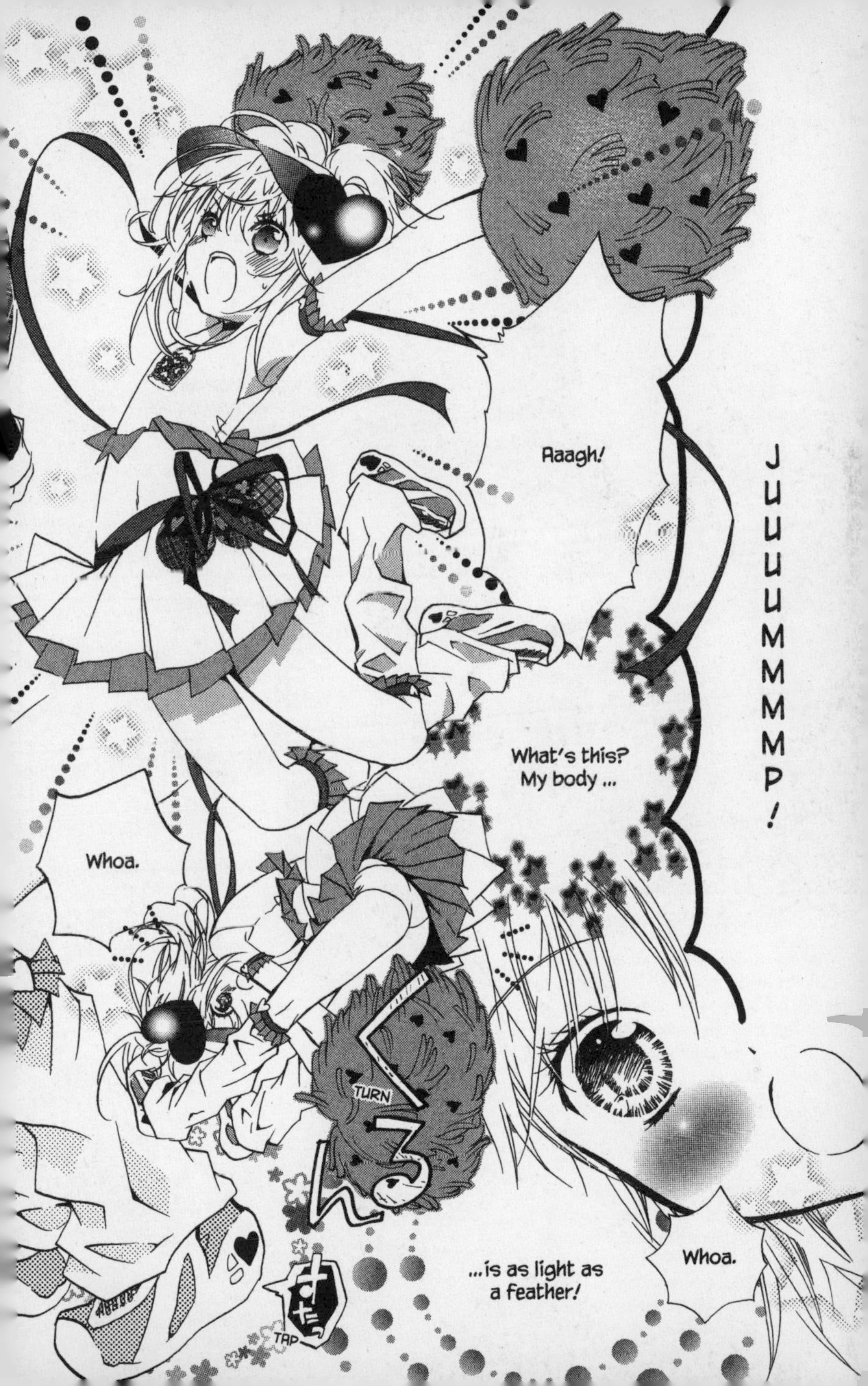
JUUUUMMMMP!
Aaagh!
What's this? My body ...
...is as light as a feather!
Whoa.
TURN
Whoa.
TAP

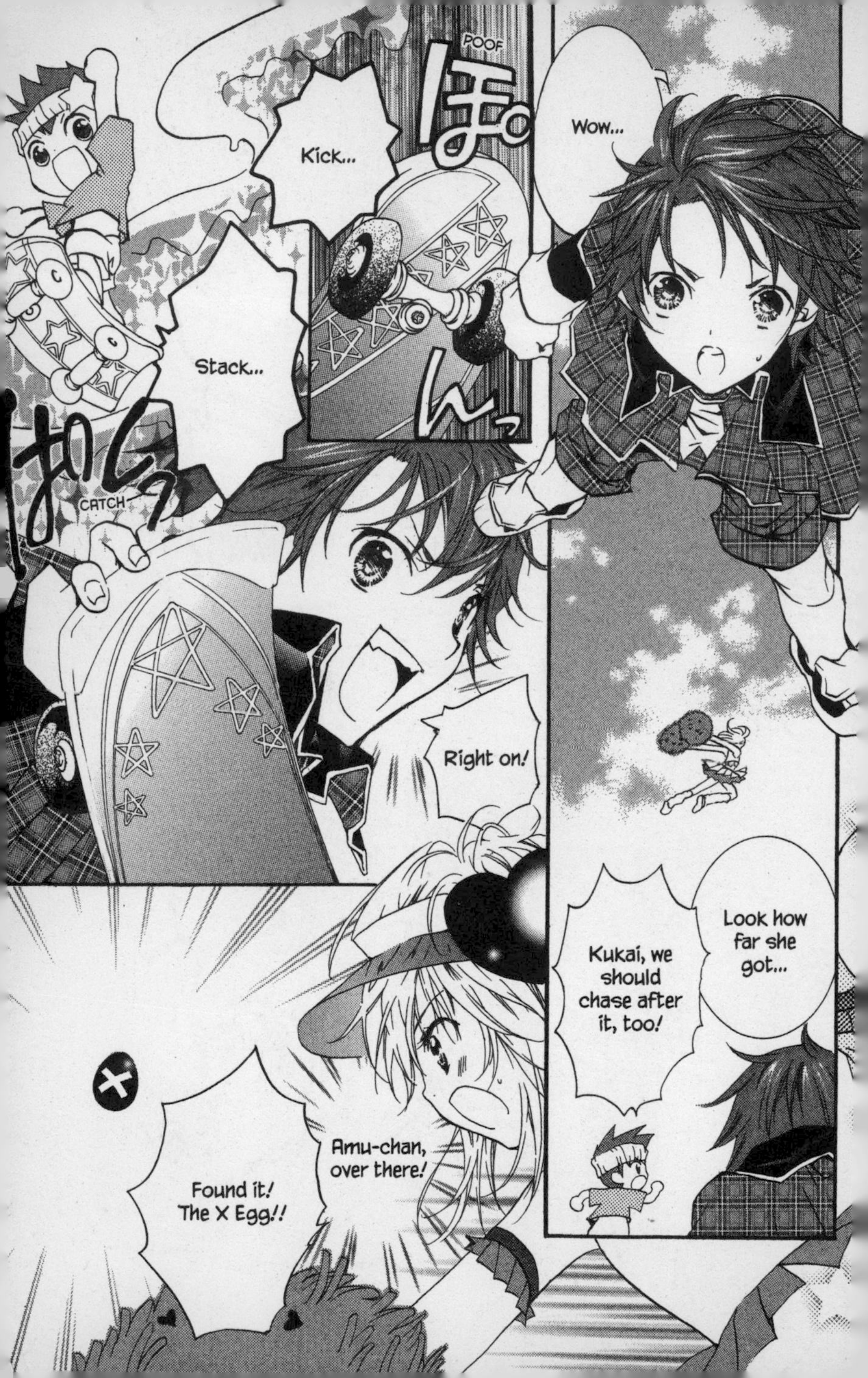
Wow...
POOF
Kick...
Stack...
CATCH
Right on!
Look how far she got...
Kukai, we should chase after it, too!
Amu-chan, over there!
Found it! The X Egg!!

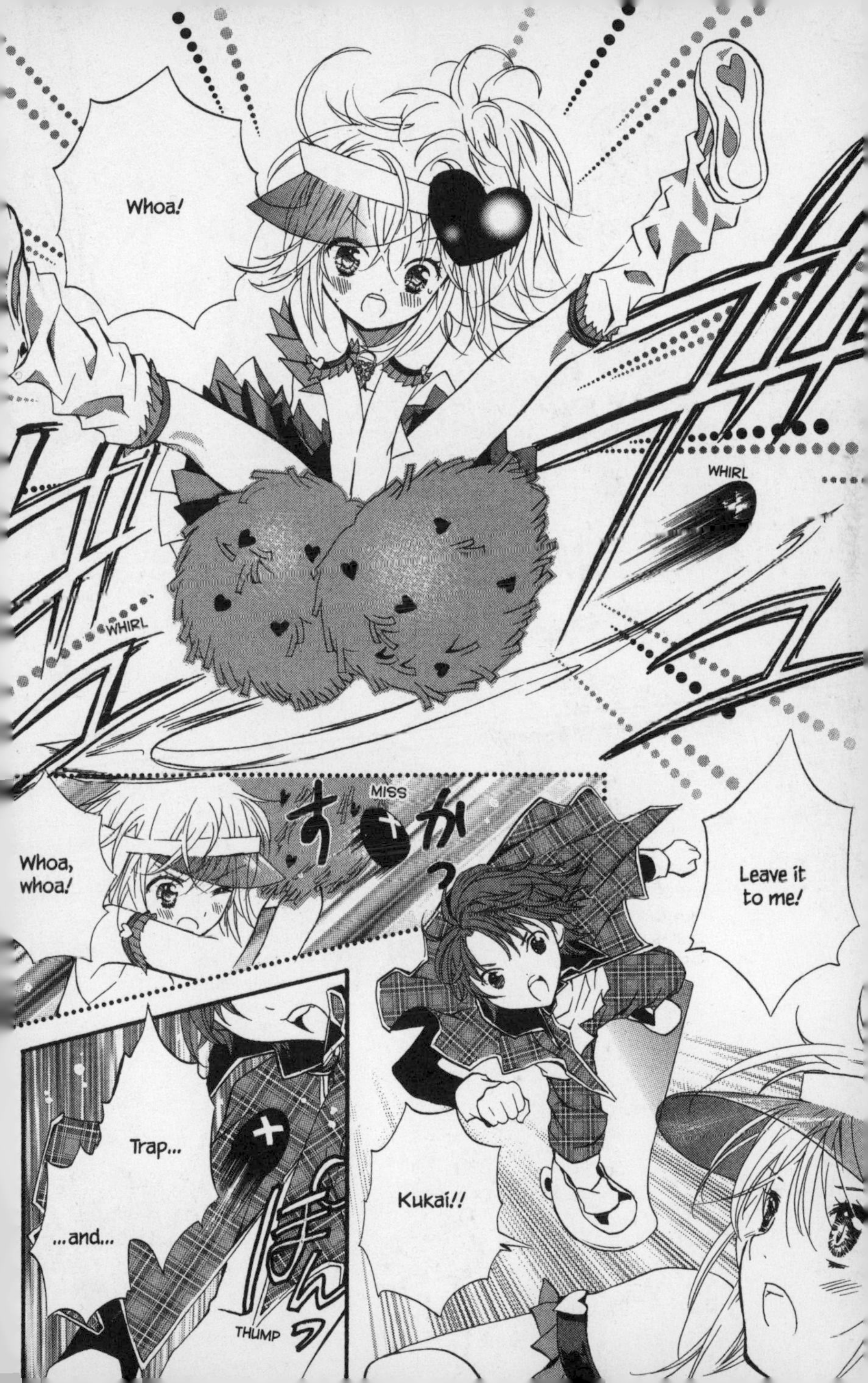
Whoa!
WHIRL
WHIRL
Leave it to me!
MISS
すかっ
Whoa, whoa!
Kukai!!
Trap...
...and...
ぽんっ
THUMP

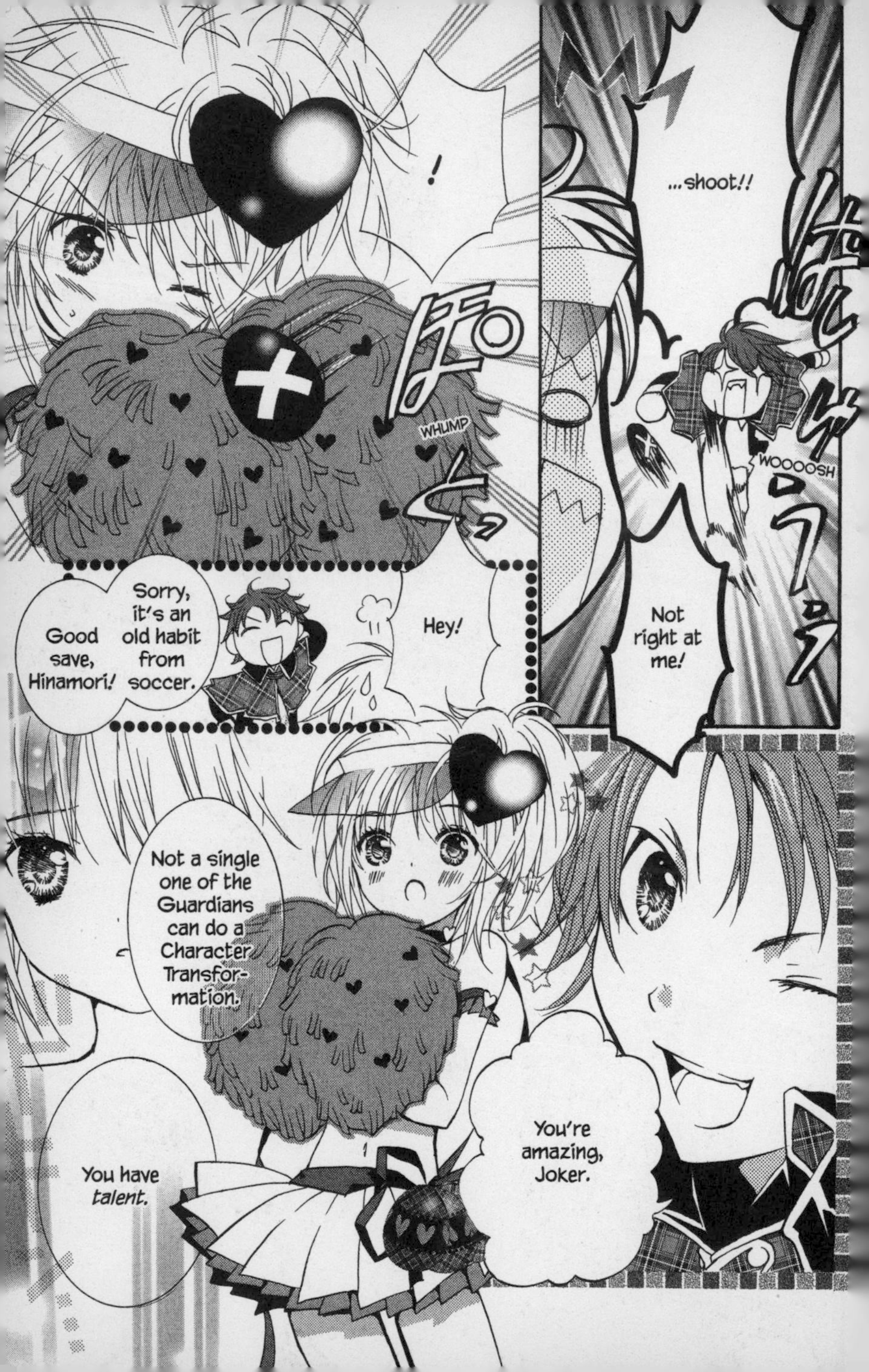
...shoot!!
WOOOOSH
Not right at me!
!
WHUMP
Hey!
Sorry, it's an old habit from soccer.
Good save, Hinamori!
You're amazing, Joker.
Not a single one of the Guardians can do a Character Transformation.
You have *talent*.

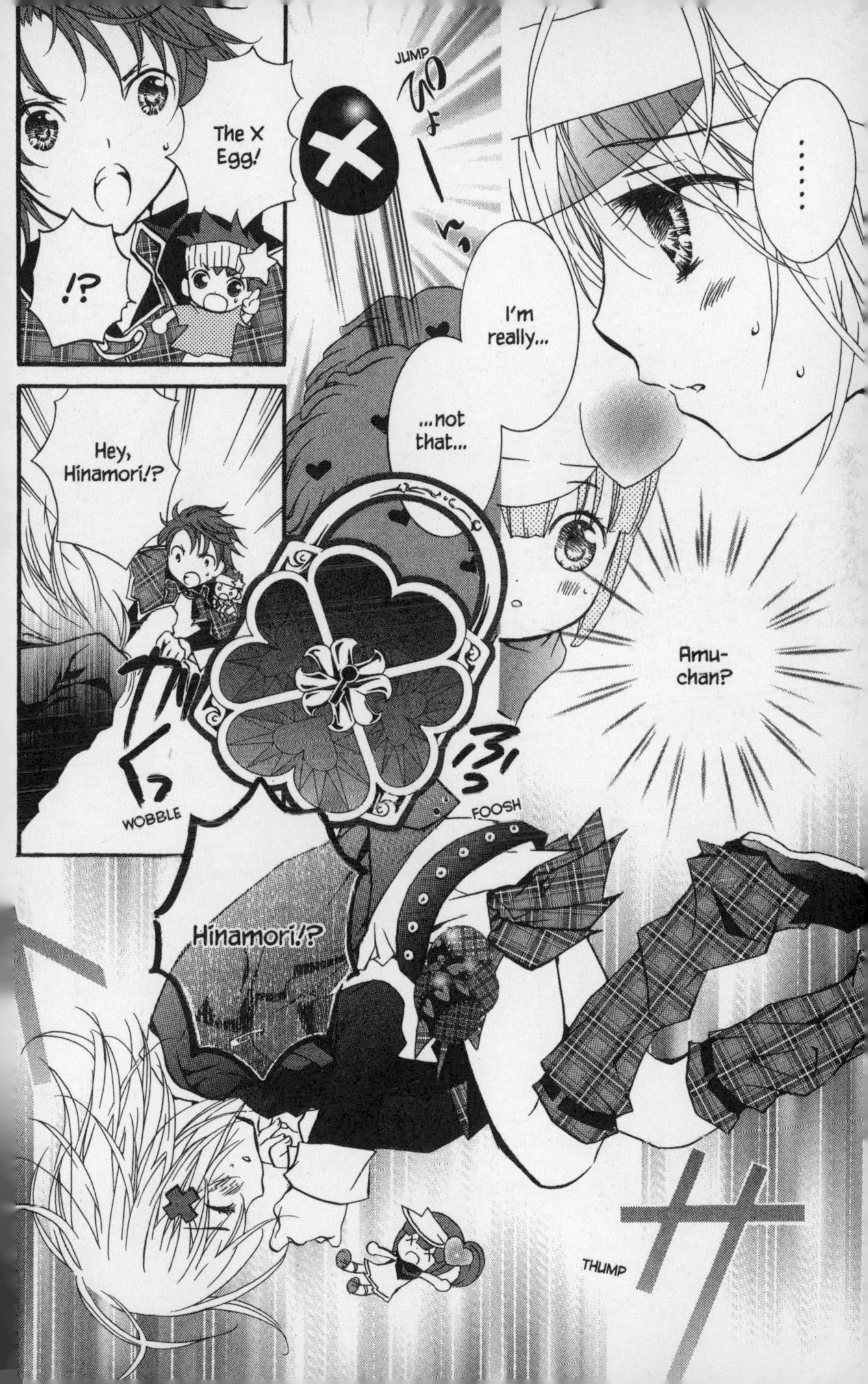
......
I'm really...
...not that...
JUMP
Amu-chan?
The X Egg!
!?
Hey, Hinamori!?
WOBBLE
FOOSH
Hinamori!?
THUMP

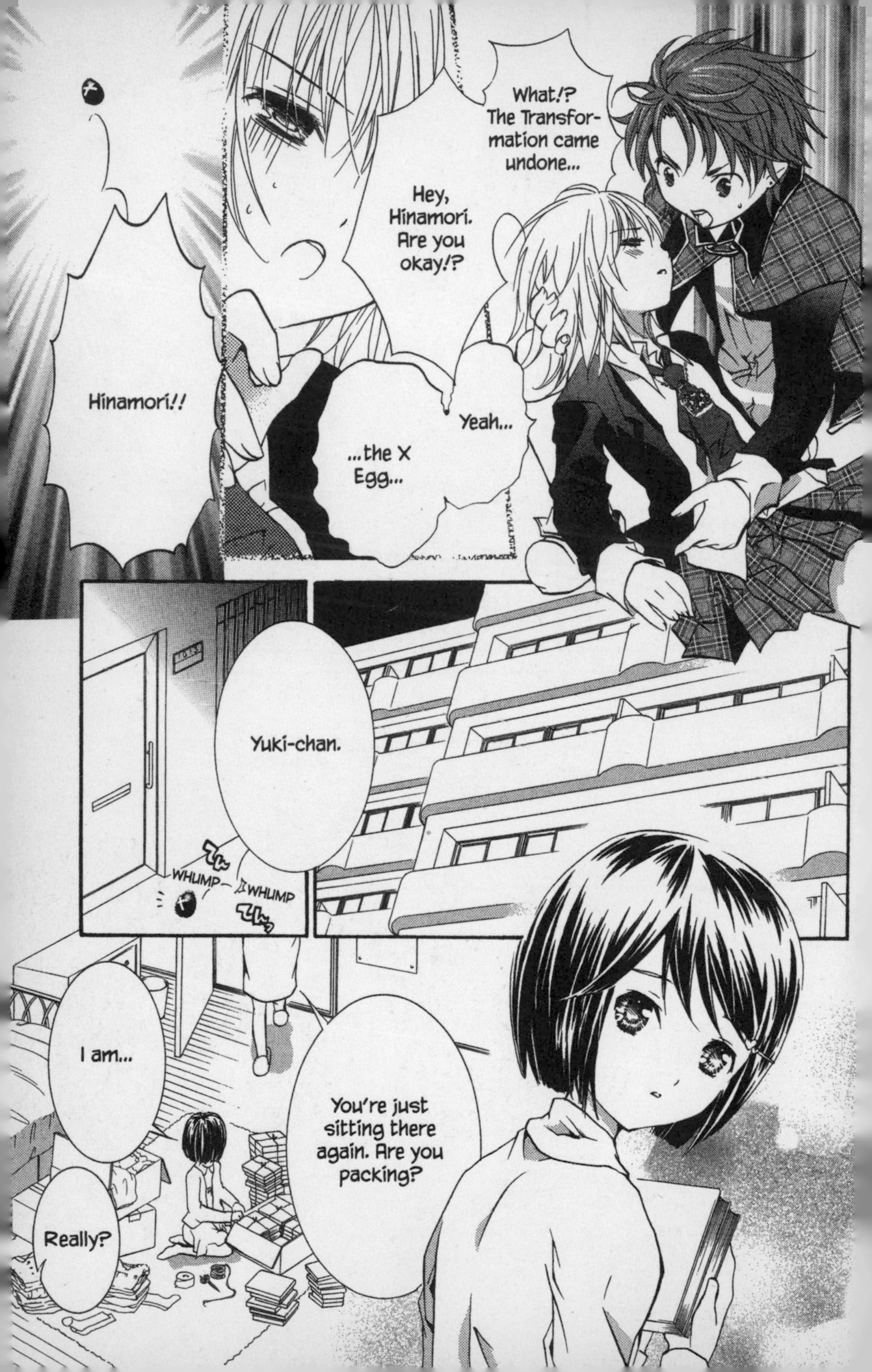
What!? The Transformation came undone...
Hey, Hinamori. Are you okay!?
Yeah...
...the X Egg...
Hinamori!!
Yuki-chan.
WHUMP
WHUMP
You're just sitting there again. Are you packing?
I am...
Really?

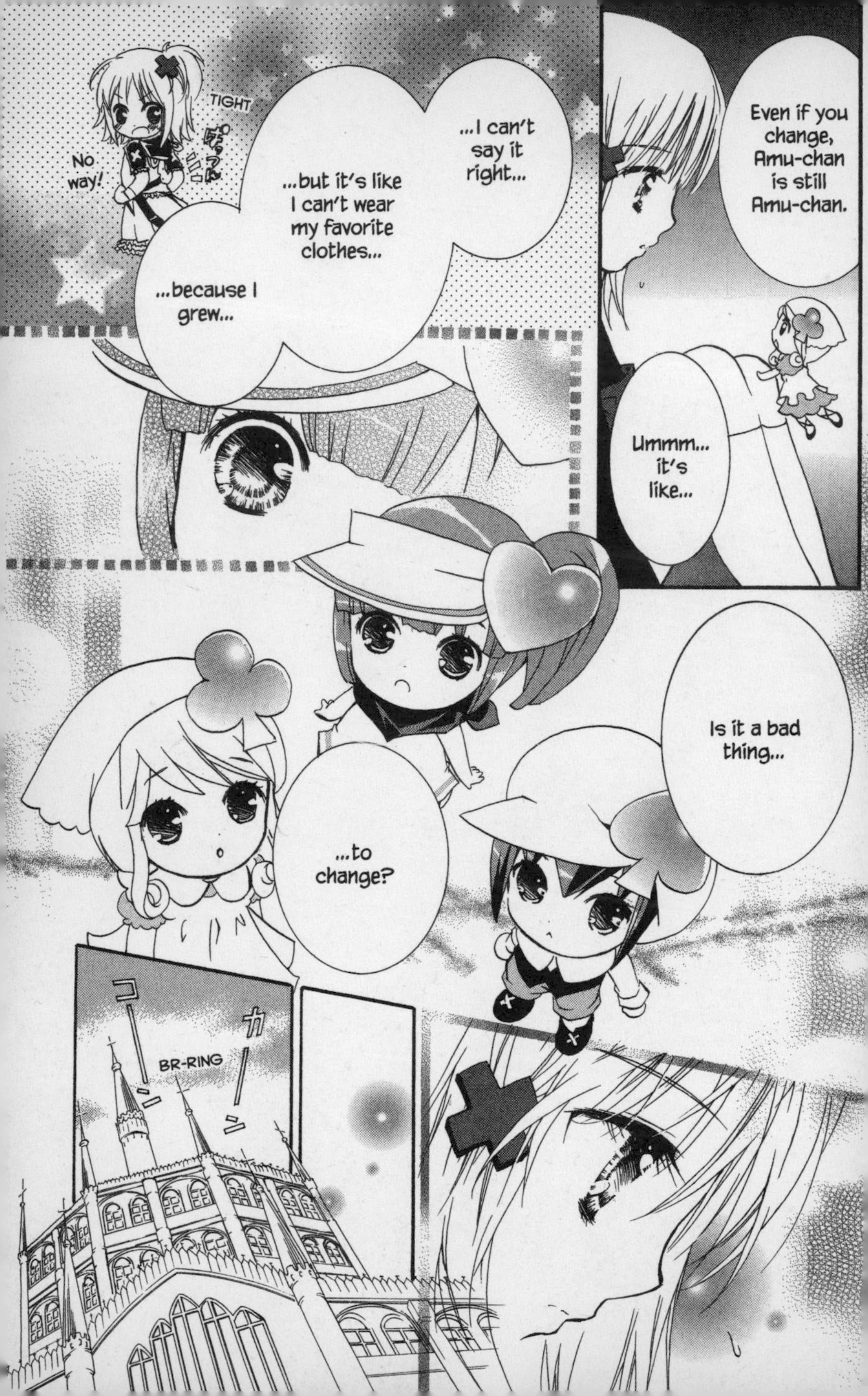
Even if you change, Amu-chan is still Amu-chan.
Ummm... it's like...
...I can't say it right...
...but it's like I can't wear my favorite clothes...
...because I grew...
TIGHT
No way!
Is it a bad thing...
...to change?
カーン
コーン
BR-RING

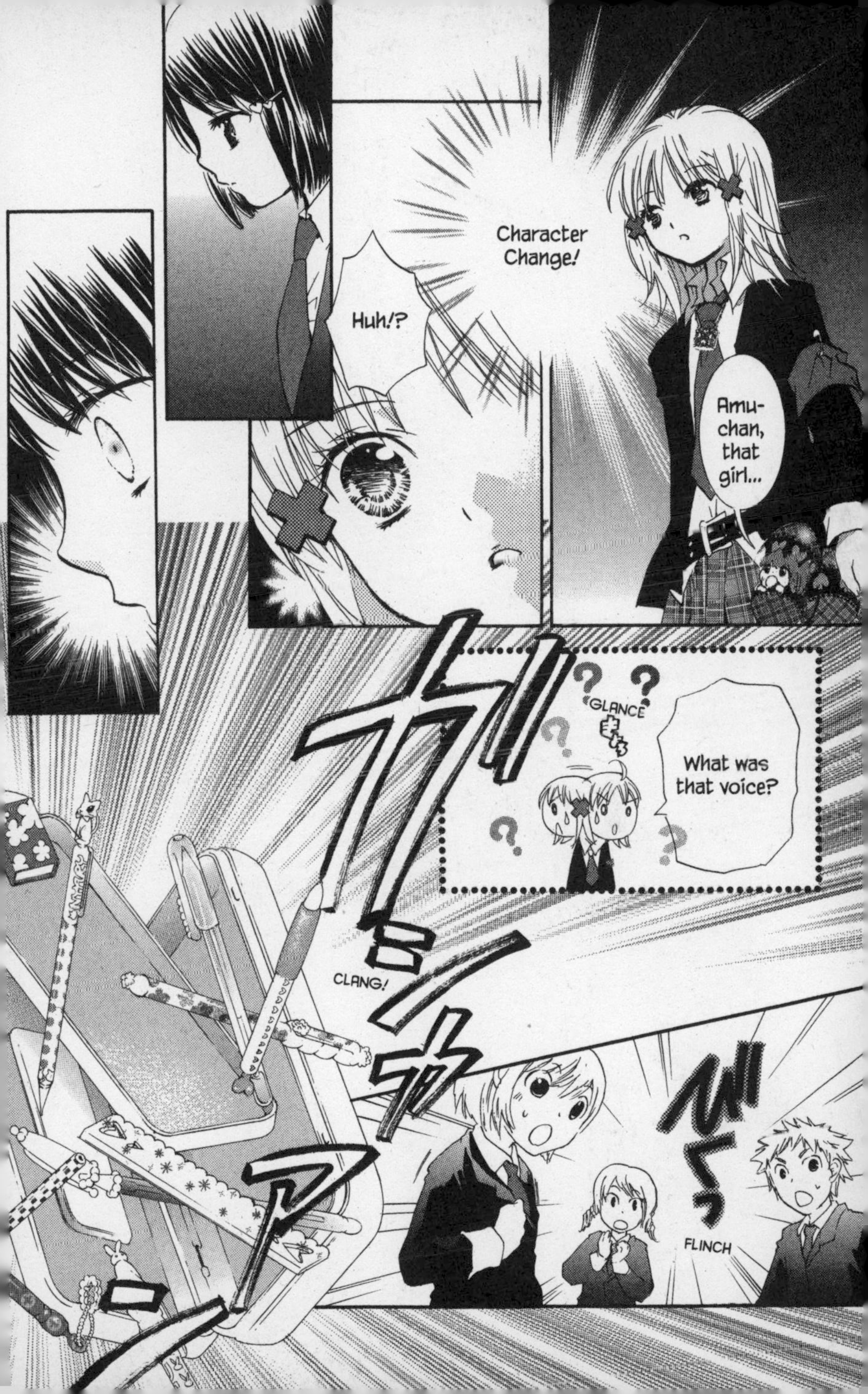

Character Change!
Amu-chan, that girl...
Huh!?
GLANCE
What was that voice?
CLANG!
FLINCH

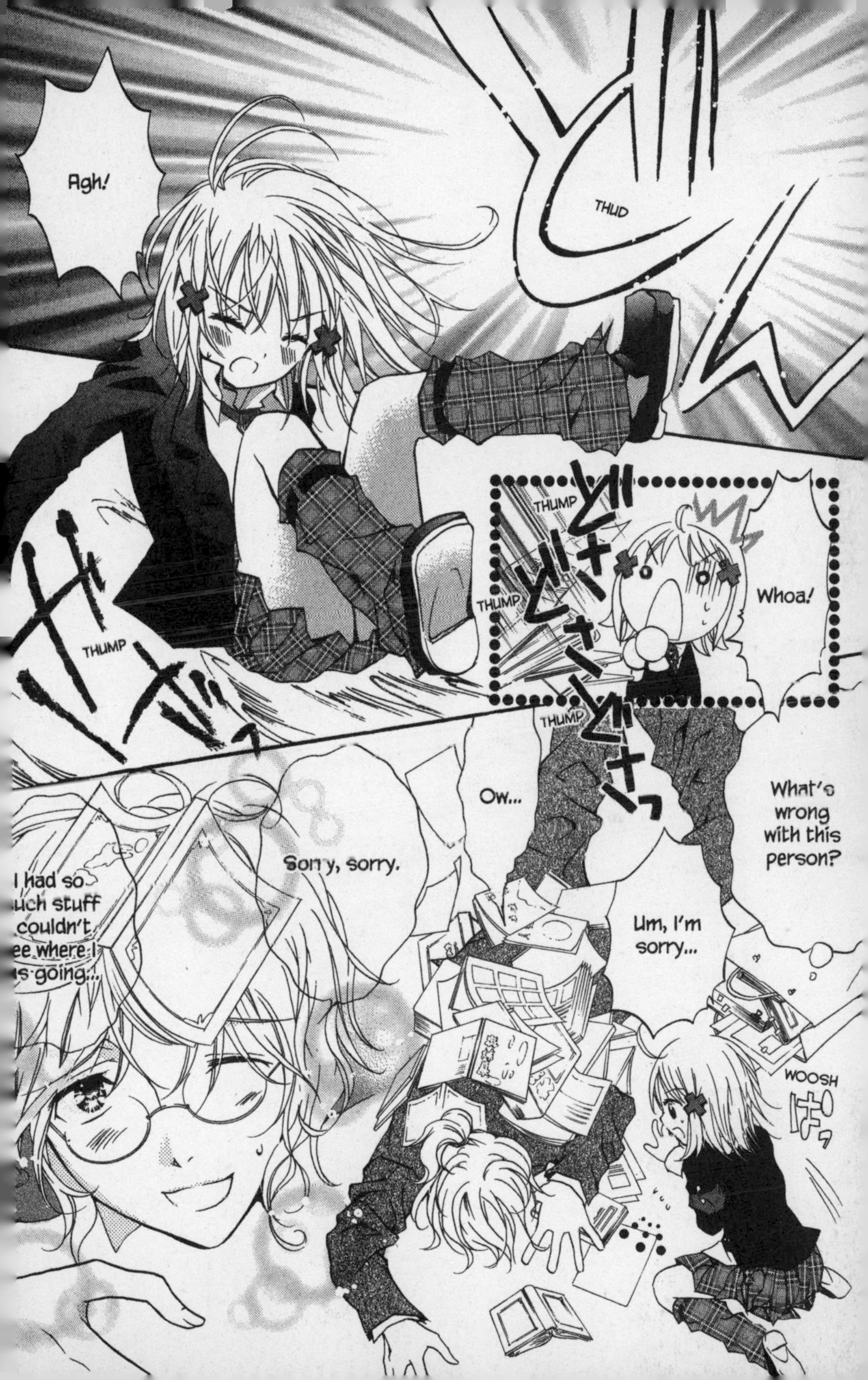
THUD
Agh!
THUMP
Whoa!
THUMP
THUMP
THUMP
What's wrong with this person?
Ow...
Um, I'm sorry...
Sorry, sorry.
WOOSH
I had so uch stuff couldn't ee where I as going...

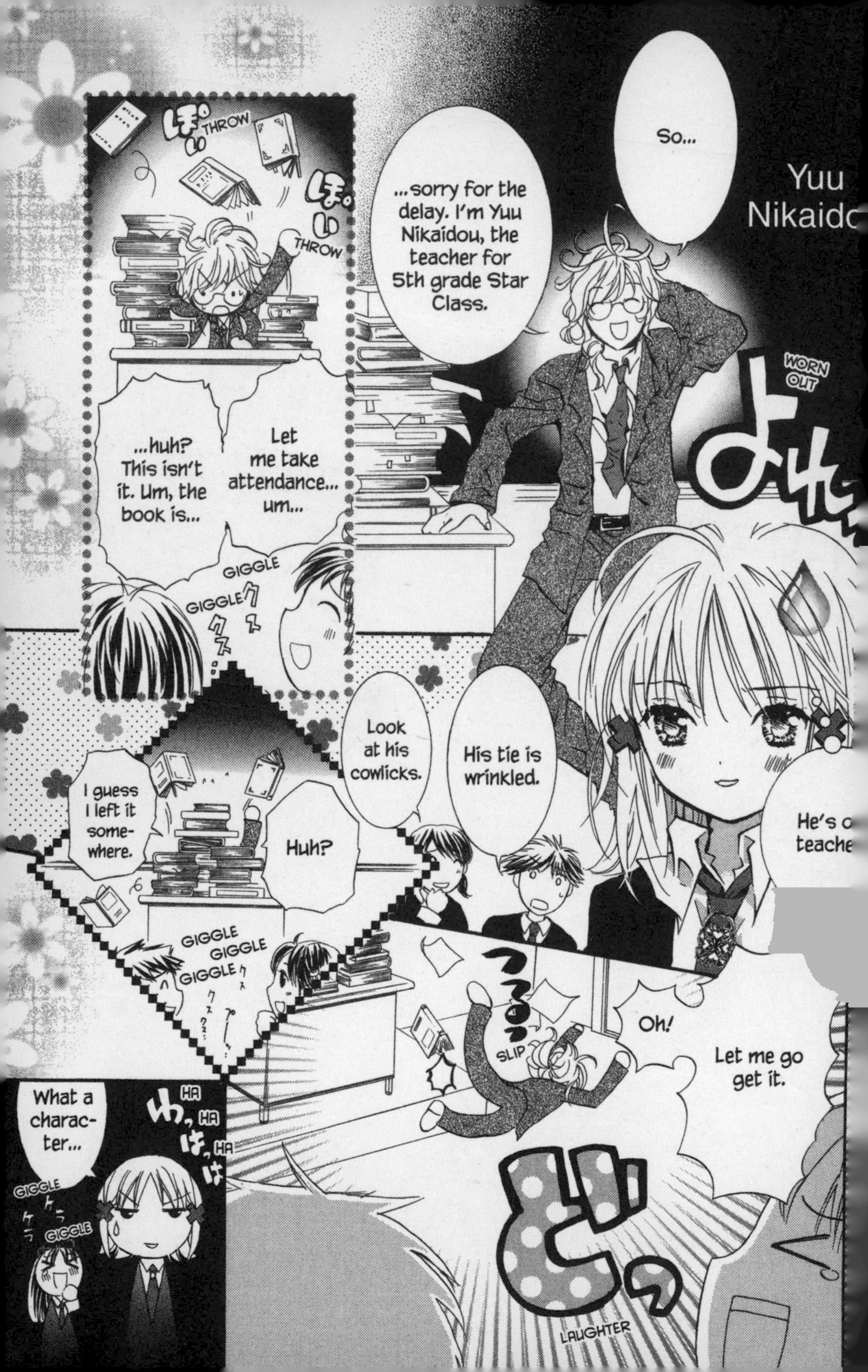

Yuu Nikaido
So...
...sorry for the delay. I'm Yuu Nikaidou, the teacher for 5th grade Star Class.
WORN OUT
THROW
THROW
Let me take attendance... um...
...huh? This isn't it. Um, the book is...
GIGGLE
GIGGLE
He's o teache
His tie is wrinkled.
Look at his cowlicks.
Huh?
I guess I left it somewhere.
GIGGLE
GIGGLE
GIGGLE
Oh!
Let me go get it.
SLIP
LAUGHTER
What a character...
HA
HA
HA
GIGGLE
GIGGLE

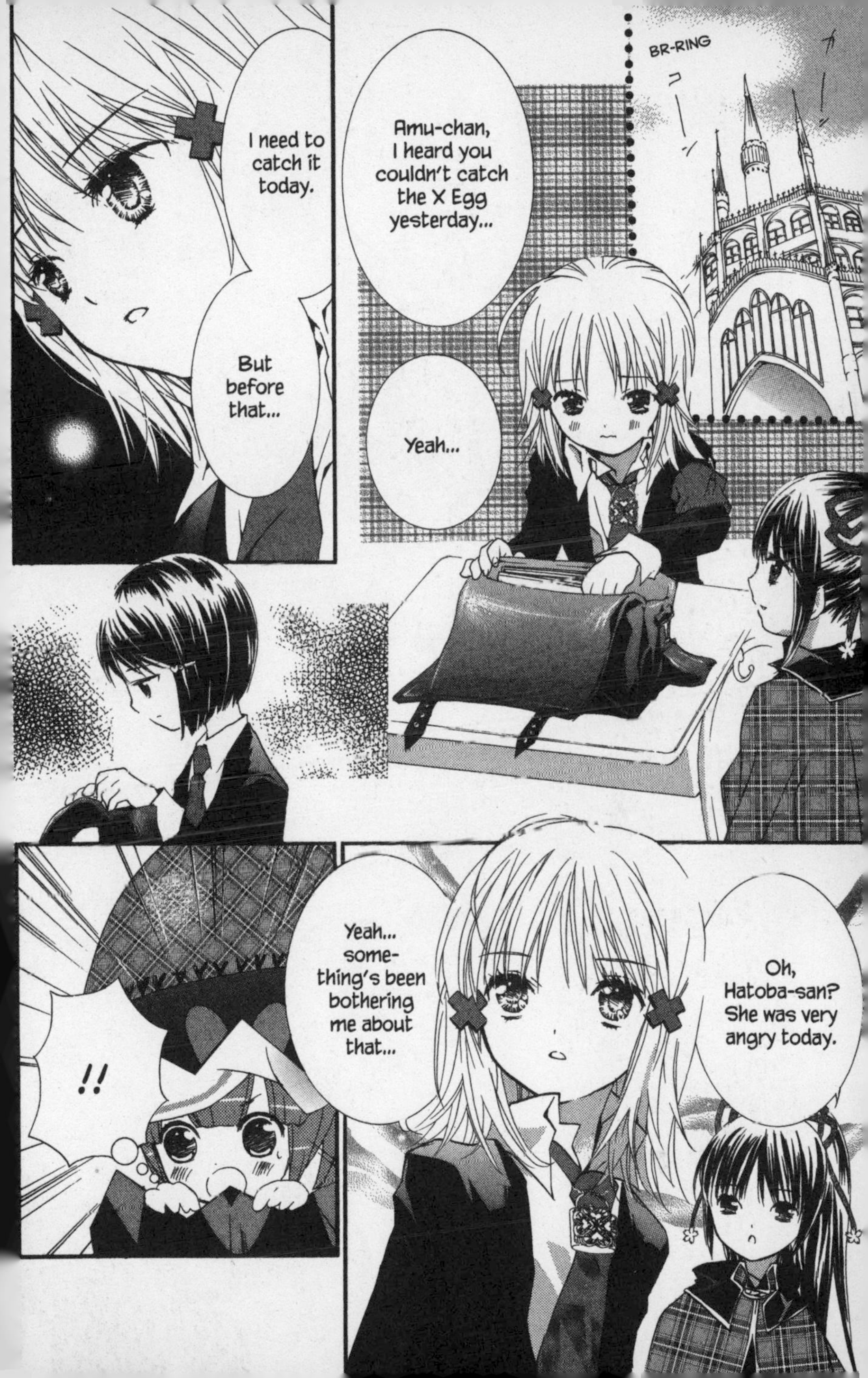
BR-RING
Amu-chan, I heard you couldn't catch the X Egg yesterday...
Yeah...
I need to catch it today.
But before that...
Oh, Hatoba-san? She was very angry today.
Yeah... some-thing's been bothering me about that...
!!

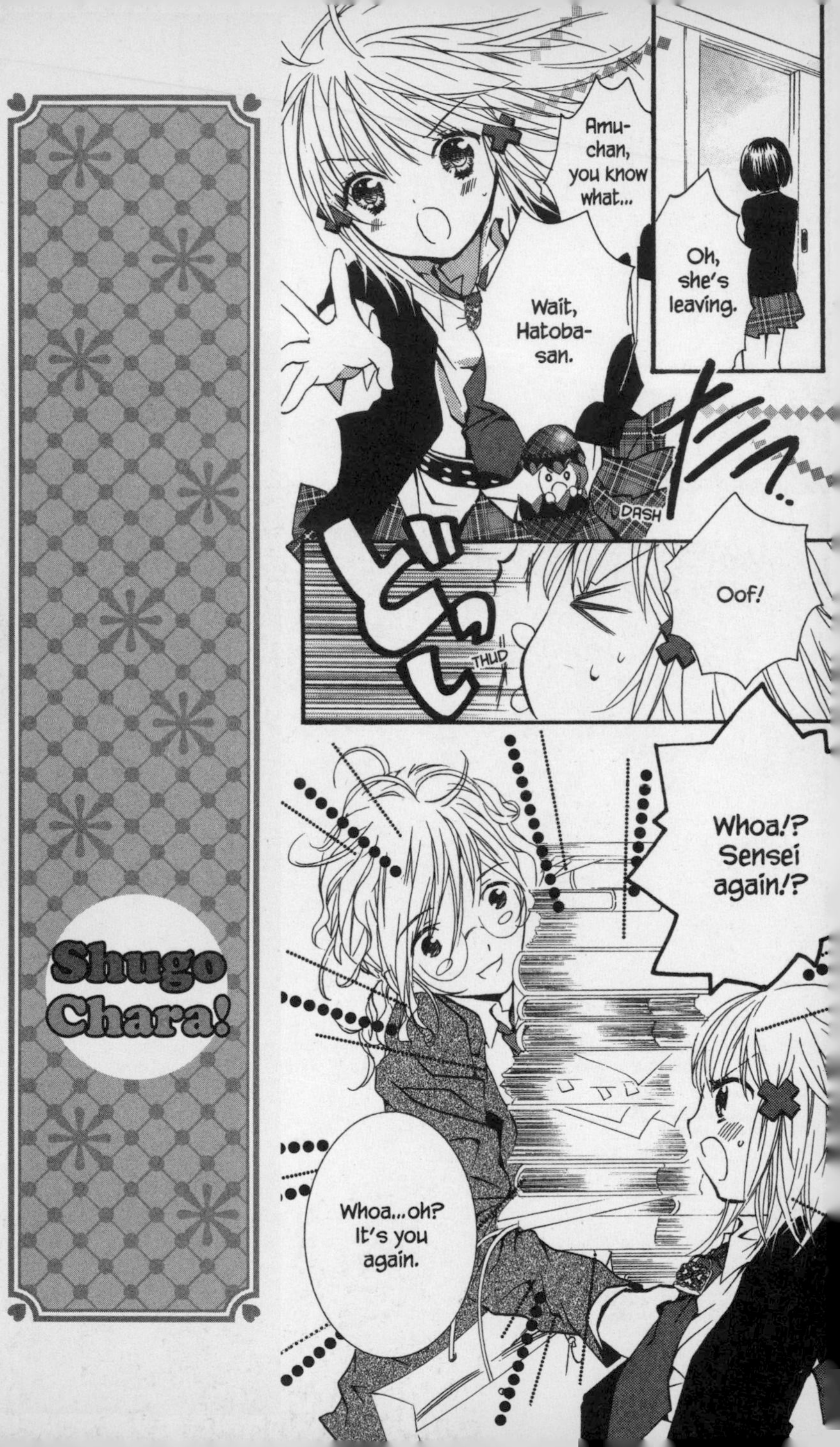
Oh, she's leaving.
Amu-chan, you know what...
Wait, Hatoba-san.
DASH
Oof!
THUD
Whoa!? Sensei again!?
Whoa...oh? It's you again.

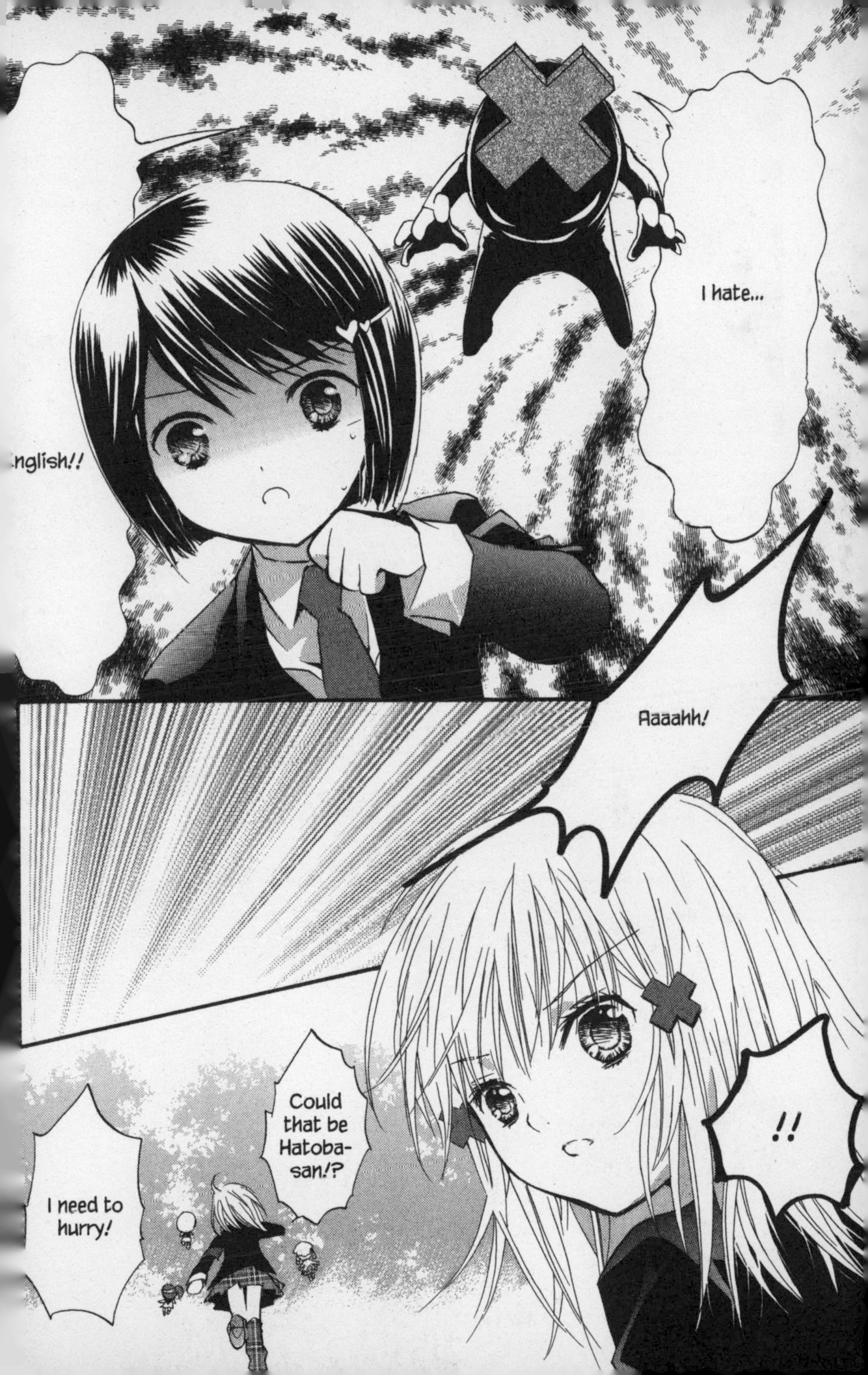
I hate...
nglish!!
Aaaahh!
!!
Could that be Hatoba-san!?
I need to hurry!

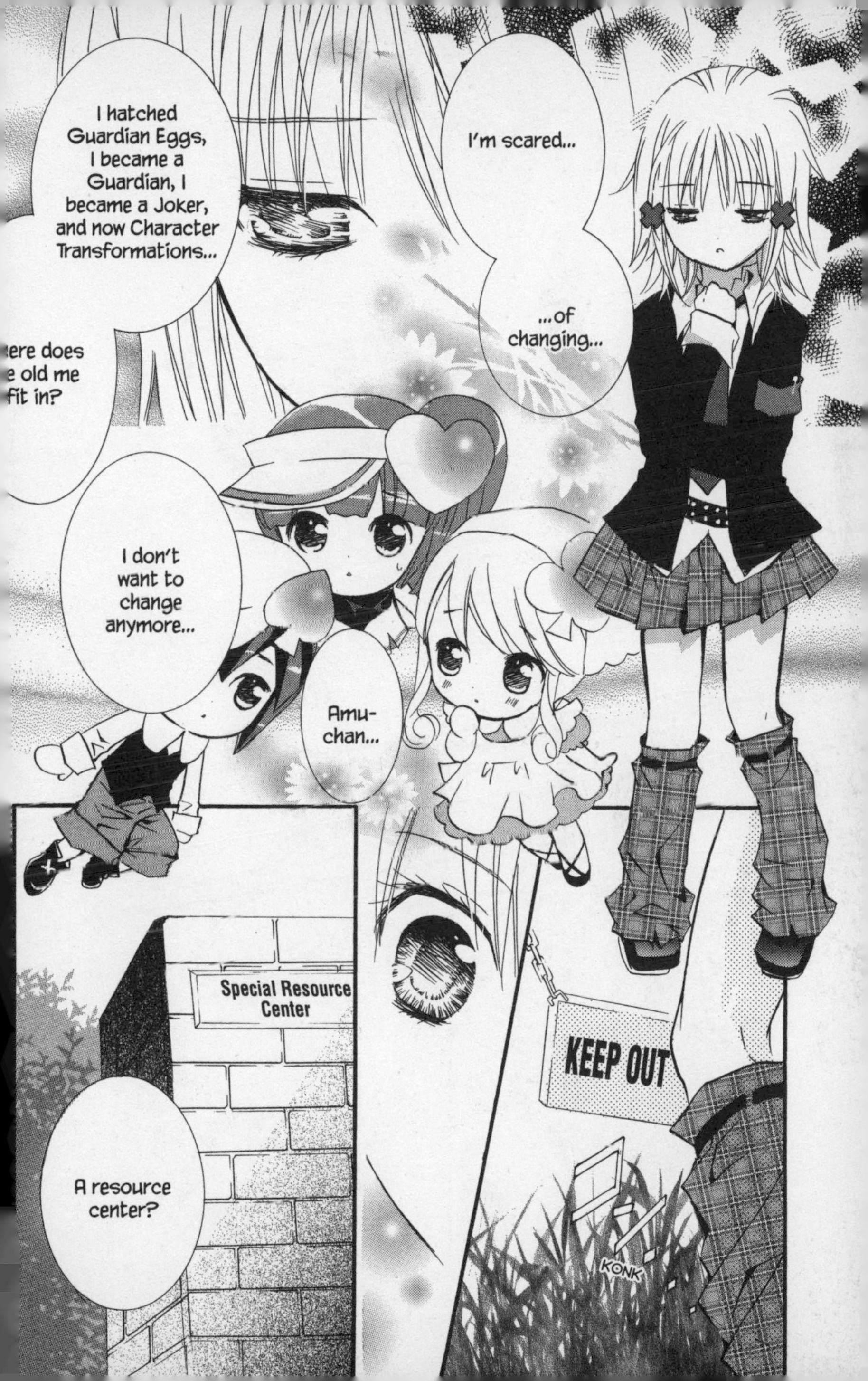
I'm scared...
...of changing...
I hatched Guardian Eggs, I became a Guardian, I became a Joker, and now Character Transformations...
ere does e old me fit in?
I don't want to change anymore...
Amu-chan...
KEEP OUT
KONK
Special Resource Center
A resource center?

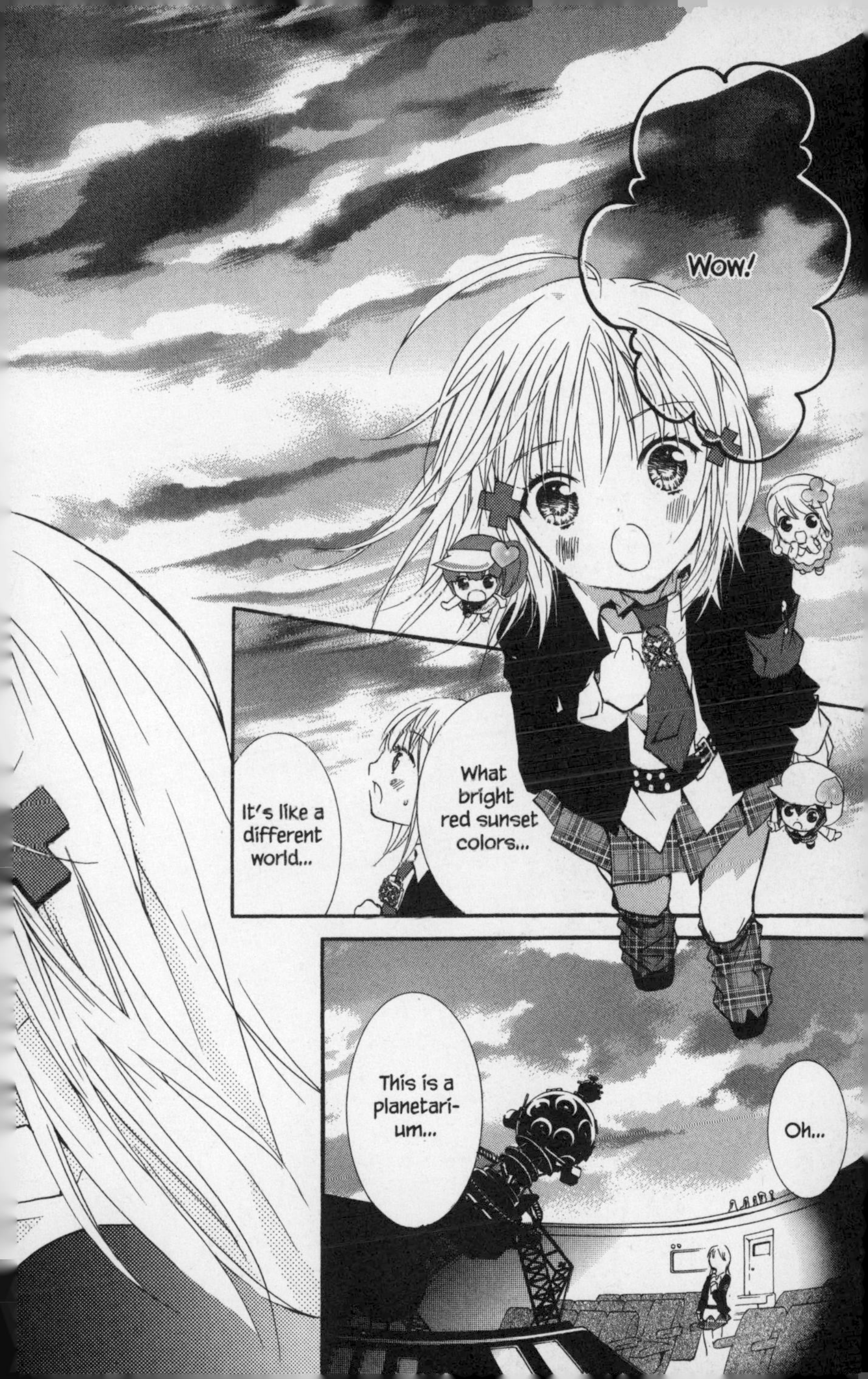
Wow!
What bright red sunset colors...
It's like a different world...
Oh...
This is a planetari-um...

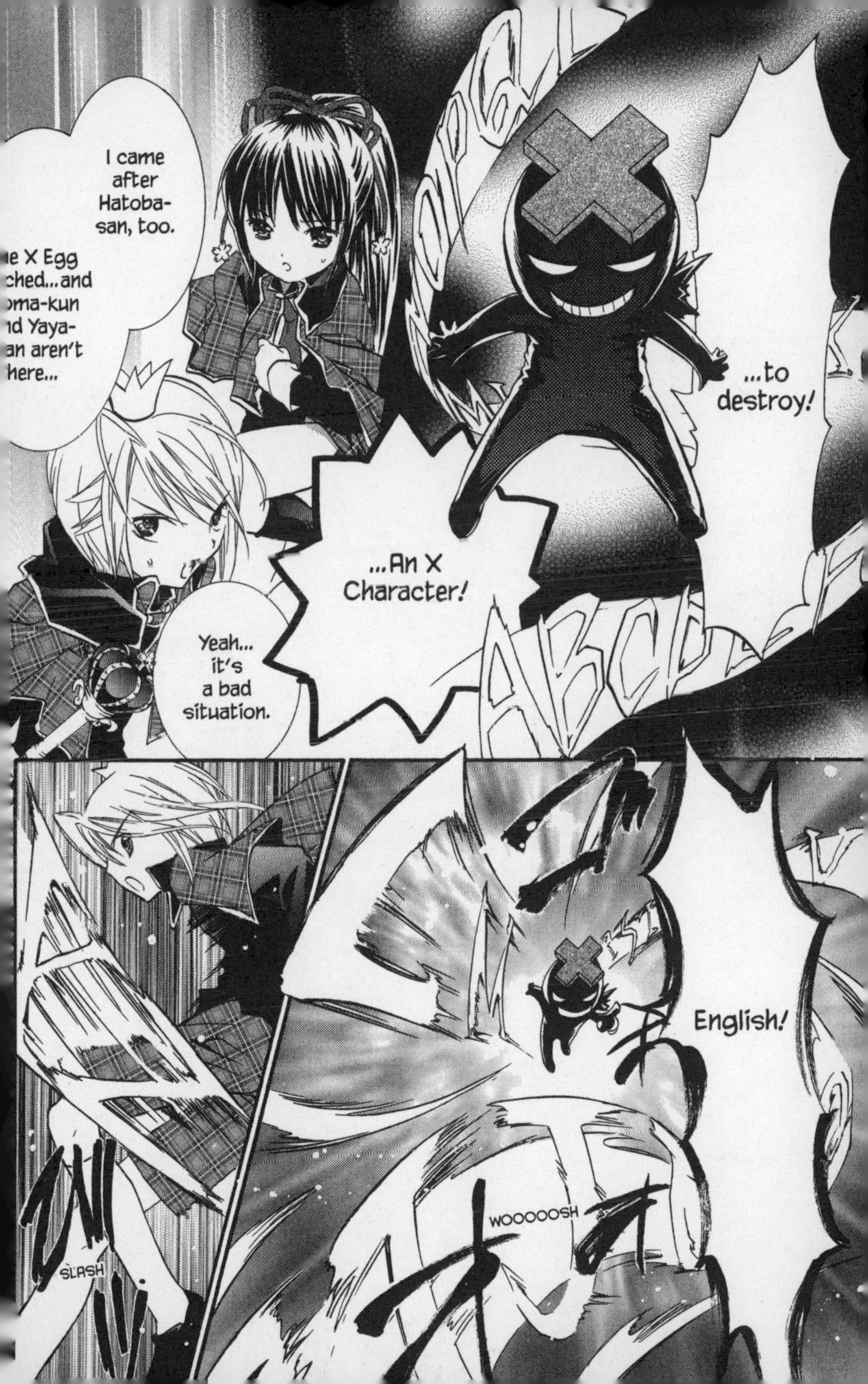
...to destroy!
I came after Hatoba-san, too.
e X Egg ched...and oma-kun nd Yaya-an aren't here...
...An X Character!
Yeah... it's a bad situation.
English!
WOOOOOSH
SLASH

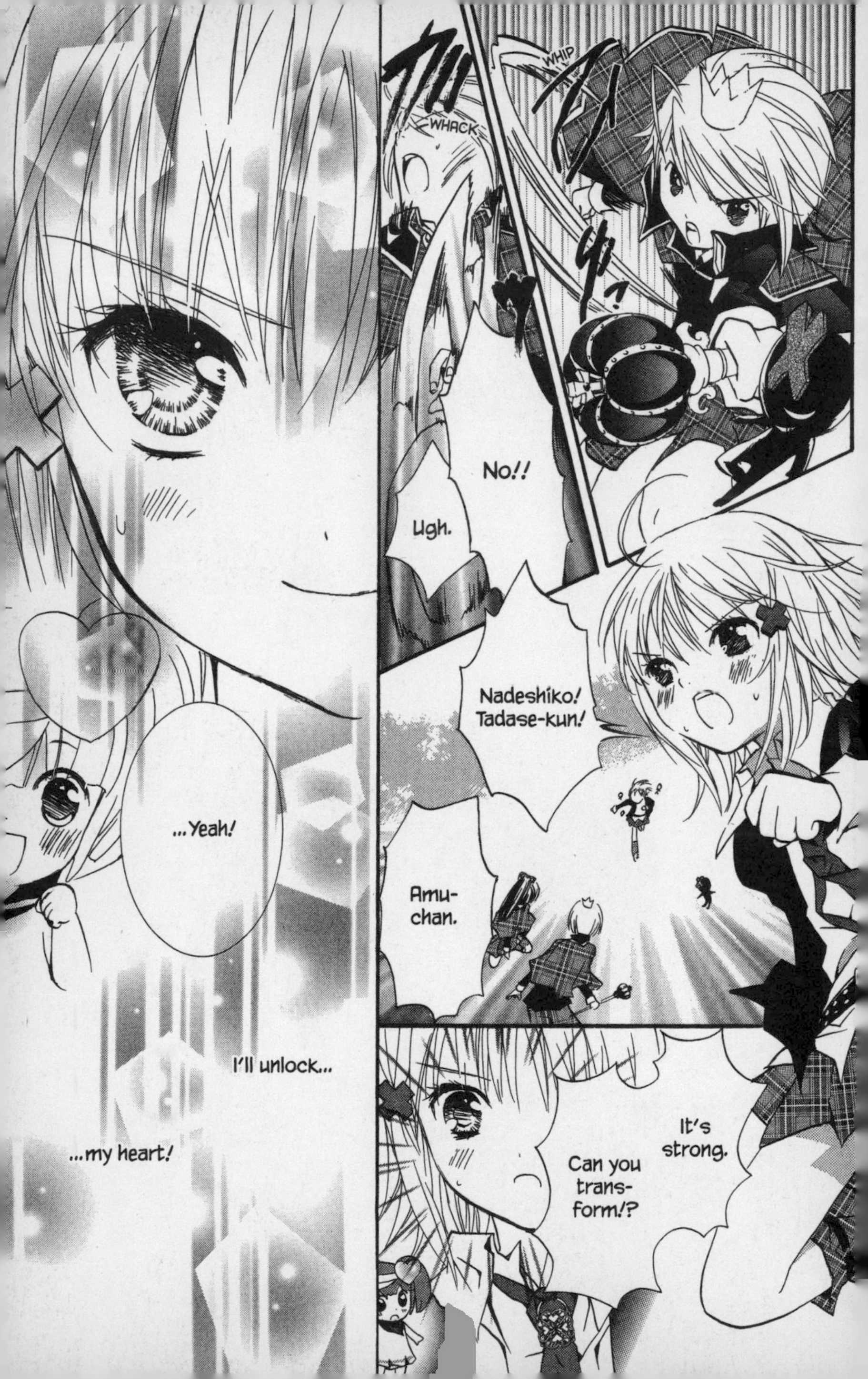
WHIP
WHACK
No!!
Ugh.
Nadeshiko! Tadase-kun!
Amu-chan.
It's strong.
Can you transform!?
...Yeah!
I'll unlock...
...my heart!

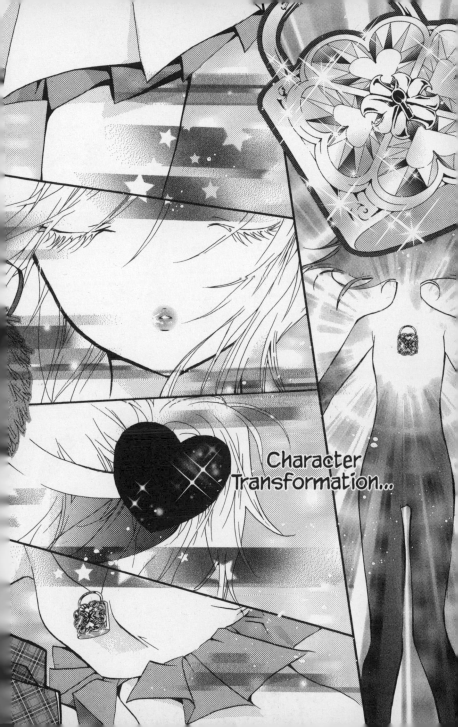

Character
Transformation...

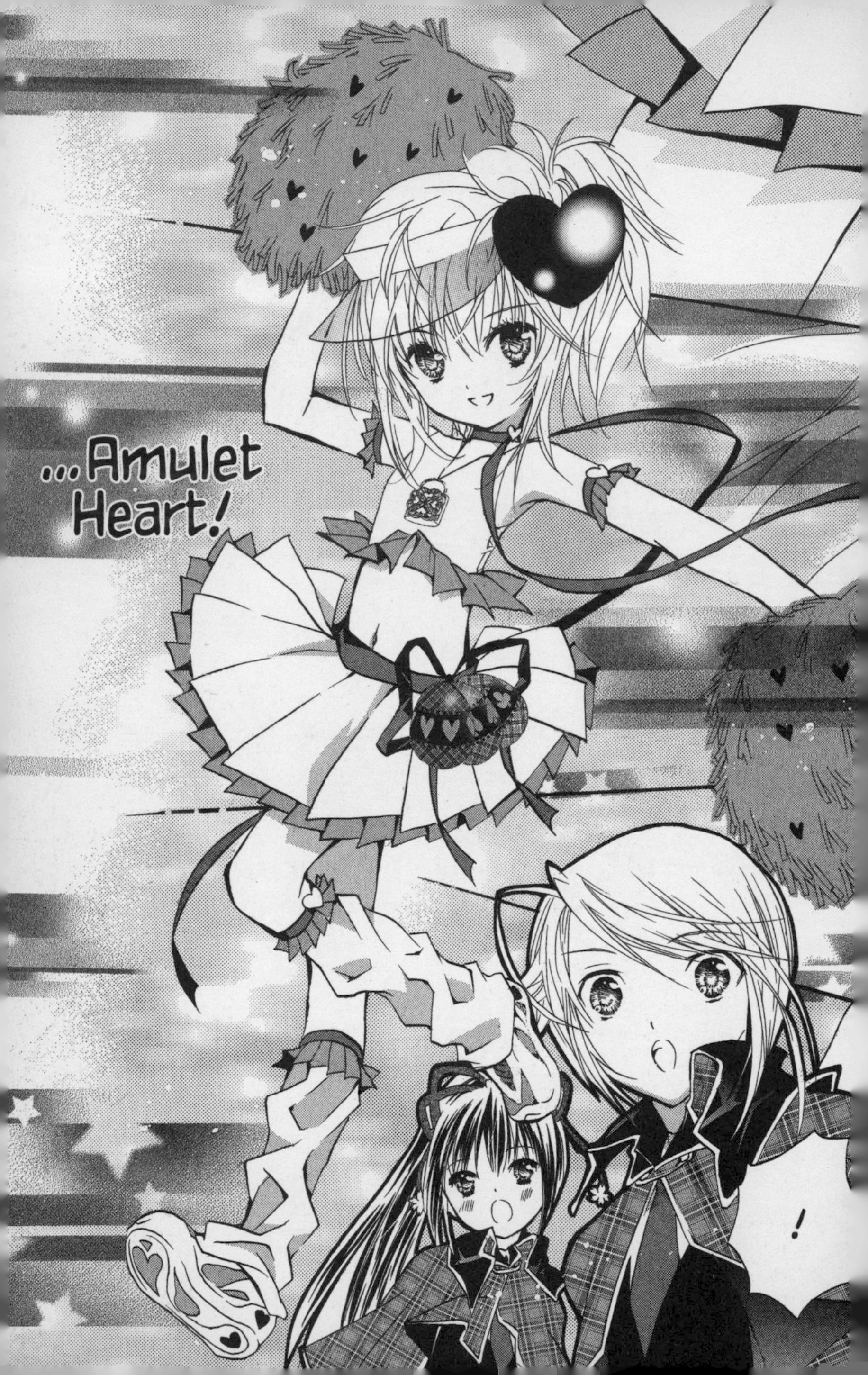
...Amulet Heart!
!

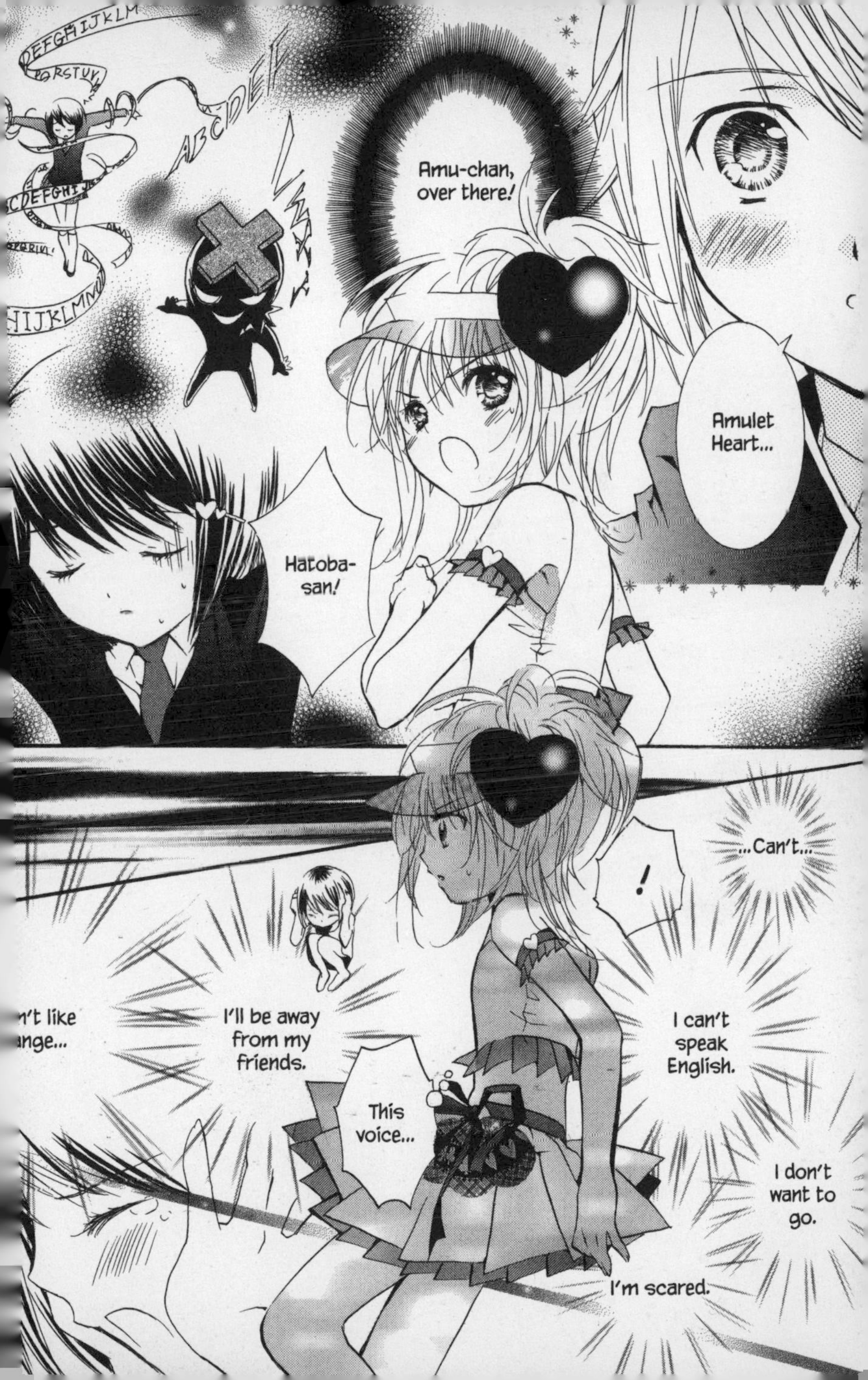
Amulet Heart...
Amu-chan, over there!
Hatoba-san!
...Can't...
!
I can't speak English.
I don't want to go.
I'm scared.
This voice...
I'll be away from my friends.
n't like
ange...

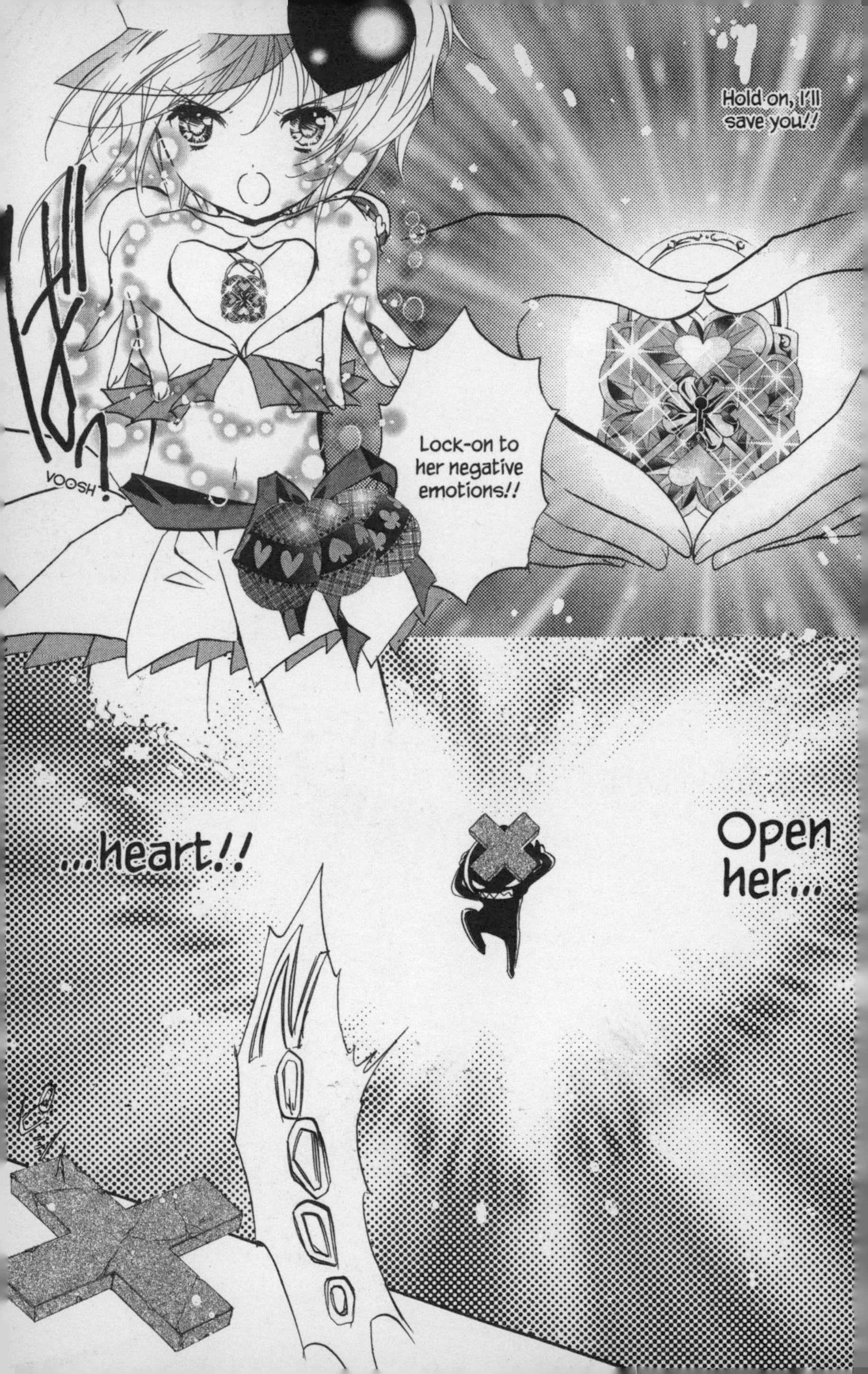
Hold on, I'll save you!!
Lock-on to her negative emotions!!
VOOSH!
Open her...
...heart!!

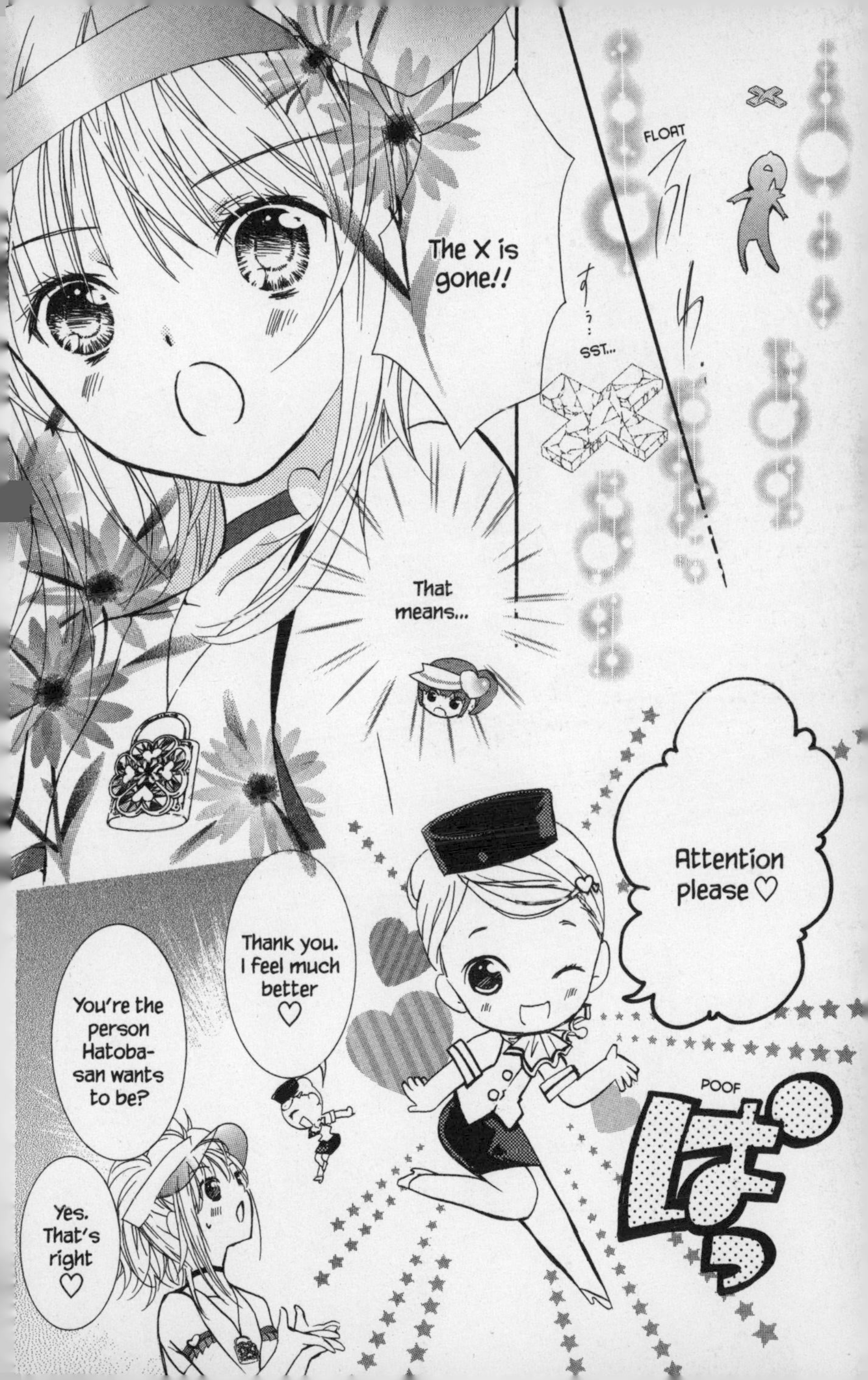
FLOAT
SST...
The X is gone!!
That means...
Attention please ♡
POOF
Thank you. I feel much better ♡
You're the person Hatoba-san wants to be?
Yes. That's right ♡

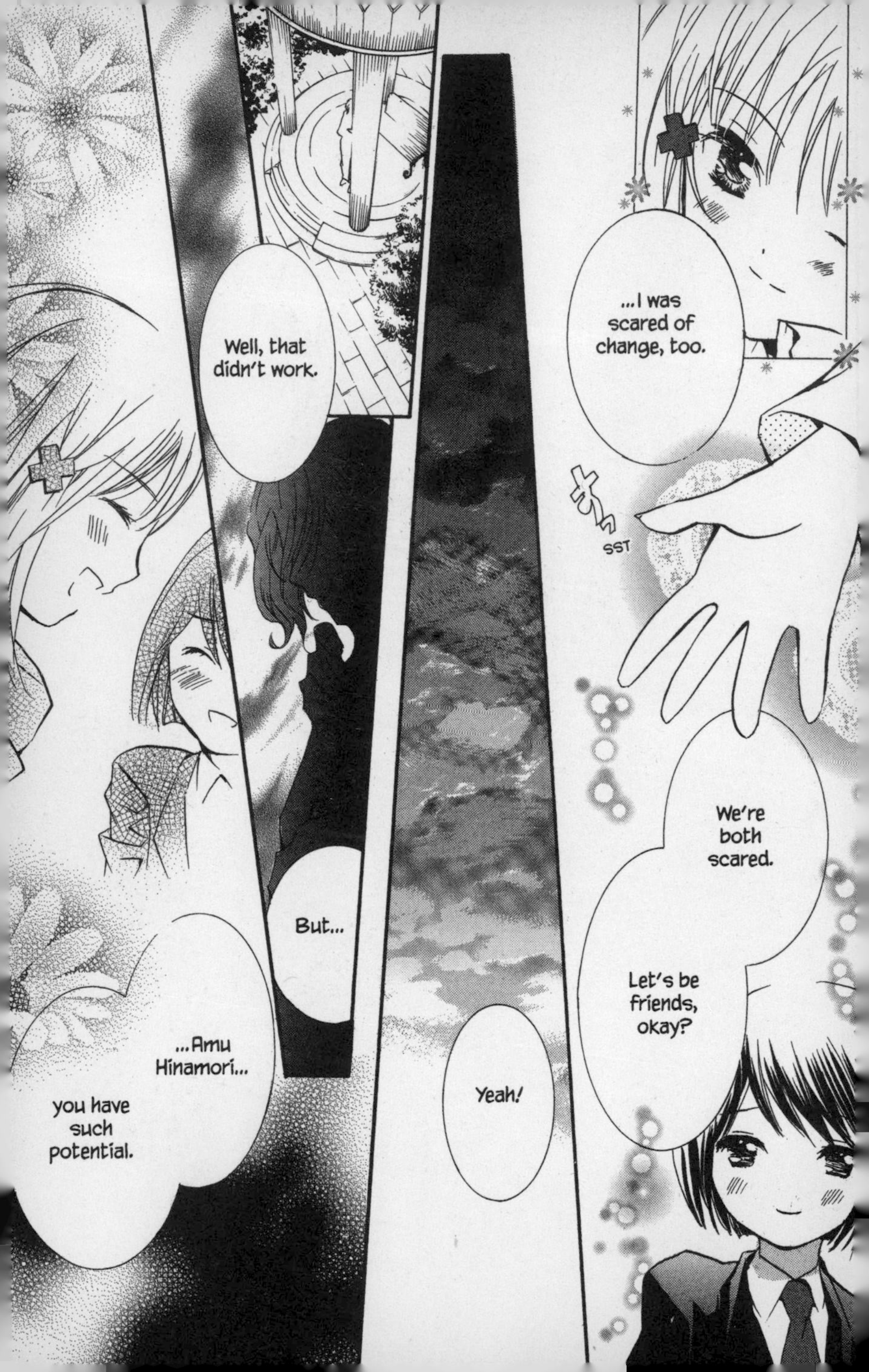
...I was scared of change, too.
SST
We're both scared.
Let's be friends, okay?
Yeah!
Well, that didn't work.
But...
...Amu Hinamori...
you have such potential.

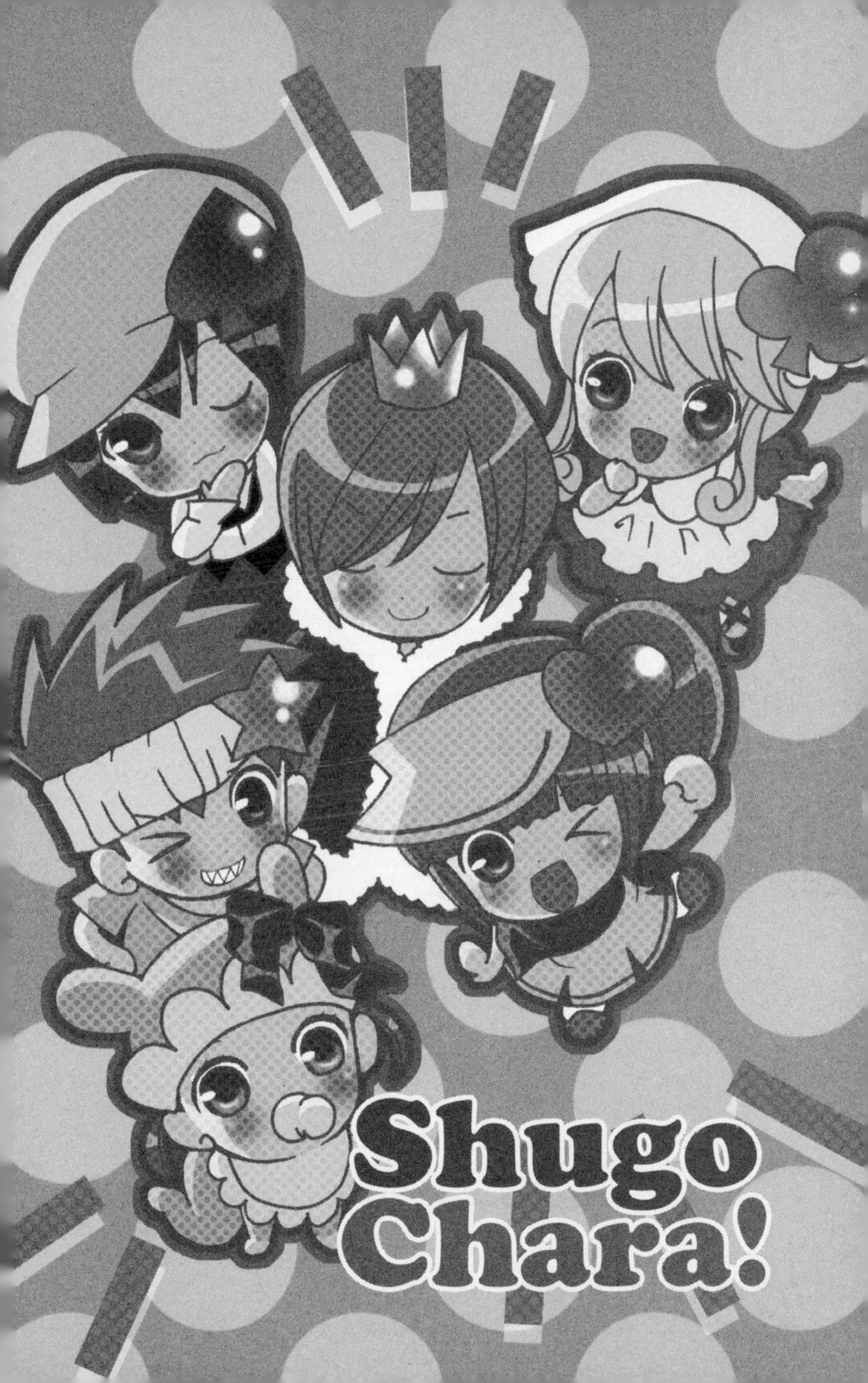
Shugo
Chara!

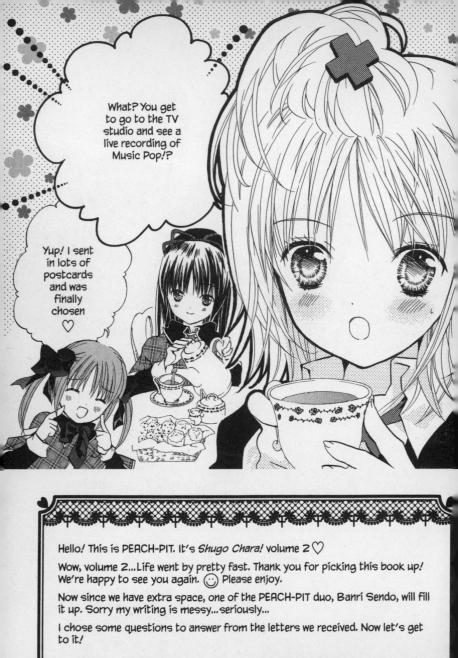

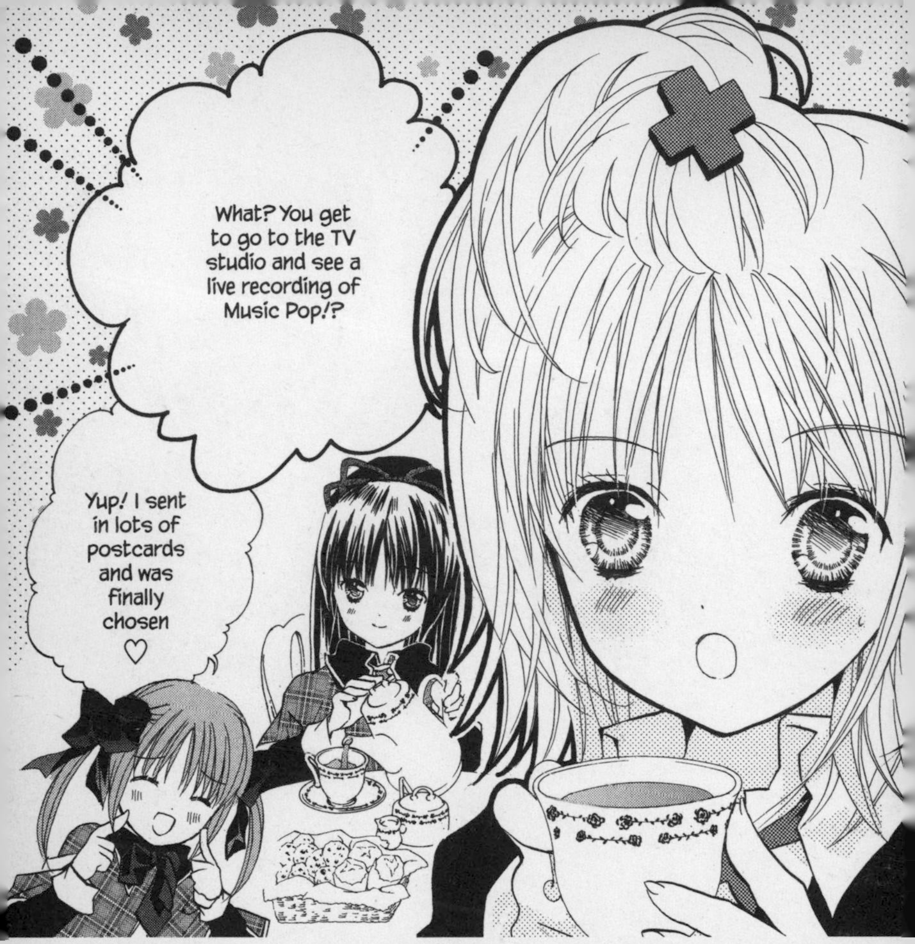
What? You get to go to the TV studio and see a live recording of Music Pop!?
Yup! I sent in lots of postcards and was finally chosen ♡

Hello! This is PEACH-PIT. It's *Shugo Chara!* volume 2 ♡

Wow, volume 2...Life went by pretty fast. Thank you for picking this book up! We're happy to see you again. ☺ Please enjoy.

Now since we have extra space, one of the PEACH-PIT duo, Banri Sendo, will fill it up. Sorry my writing is messy...seriously...

I chose some questions to answer from the letters we received. Now let's get to it!

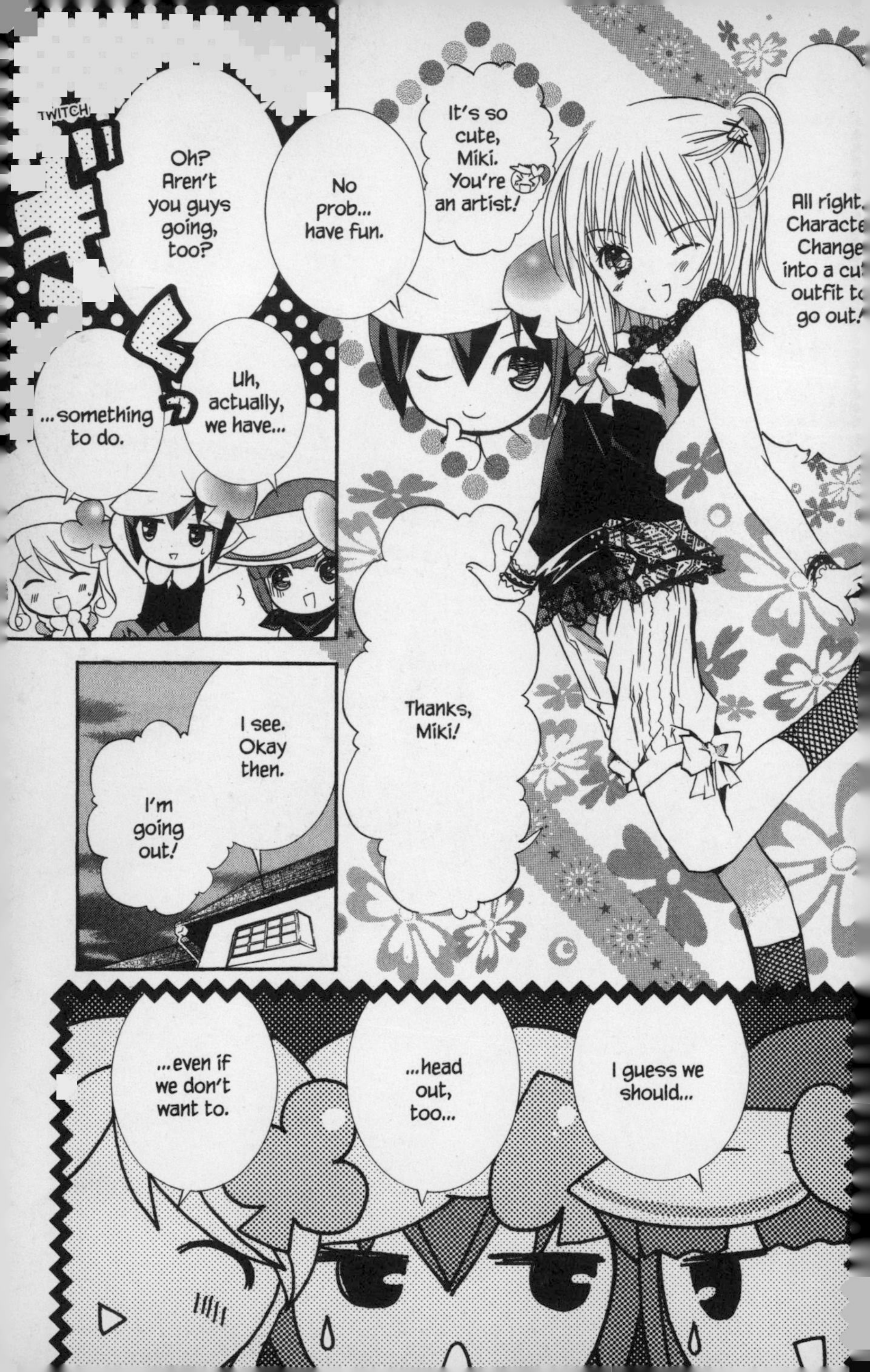
All right, Characte Change into a cu outfit t go out!
It's so cute, Miki. You're an artist!
No prob... have fun.
Thanks, Miki!
TWITCH
Oh? Aren't you guys going, too?
Uh, actually, we have...
...something to do.
I see. Okay then.
I'm going out!
I guess we should...
...head out, too...
...even if we don't want to.

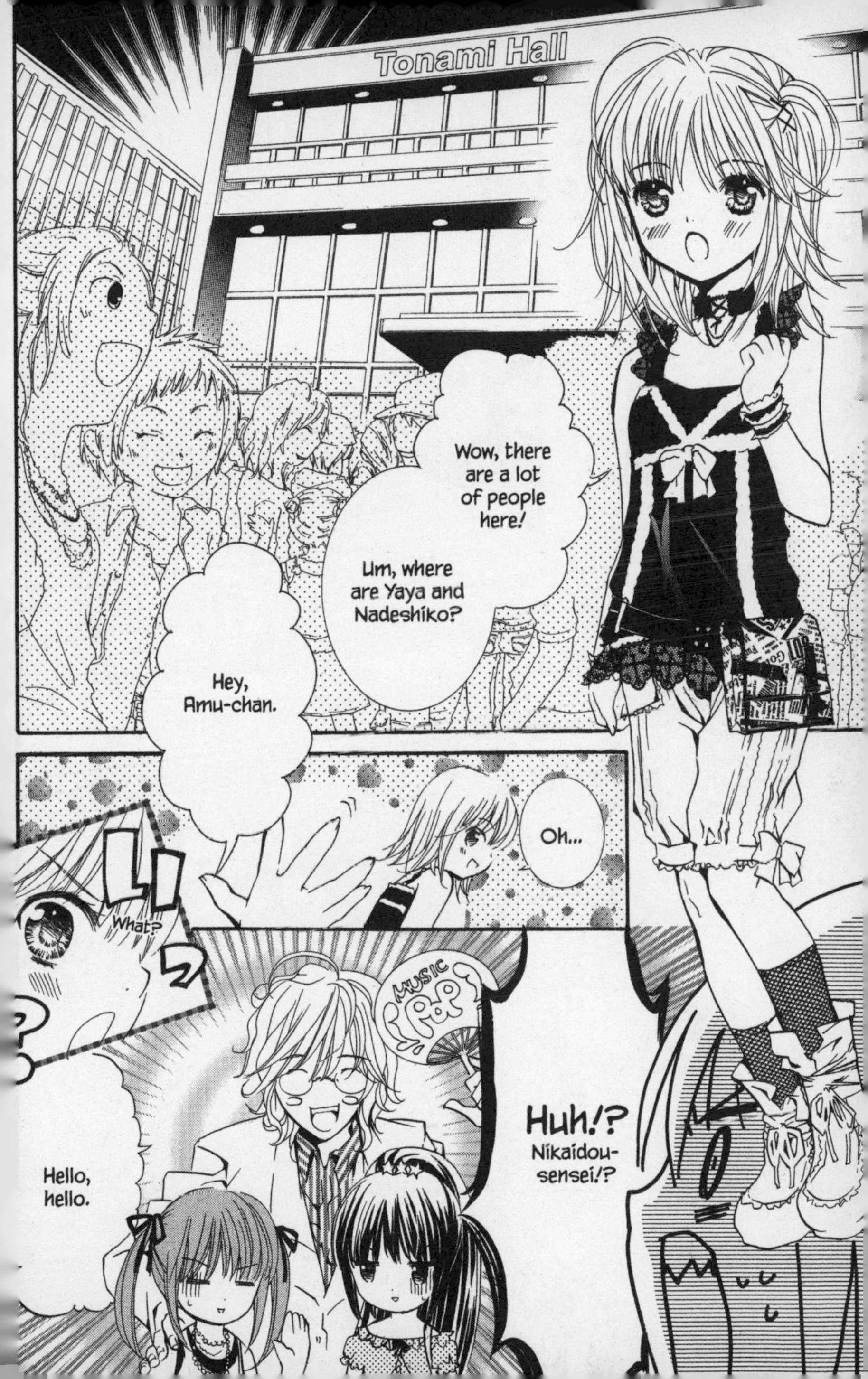
Tonami Hall
Wow, there are a lot of people here!
Um, where are Yaya and Nadeshiko?
Hey, Amu-chan.
Oh...
What?
Huh!? Nikaidou-sensei!?
MUSIC POP
Hello, hello.

SMILE

Are you three alone? No adults?

Hmm? What are you whispering about?

Hey, why is he here, too!?

Ummm... uh...

Hmm...I don't approve of you kids being alone.

Urgh...

Uh...we bumped into him.

I guess he applied for this, too...

Oh! Popcorn! Is it chocolate flavored?

And so he sits with us...

Uh...did you want some?

Yay, we got good seats.

MUSIC NEW

I can't do anything!

He's your teacher. Do something!

Urgh! He's so in the way!

Huh?

Think about it. Percentage-wise, there are only a few who can become a star.

Realistically speaking... right?

はっ
WOOSH

Oh, it got dark!

Thank you for waiting.

Music Pop...

...is about to start!

FLASH

ゆうき
YEAH

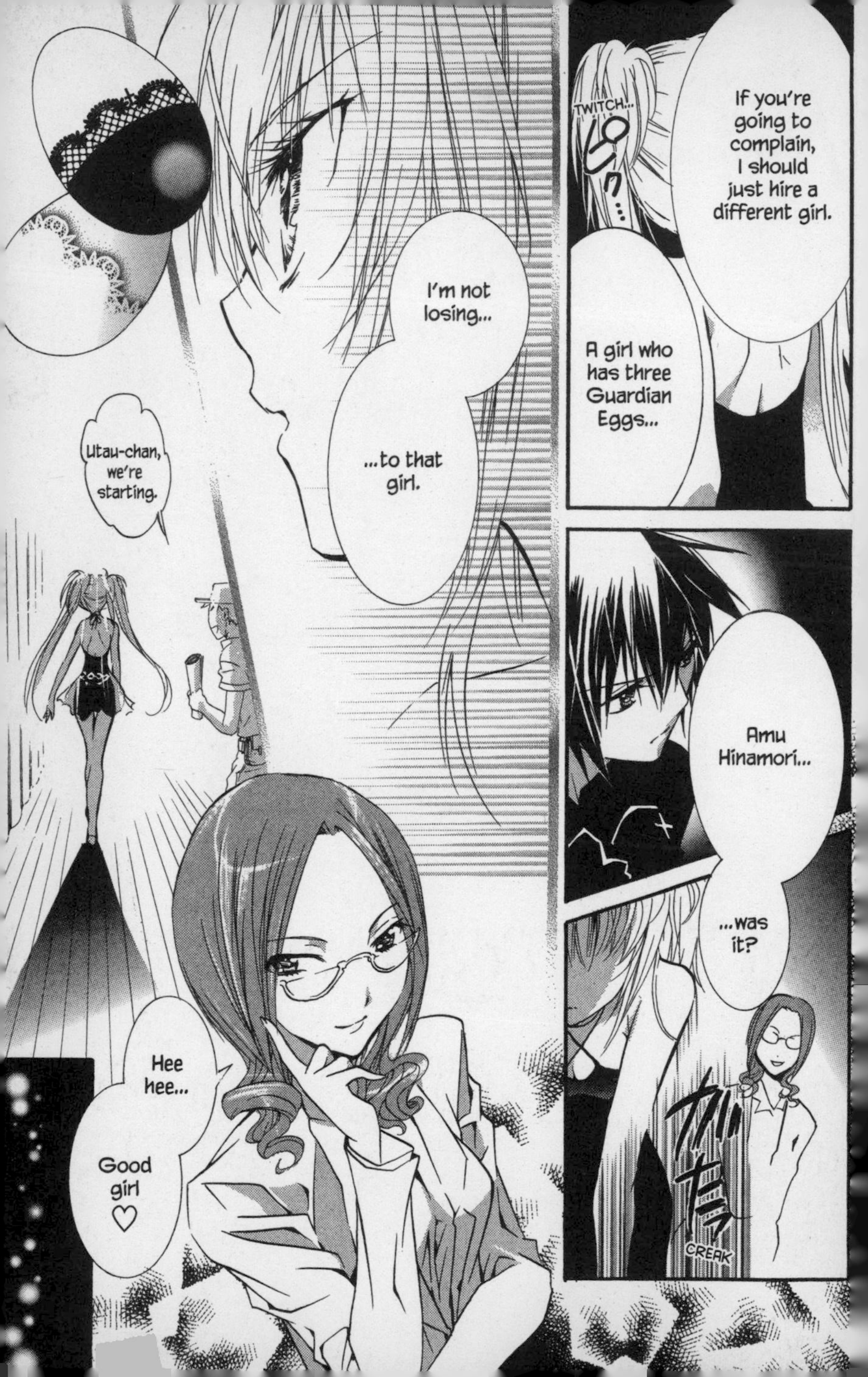
If you're going to complain, I should just hire a different girl.
TWITCH...
A girl who has three Guardian Eggs...
Amu Hinamori...
...was it?
CREAK
I'm not losing...
...to that girl.
Utau-chan, we're starting.
Hee hee...
Good girl ♡

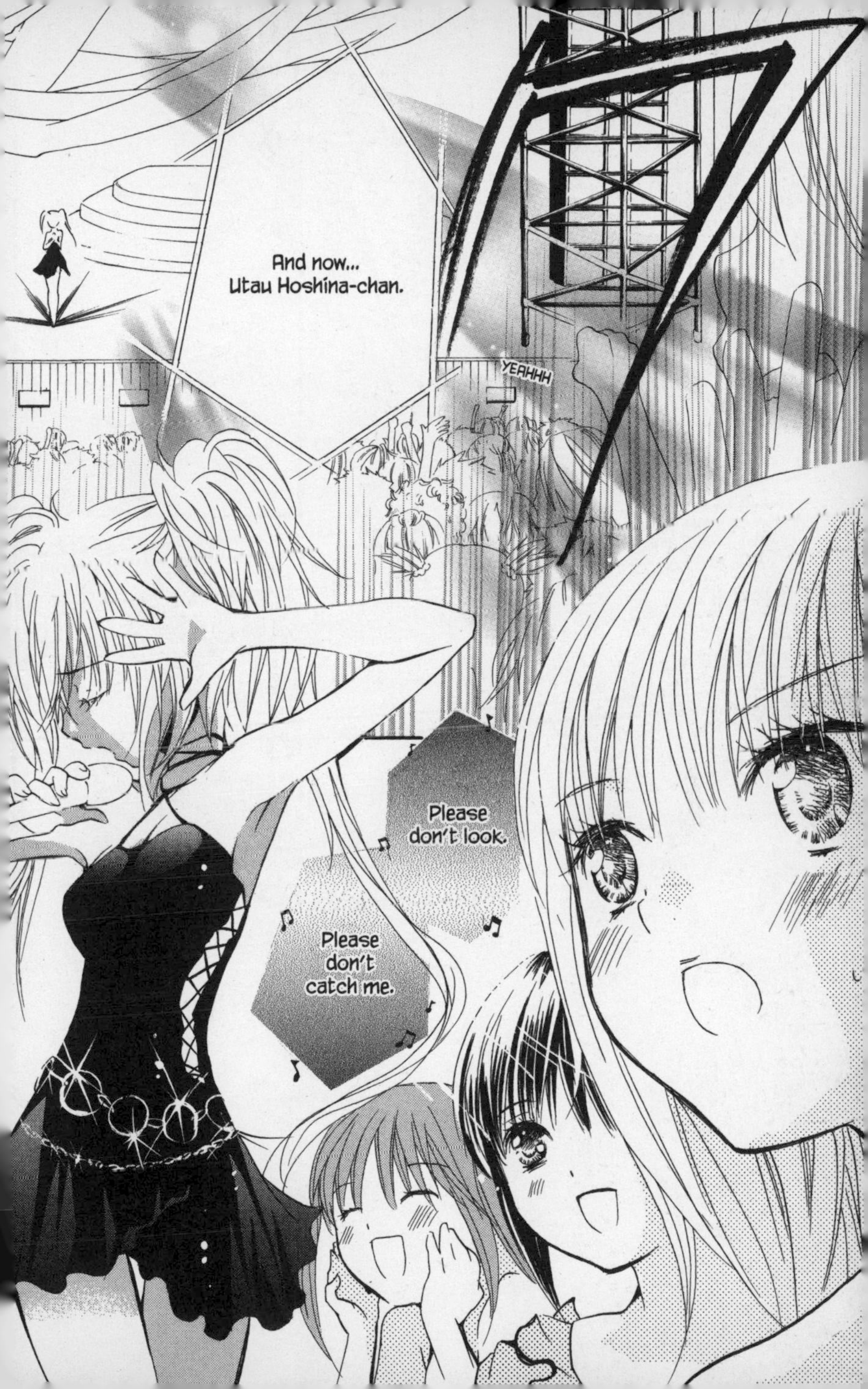
And now... Utau Hoshina-chan.
YEAHHH
Please don't look.
Please don't catch me.

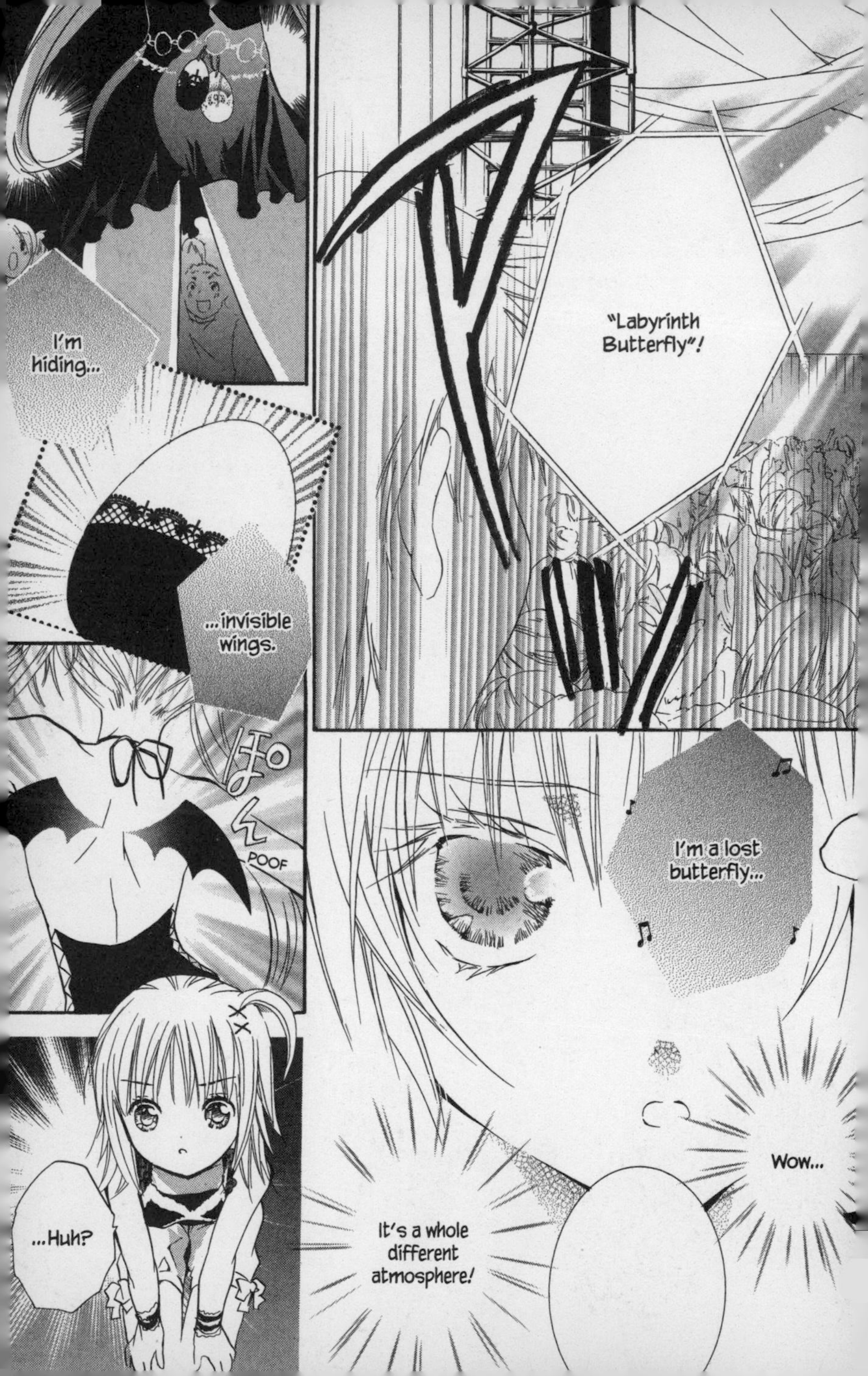
"Labyrinth Butterfly"!
I'm a lost butterfly...
Wow...
It's a whole different atmosphere!
I'm hiding...
...invisible wings.
POOF
...Huh?

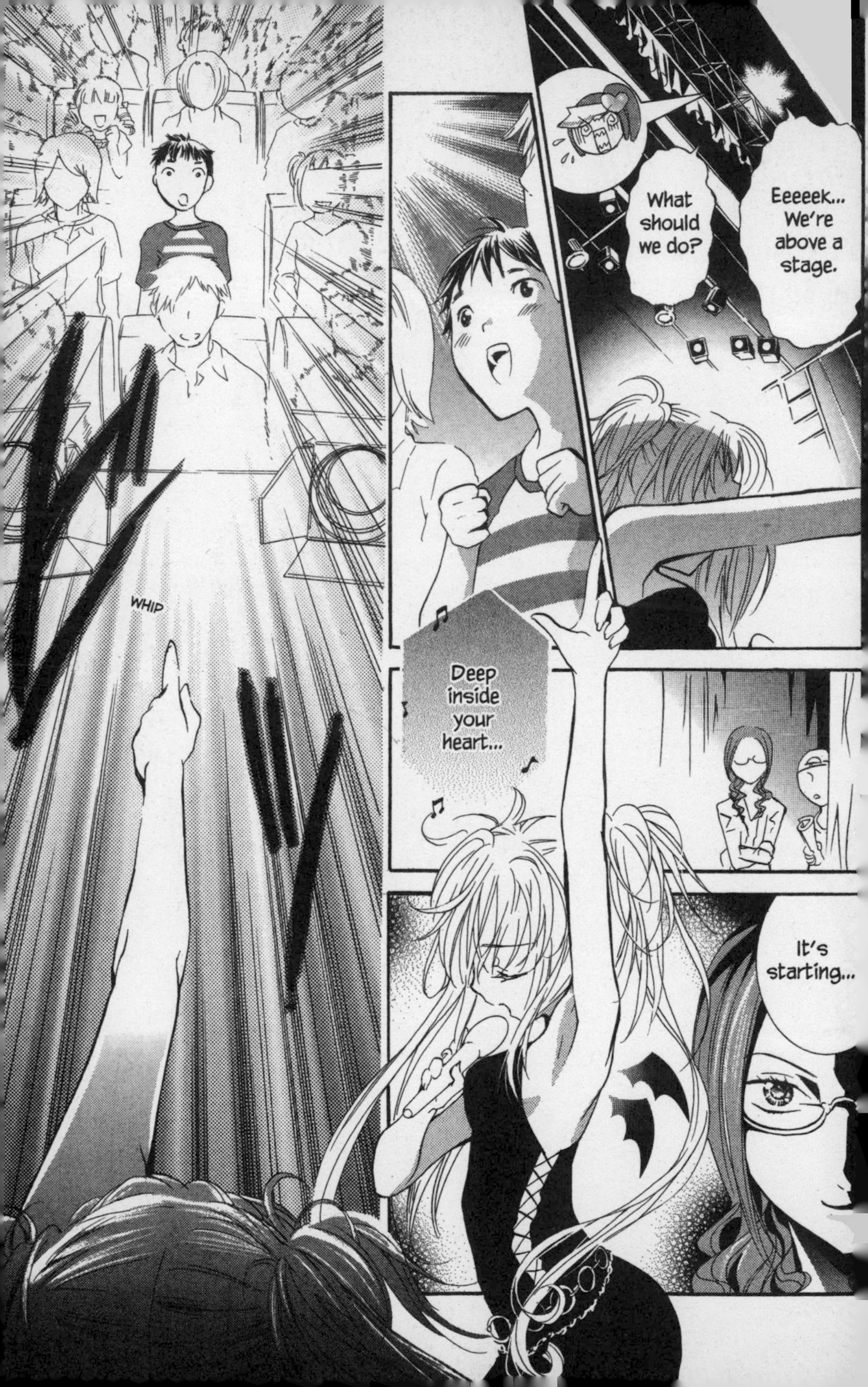
Eeeeek... We're above a stage.
What should we do?
Deep inside your heart...
It's starting...
WHIP

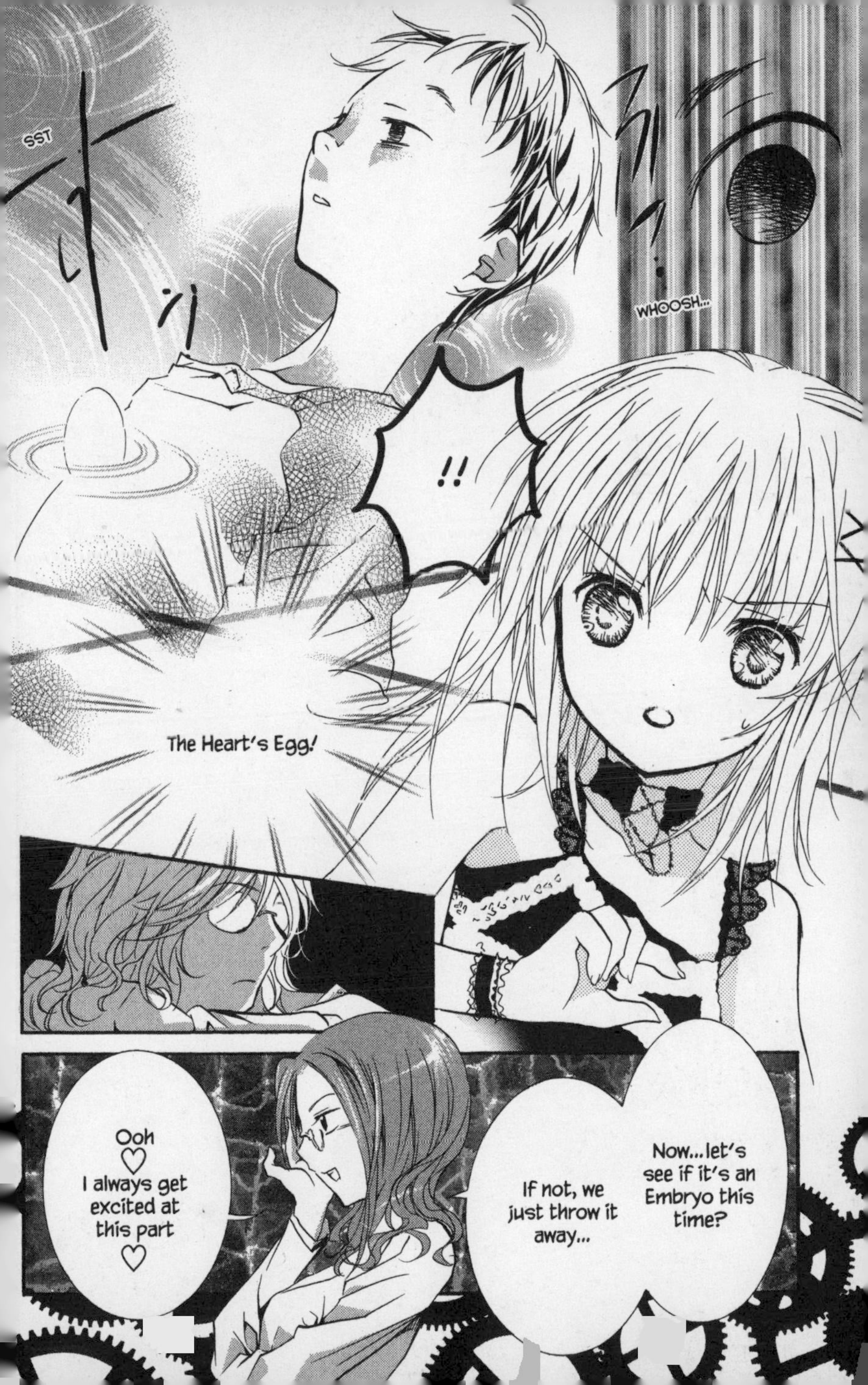
WHOOSH...
SST
!!
The Heart's Egg!
Now...let's see if it's an Embryo this time?
If not, we just throw it away...
Ooh ♡ I always get excited at this part ♡

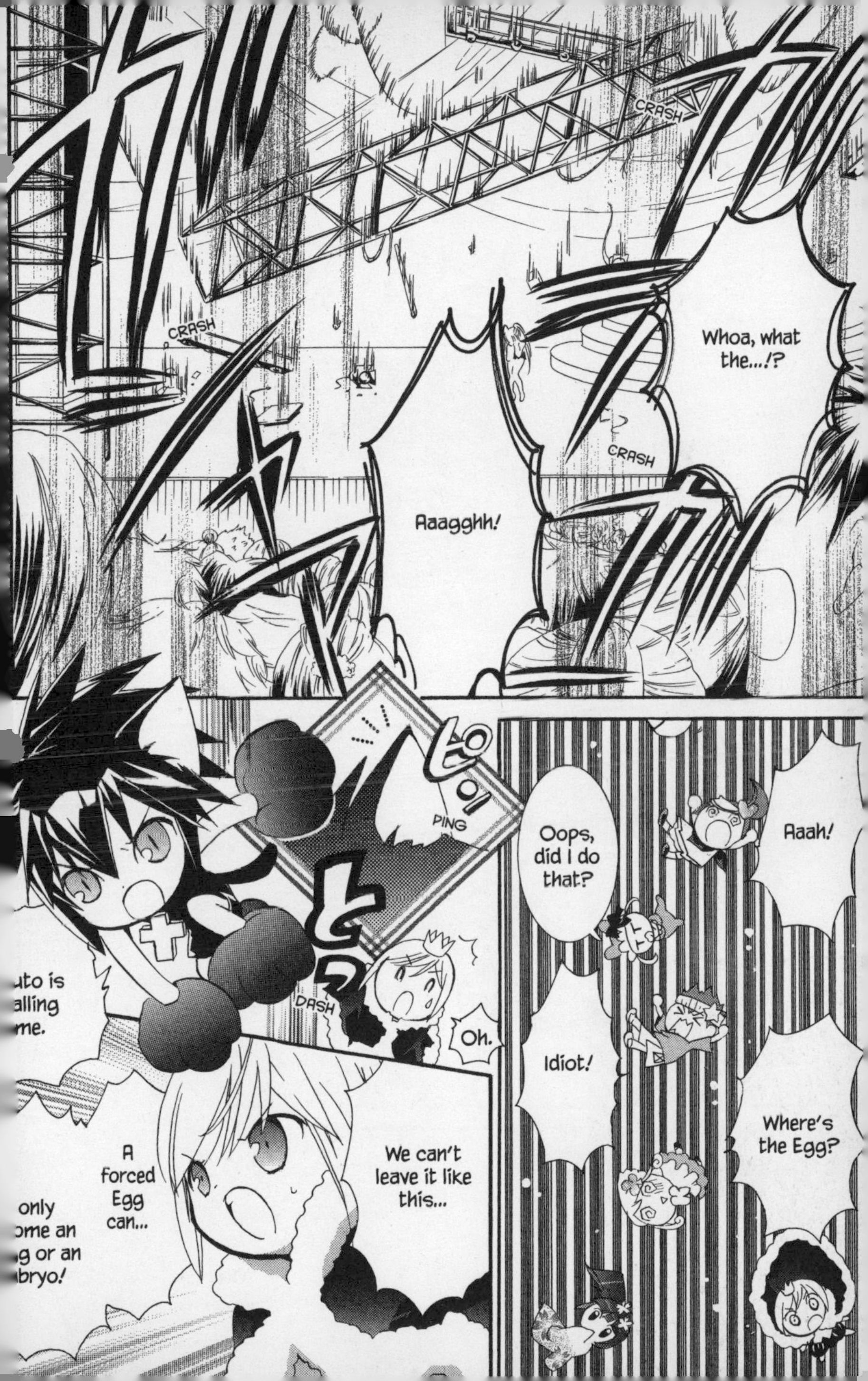
CRASH
Whoa, what the...!?
CRASH
CRASH
Aaagghh!
Aaah!
Oops, did I do that?
Where's the Egg?
Idiot!
PING
DASH
Oh.
uto is alling me.
We can't leave it like this...
A forced Egg can...
only ome an g or an bryo!

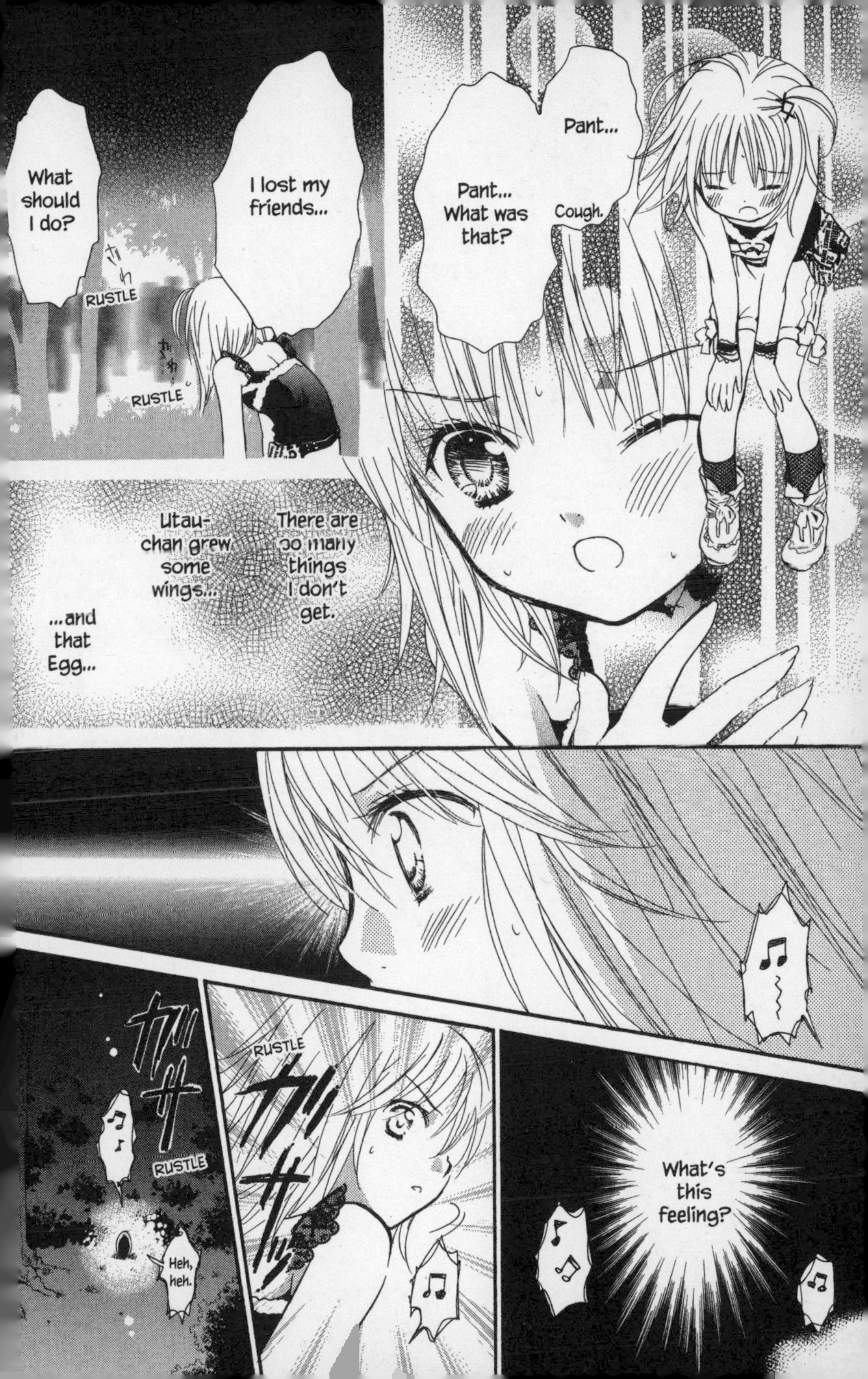
Pant...
Pant... What was that?
Cough.
I lost my friends...
What should I do?
RUSTLE
RUSTLE
There are so many things I don't get.
Utau-chan grew some wings...
...and that Egg...
What's this feeling?
RUSTLE
RUSTLE
Heh, heh.

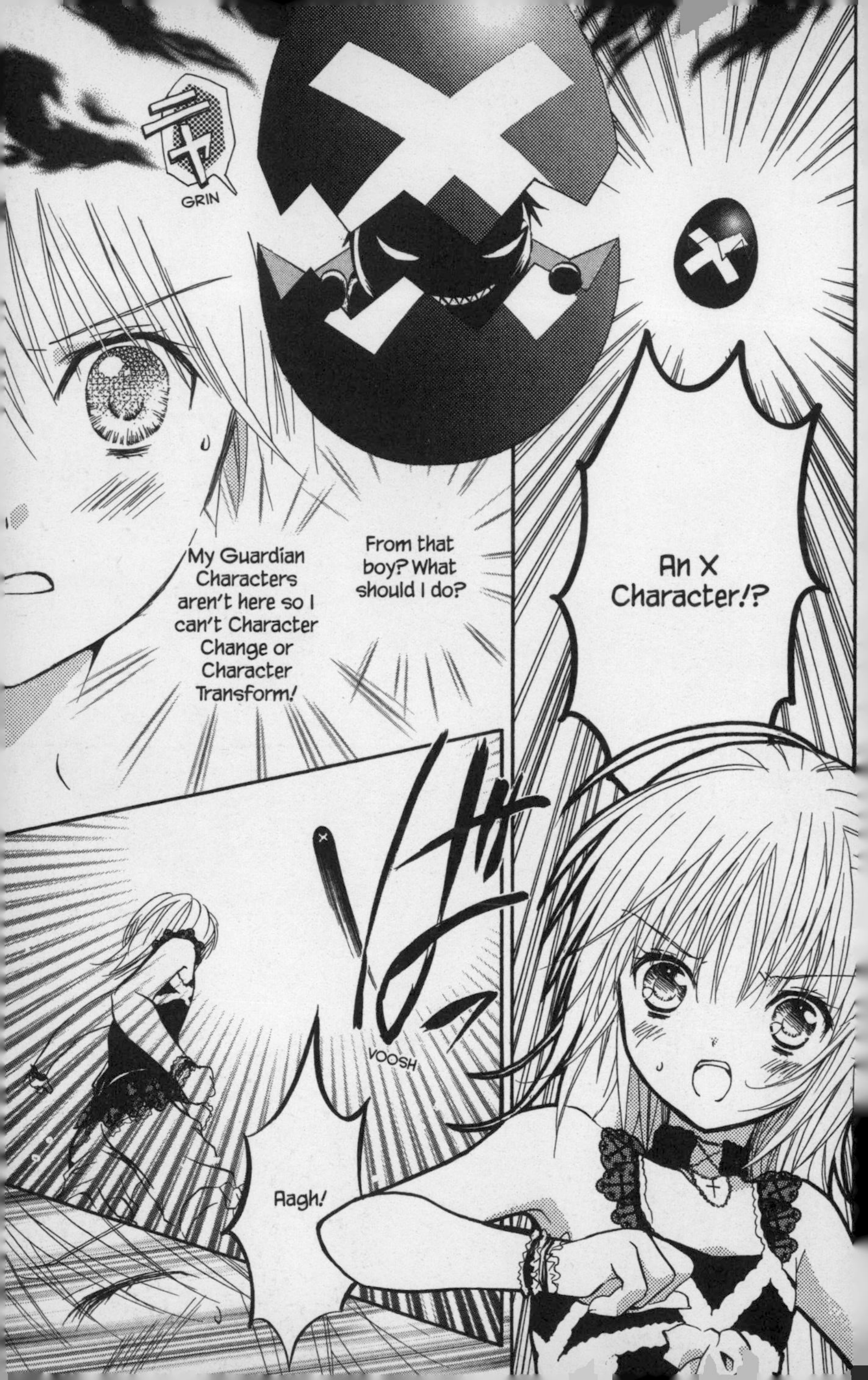
An X
Character!?
GRIN
From that boy? What should I do?
My Guardian Characters aren't here so I can't Character Change or Character Transform!
VOOSH
Aagh!

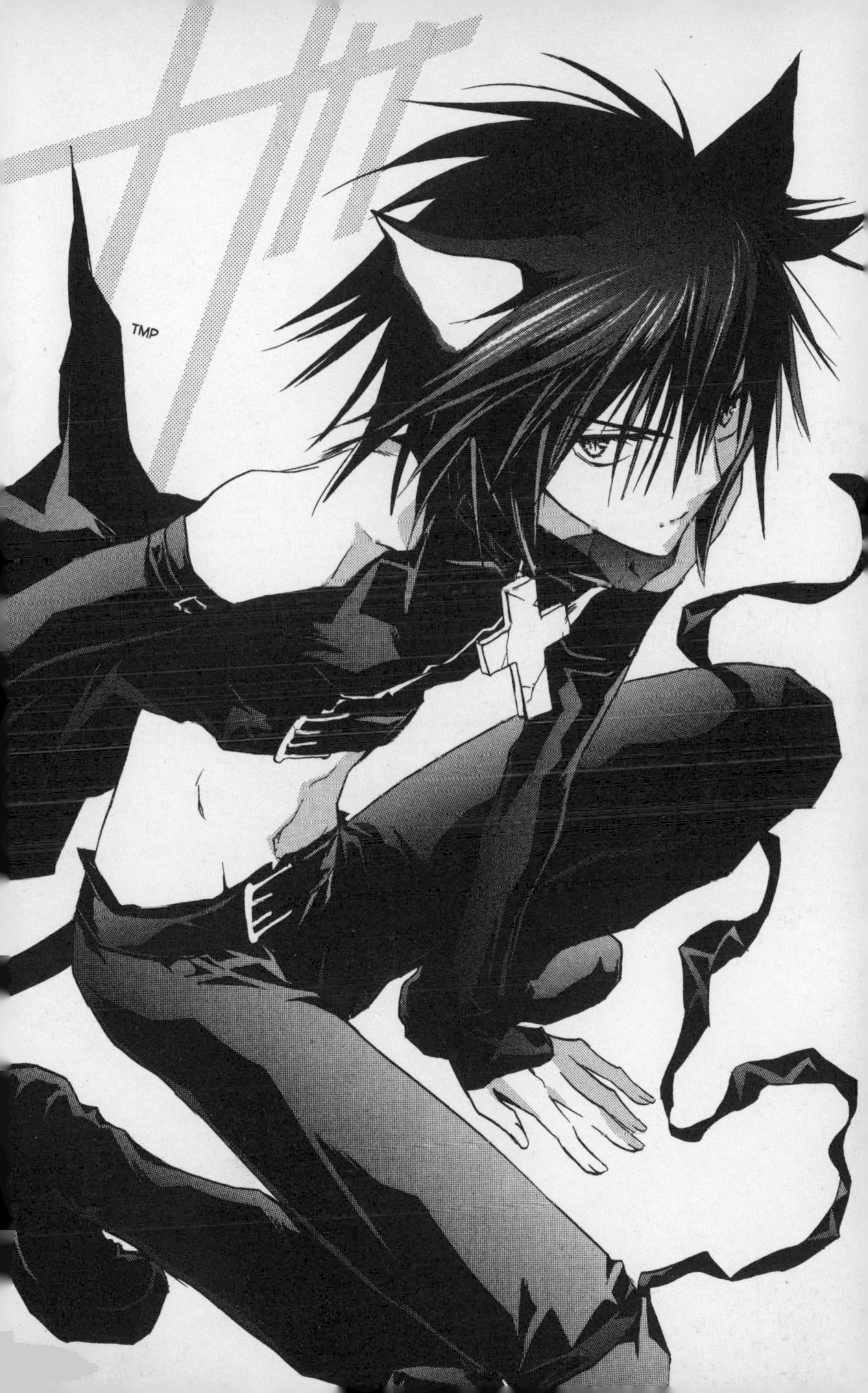
TMP

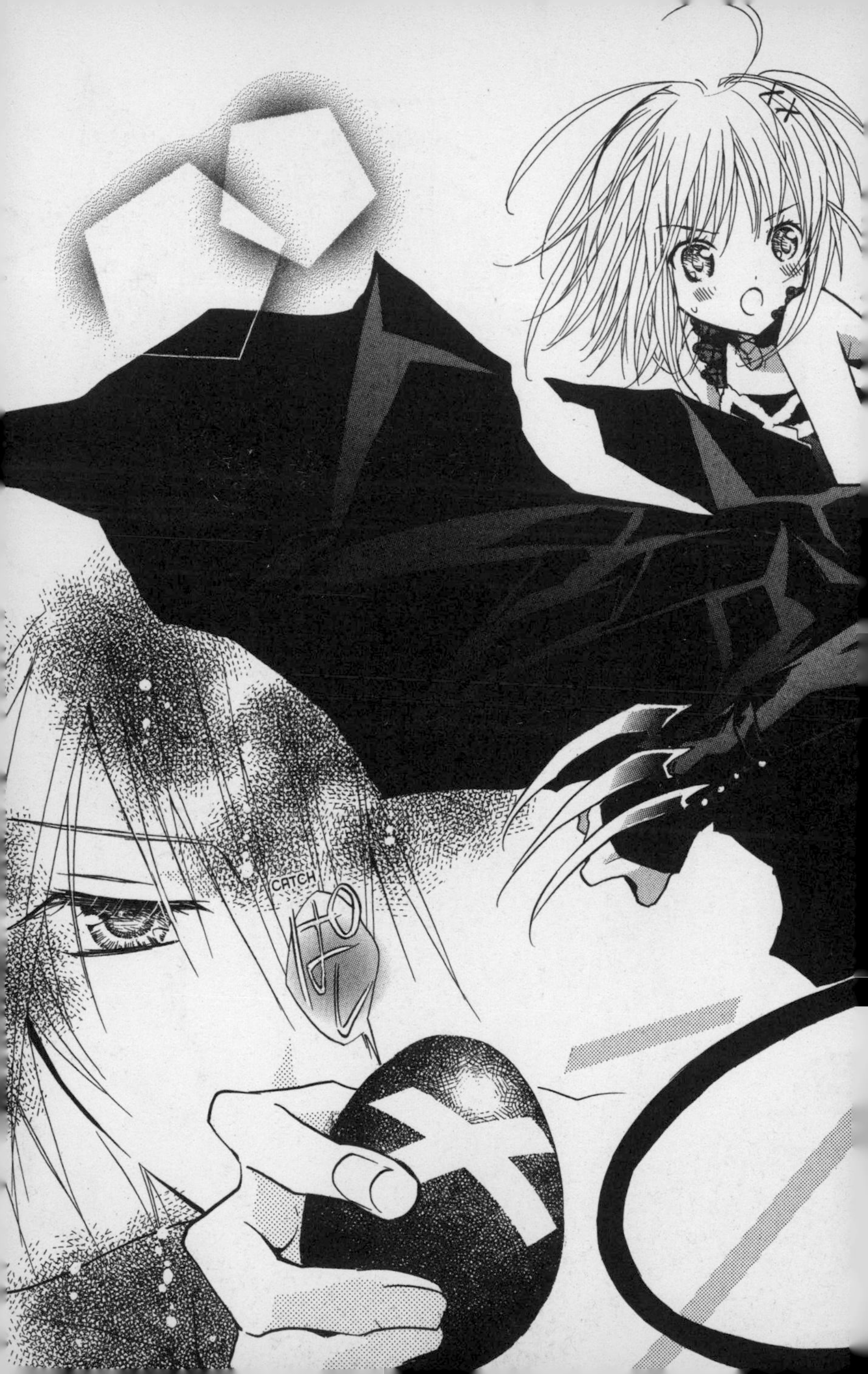
CATCH

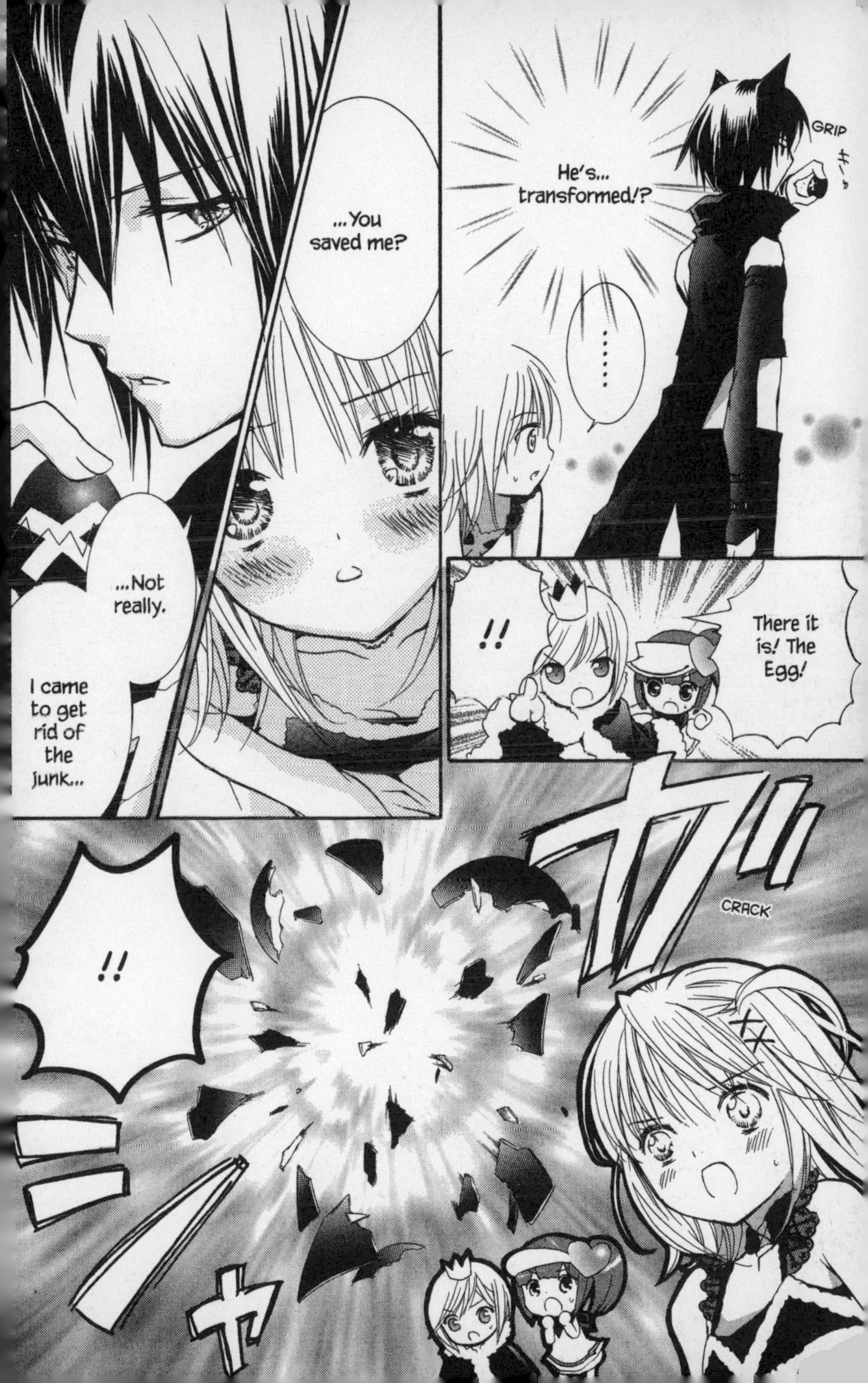
GRIP
He's... transformed!?
......
There it is! The Egg!
!!
...You saved me?
...Not really.
I came to get rid of the junk...
CRACK
!!

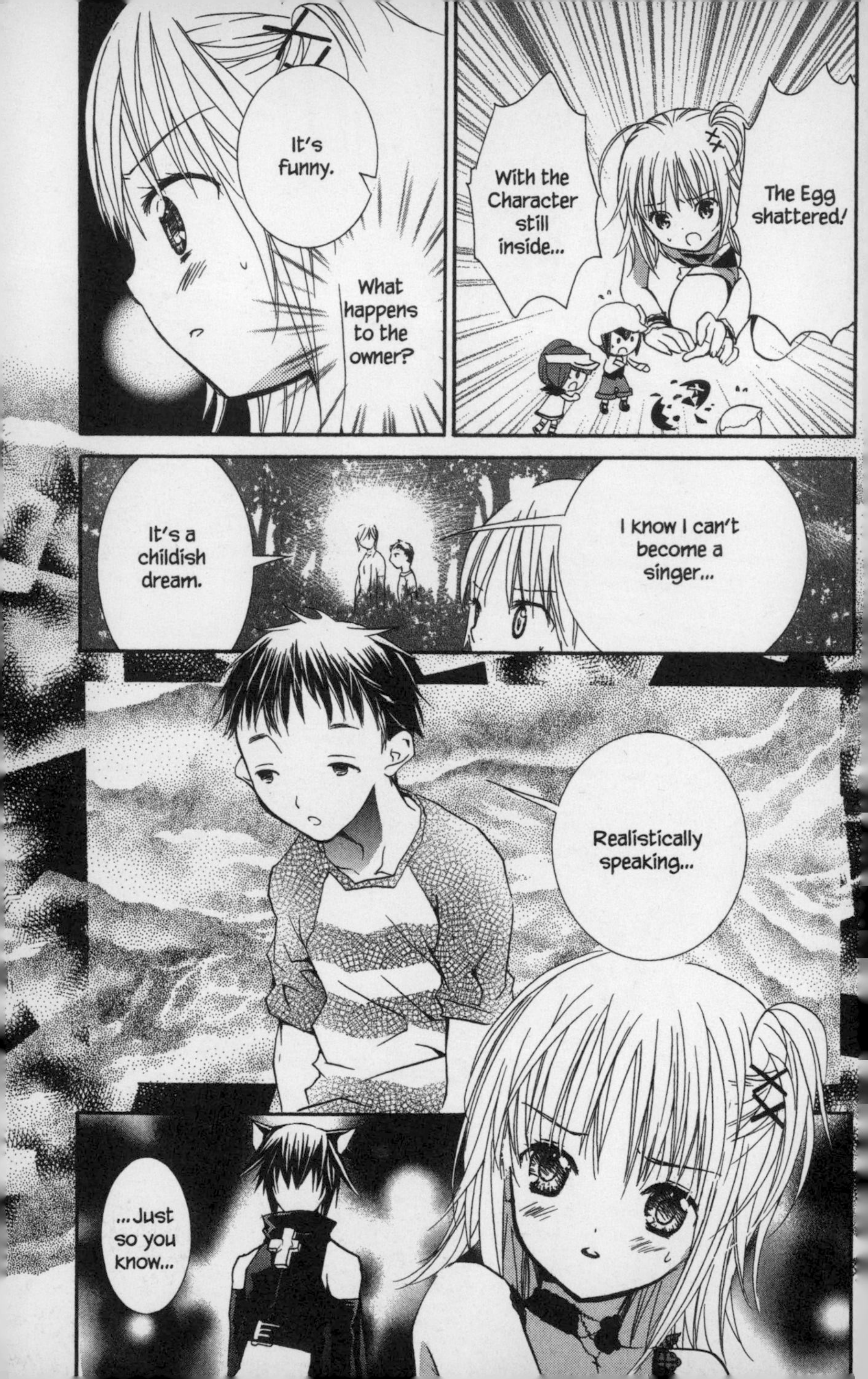
The Egg shattered!
With the Character still inside...
It's funny.
What happens to the owner?
I know I can't become a singer...
It's a childish dream.
Realistically speaking...
...Just so you know...

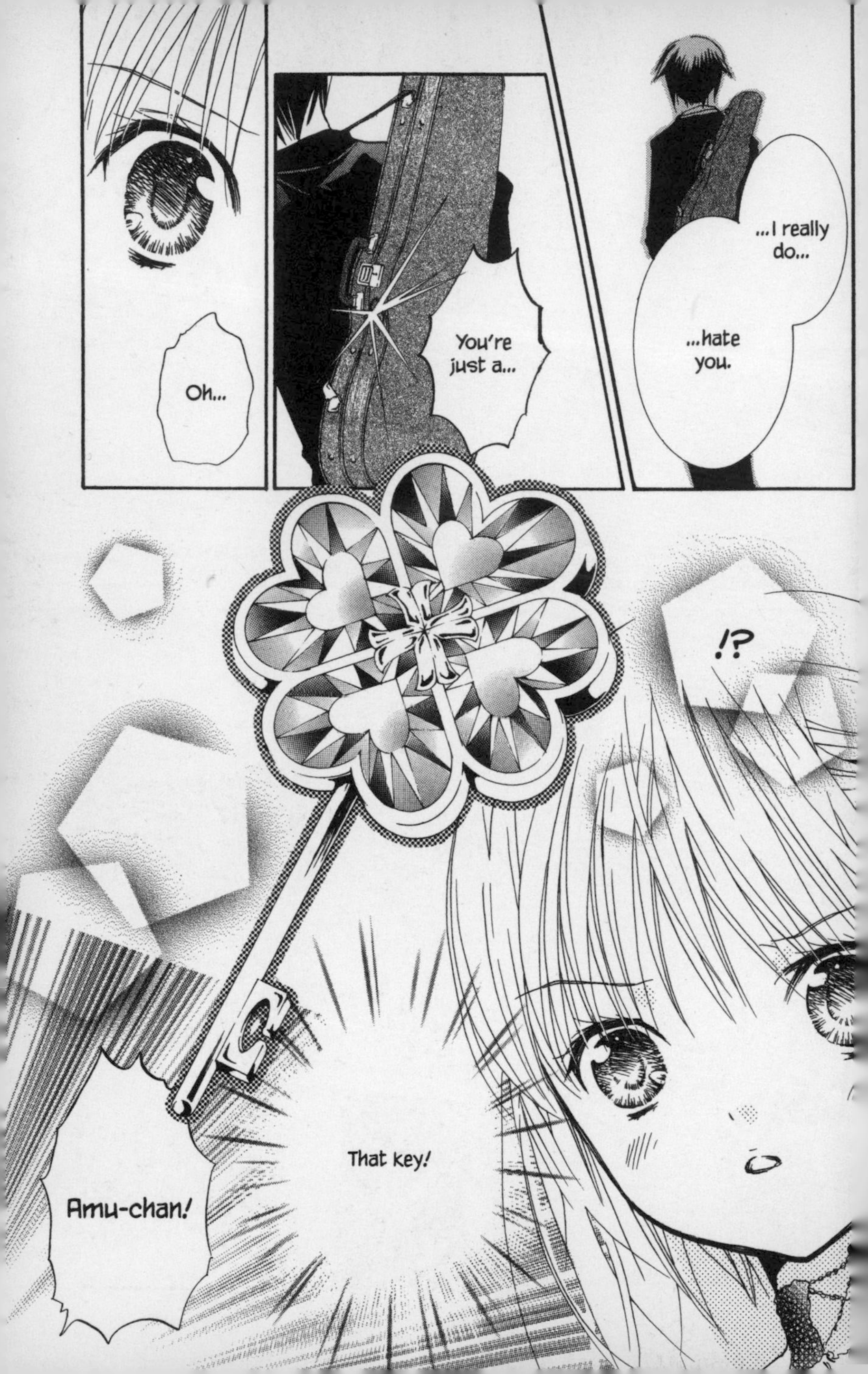
...I really do...
...hate you.
You're just a...
Oh...
!?
That key!
Amu-chan!

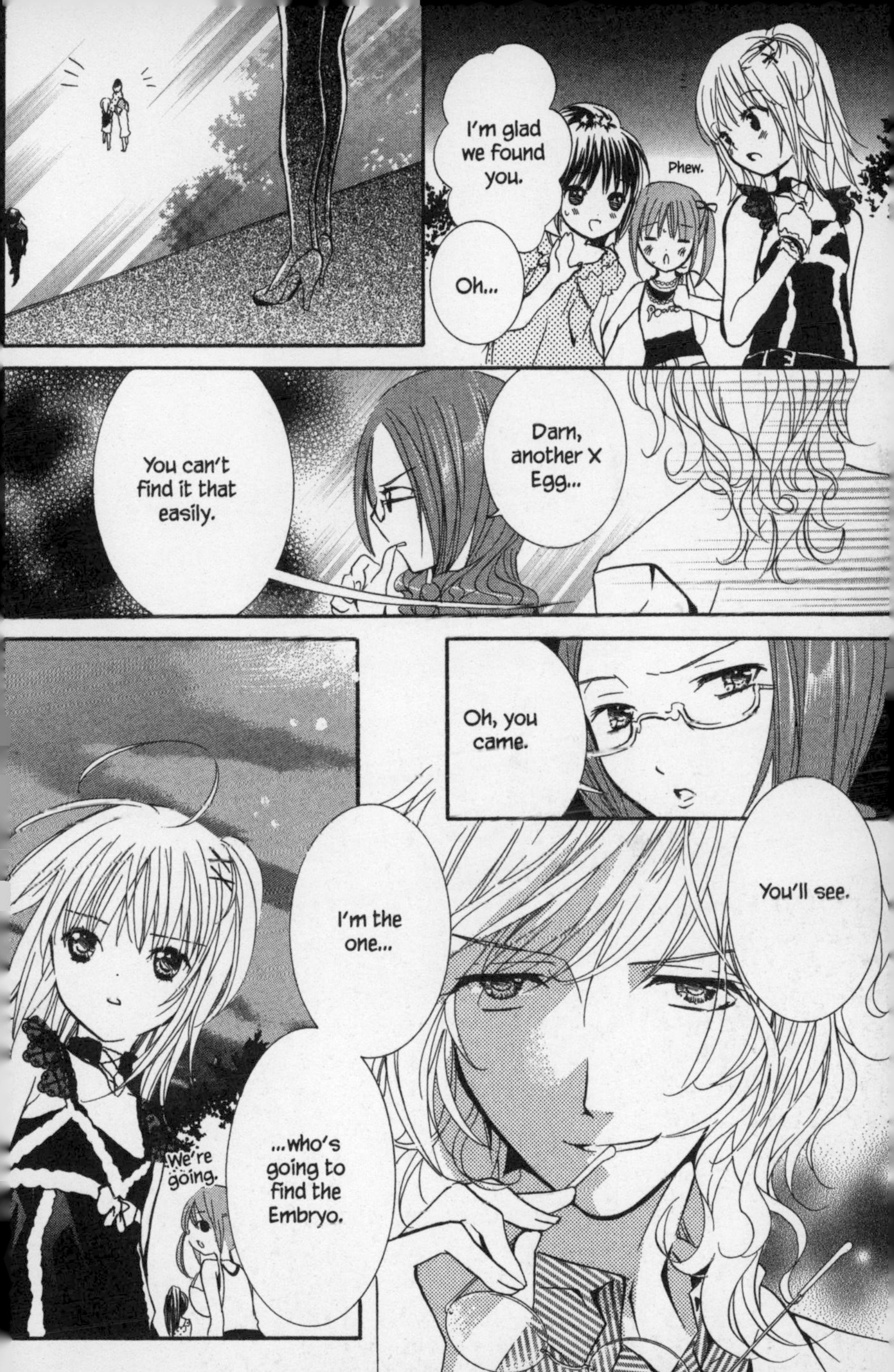
I'm glad we found you.
Phew.
Oh...
Darn, another X Egg...
You can't find it that easily.
Oh, you came.
You'll see.
I'm the one...
...who's going to find the Embryo.
We're going.

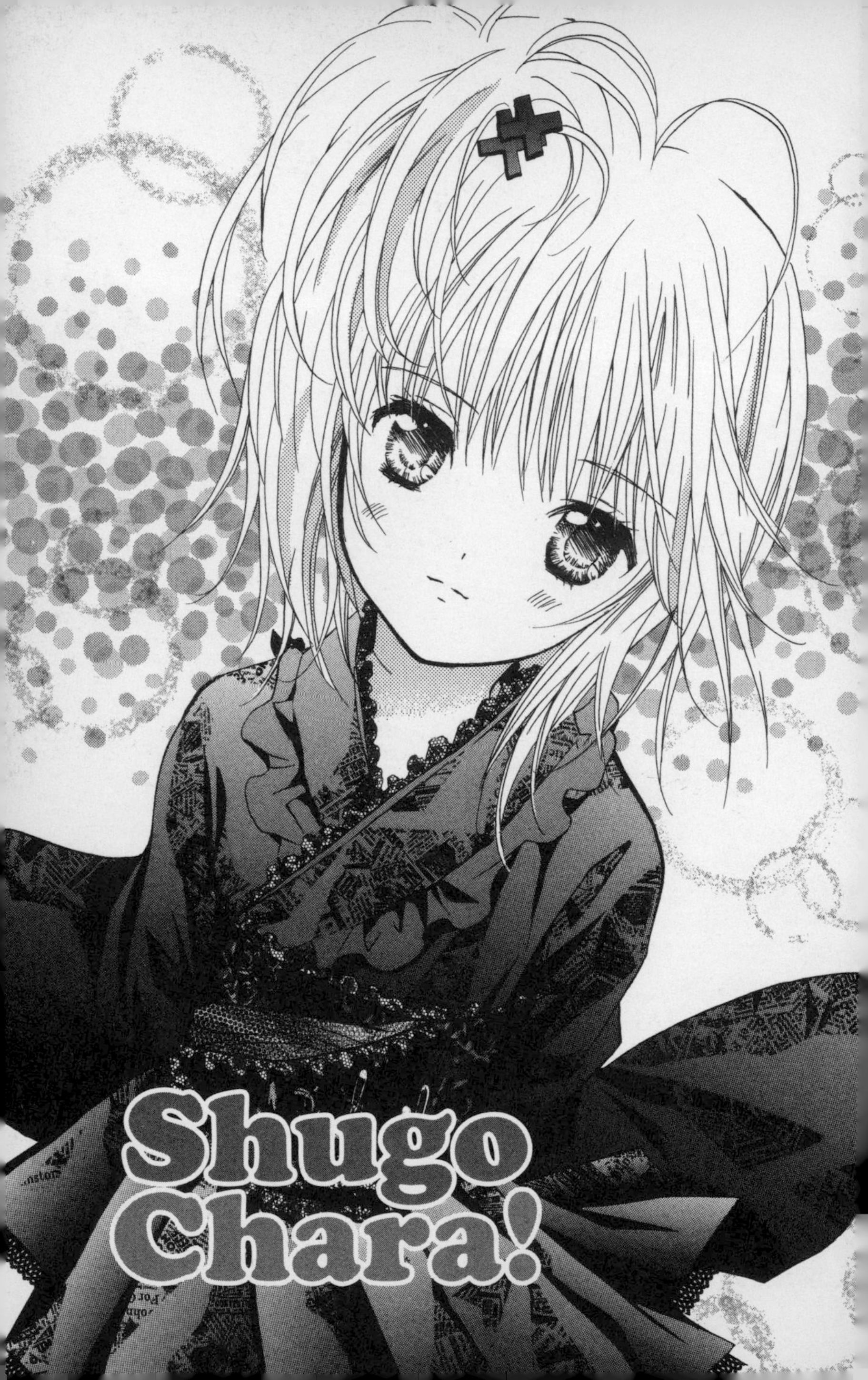
Shugo
Chara!

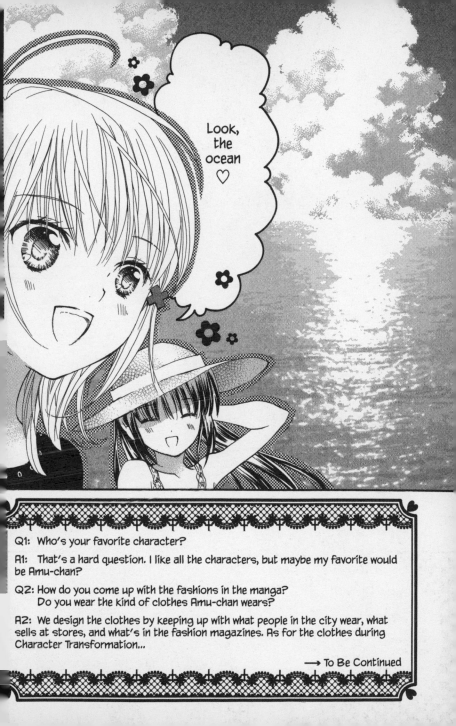

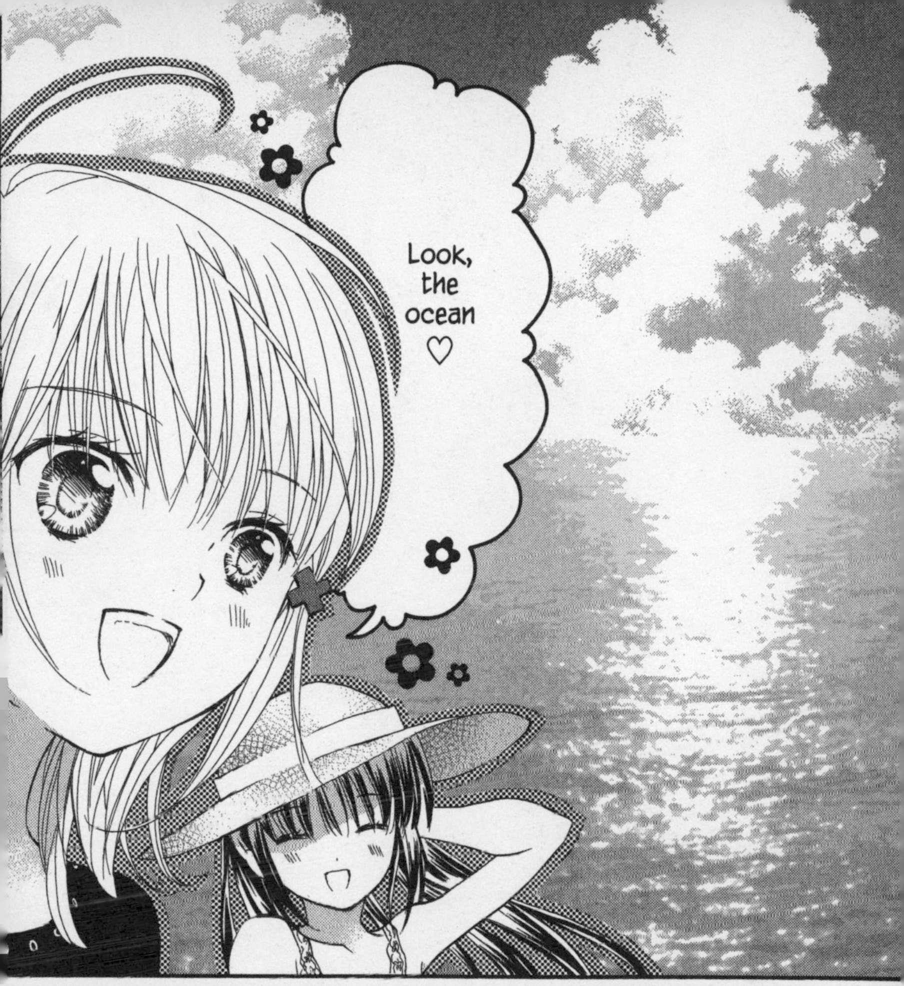
Look, the ocean ♡

Q1: Who's your favorite character?

A1: That's a hard question. I like all the characters, but maybe my favorite would be Amu-chan?

Q2: How do you come up with the fashions in the manga?
Do you wear the kind of clothes Amu-chan wears?

A2: We design the clothes by keeping up with what people in the city wear, what sells at stores, and what's in the fashion magazines. As for the clothes during Character Transformation...

⟶ To Be Continued

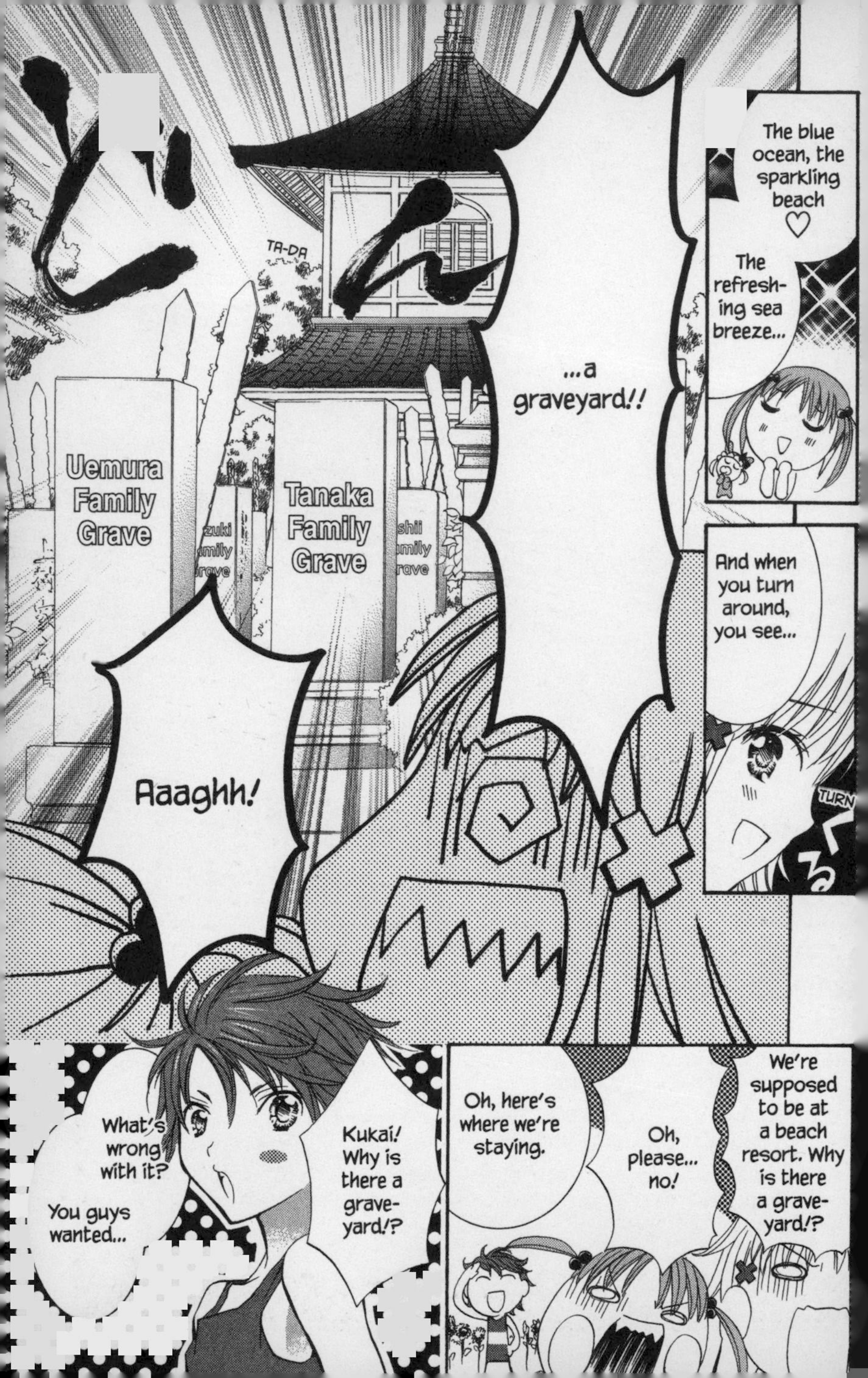
The blue ocean, the sparkling beach ♡
The refresh-ing sea breeze...
And when you turn around, you see...
TURN
...a graveyard!!
TA-DA
Uemura Family Grave
Tanaka Family Grave
Aaaghh!
We're supposed to be at a beach resort. Why is there a grave-yard!?
Oh, please... no!
Oh, here's where we're staying.
Kukai! Why is there a grave-yard!?
What's wrong with it?
You guys wanted...

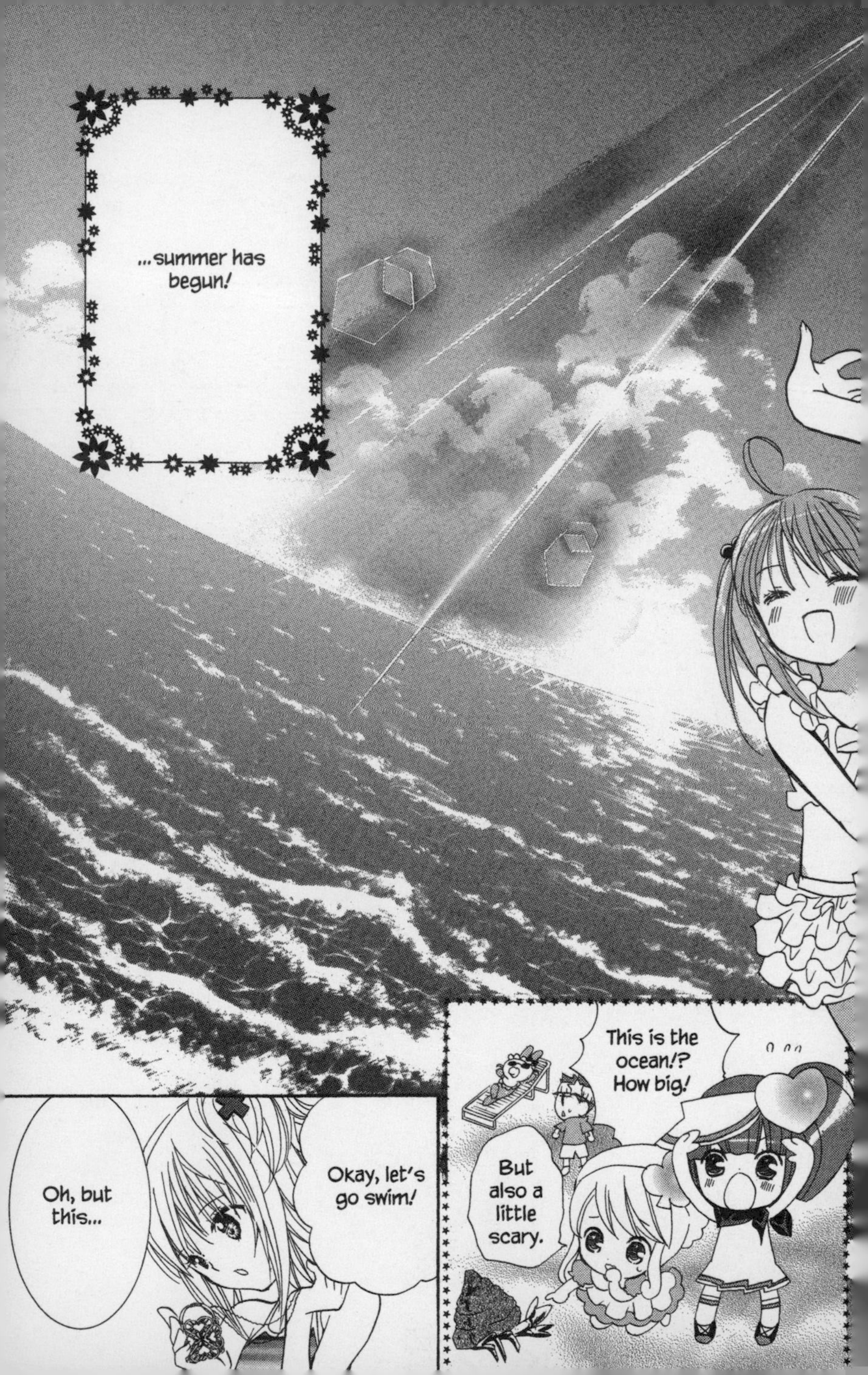
...summer has begun!
This is the ocean!? How big!
But also a little scary.
Okay, let's go swim!
Oh, but this...

That key... looked like this lock.

Why did he have it?

Hee hee...I don't want to get sun tanned.

You never participate in gym class, either...

?

I'll hold the lock for you.

Forget that guy!

No, I'm not going to think about it now!

You idiots!!!

No, I'm not. I'll be sitting here.

Huh? Nadeshiko, you're not swimming?

TWITCH

TWITCH

I don't think they had elementary school at the dawn of time...

Oh my.

But no, you're worried about UV rays!

That's what summer has been about for elementary school kids since the dawn of time!

ROOOOAAARR

GRIP

Summer vacation is about watermelons, shaved ice, popsicles... summer festivals with fireworks...

Agh, it's salty!

Take some seawater!

Ozone hole, come and get me! I'll show you what a true elementary school student is like.

AAH

SPLASH

FLASH

Oh, look! Over there!

Let's ☆ enjoy a true summer!

...and the ocean!!!

OOGA

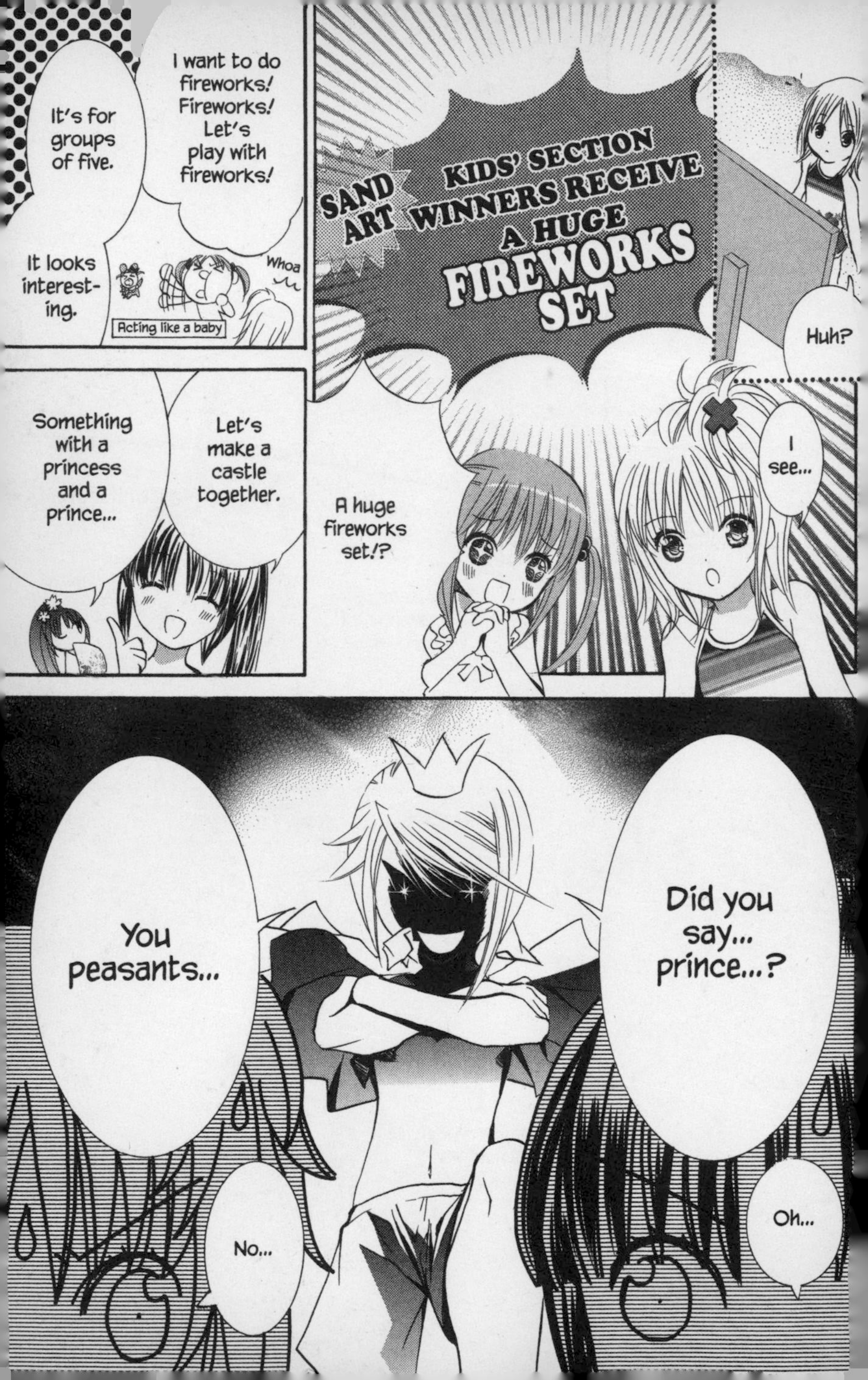
Huh?
SAND ART
KIDS' SECTION WINNERS RECEIVE A HUGE FIREWORKS SET
I see...
A huge fireworks set!?
I want to do fireworks! Fireworks! Let's play with fireworks!
It's for groups of five.
Whoa
It looks interest-ing.
Acting like a baby
Let's make a castle together.
Something with a princess and a prince...
Did you say... prince...?
You peasants...
Oh...
No...

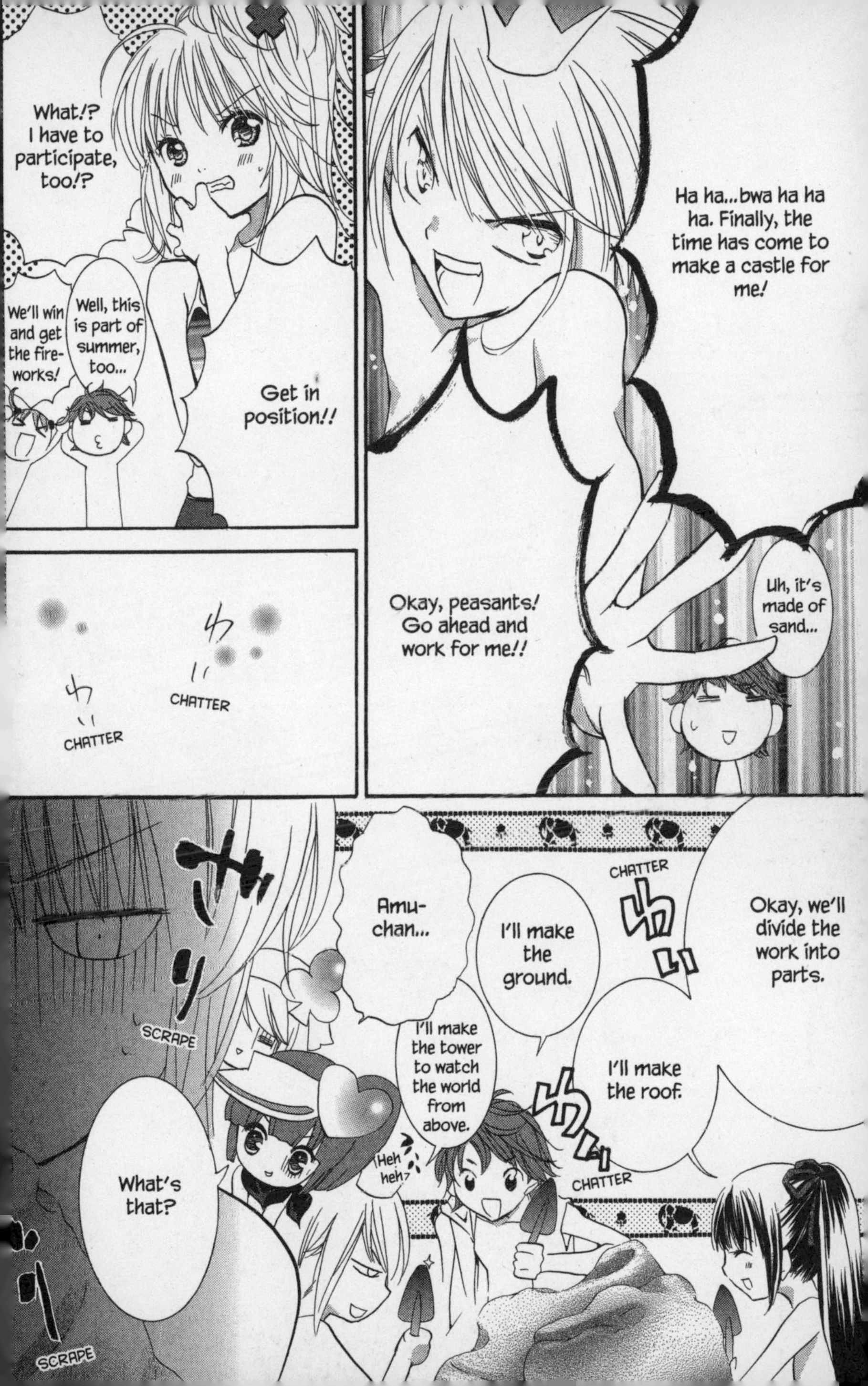
Ha ha...bwa ha ha ha. Finally, the time has come to make a castle for me!
Okay, peasants! Go ahead and work for me!!
Uh, it's made of sand...
What!? I have to participate, too!?
Well, this is part of summer, too...
We'll win and get the fire-works!
Get in position!!
CHATTER
CHATTER
Okay, we'll divide the work into parts.
CHATTER
I'll make the ground.
I'll make the roof.
Amu-chan...
I'll make the tower to watch the world from above.
CHATTER
Heh heh
What's that?
SCRAPE
SCRAPE

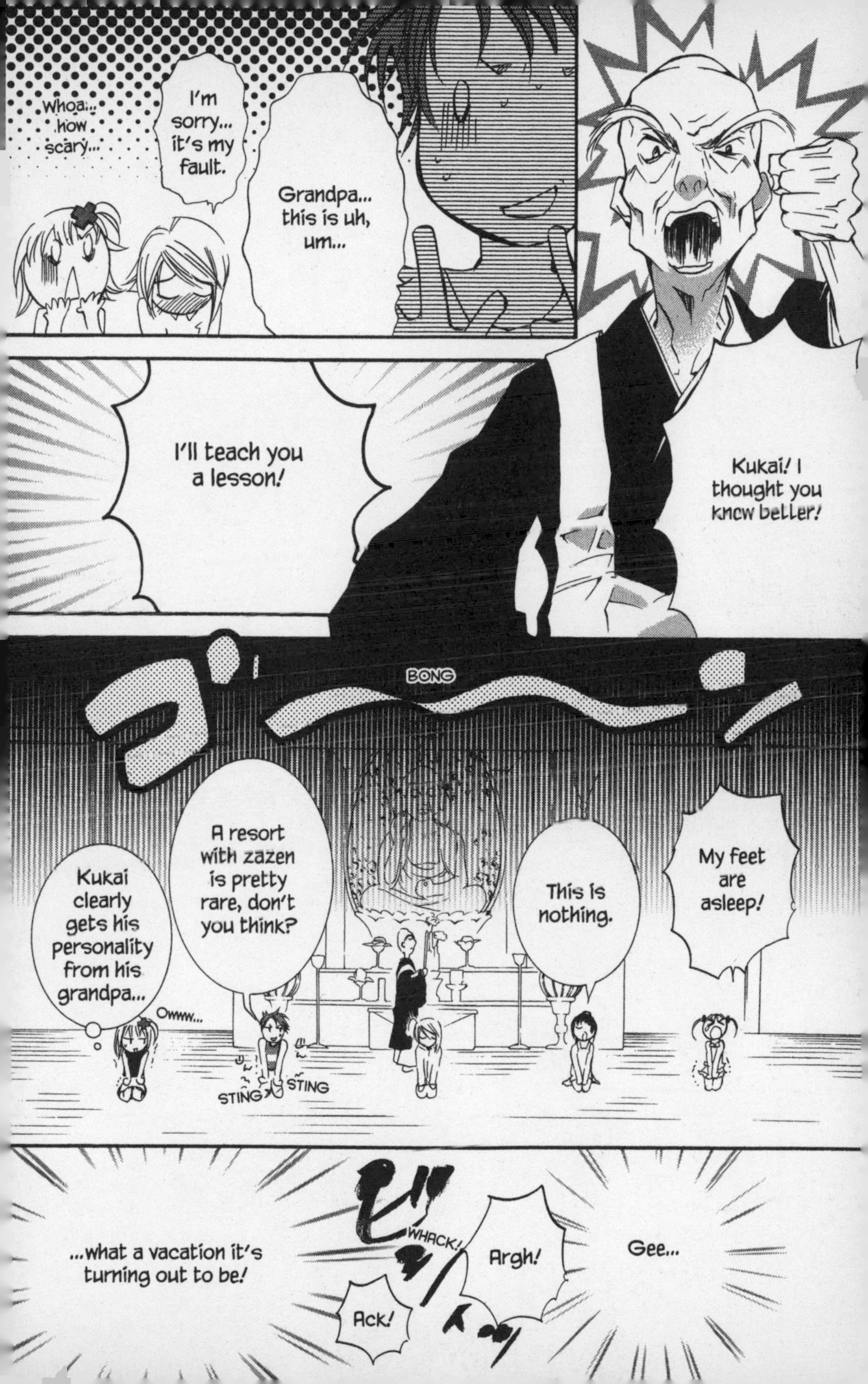
Grandpa... this is uh, um...
I'm sorry... it's my fault.
Whoa... how scary...
Kukai! I thought you knew better!
I'll teach you a lesson!
BONG
My feet are asleep!
This is nothing.
A resort with zazen is pretty rare, don't you think?
Kukai clearly gets his personality from his grandpa...
Owww...
STING
STING
Gee...
Argh!
WHACK!
Ack!
...what a vacation it's turning out to be!

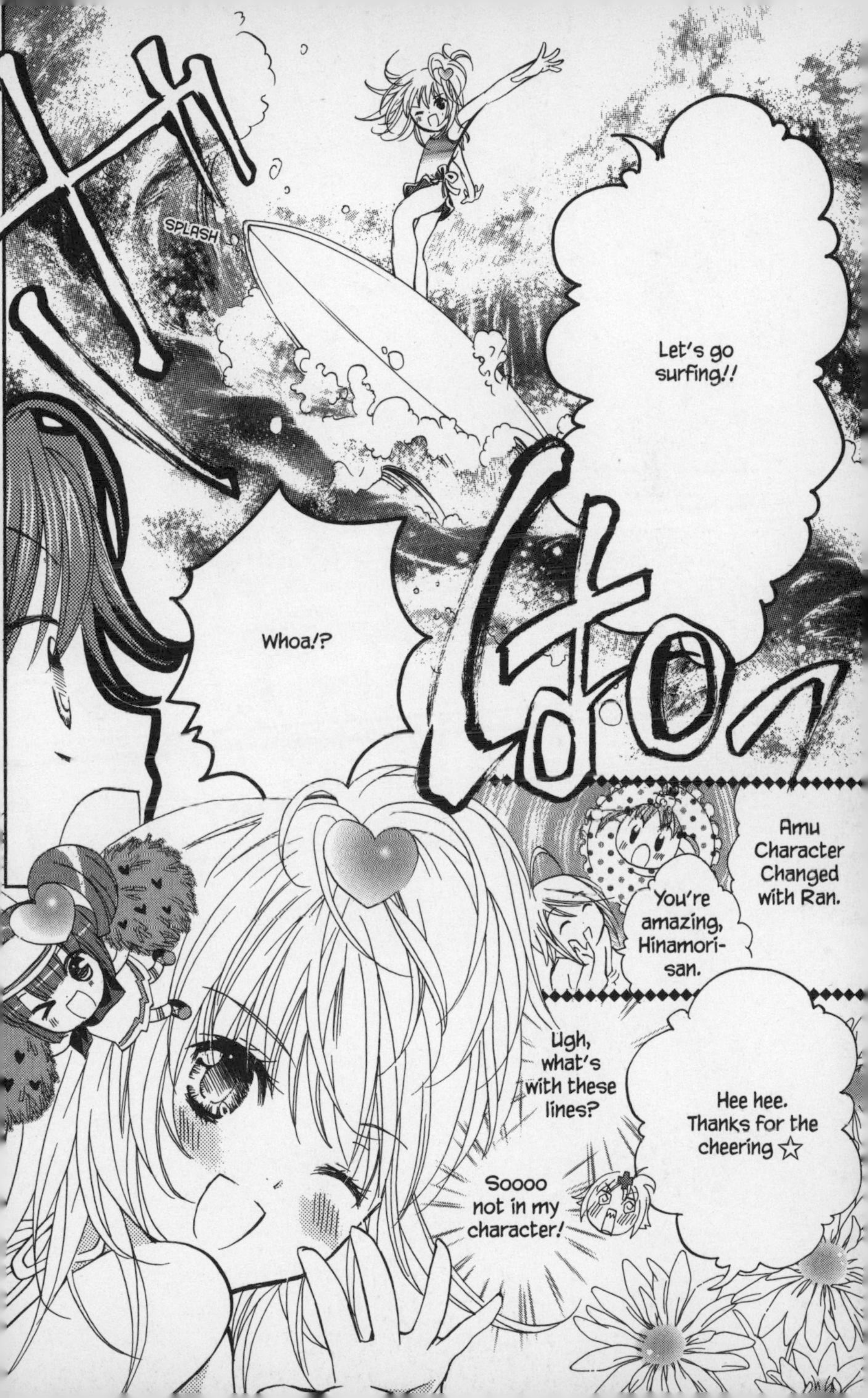
Let's go surfing!!
SPLASH
Whoa!?
Amu Character Changed with Ran.
You're amazing, Hinamori-san.
Hee hee. Thanks for the cheering ☆
Ugh, what's with these lines?
Soooo not in my character!

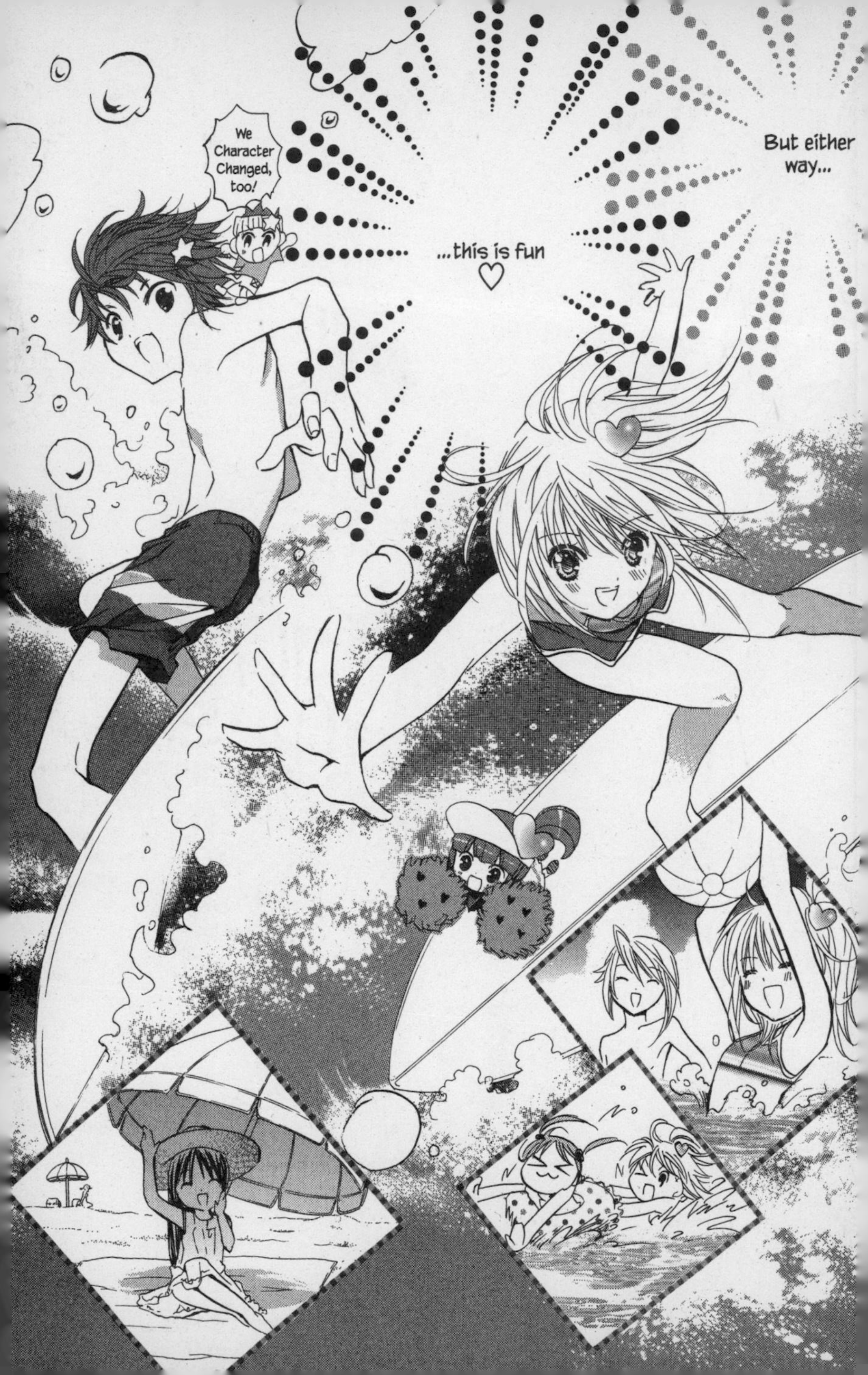
But either way...
...this is fun ♡
We Character Changed, too!

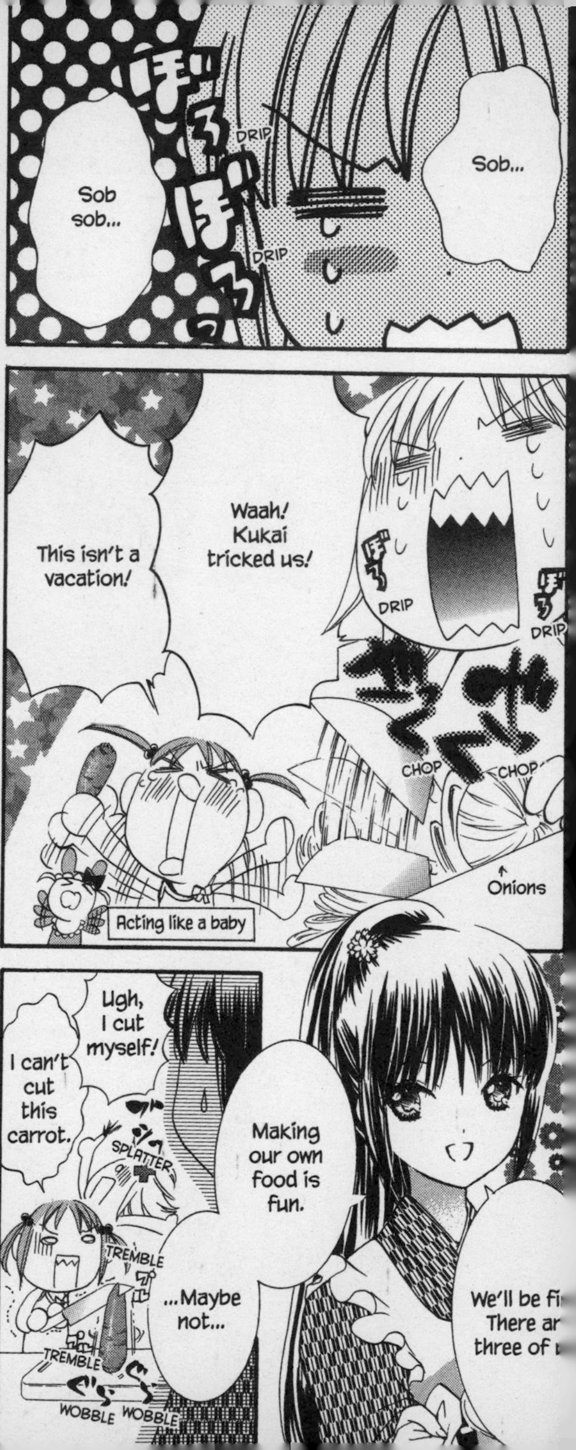
Sob...
DRIP
DRIP
Sob sob...
Waah! Kukai tricked us!
DRIP
DRIP
CHOP
CHOP
Onions
This isn't a vacation!
Acting like a baby
We'll be fi
There ar
three of u
Making our own food is fun.
...Maybe not...
Ugh, I cut myself!
I can't cut this carrot.
SPLATTER
TREMBLE
TREMBLE
WOBBLE
WOBBLE

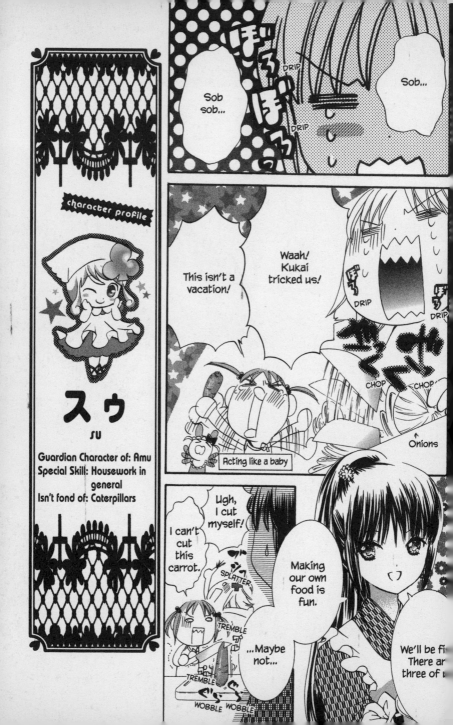

character profile

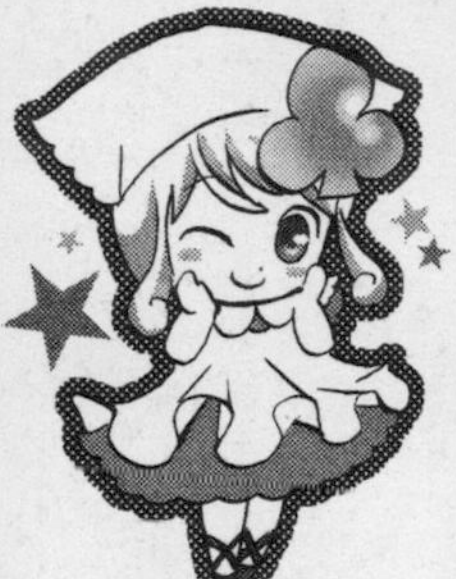

スゥ

SU

Guardian Character of: Amu
Special Skill: Housework in general
Isn't fond of: Caterpillars

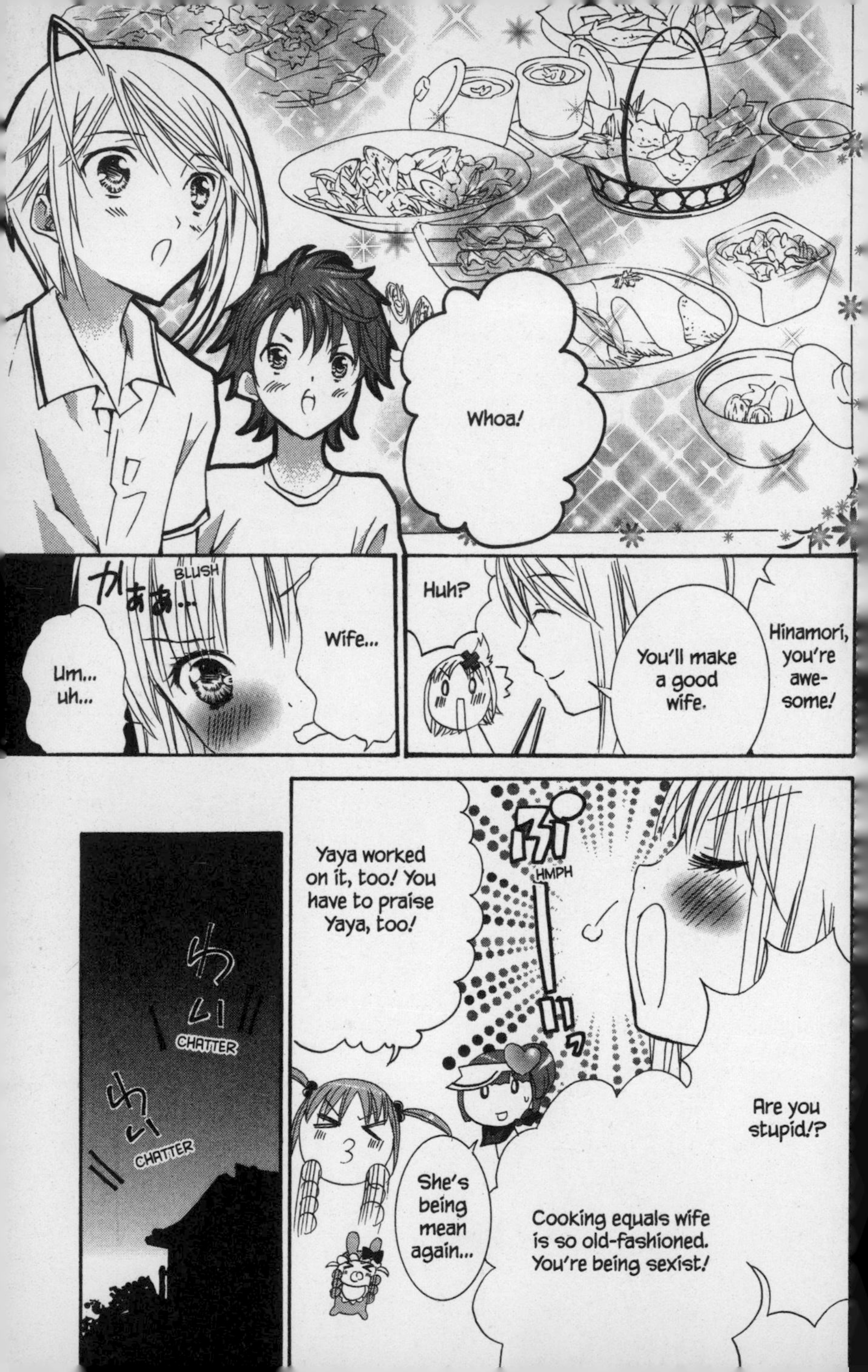
Whoa!
Hinamori, you're awesome!
You'll make a good wife.
Huh?
Wife...
BLUSH
Um... uh...
Are you stupid!?
Cooking equals wife is so old-fashioned. You're being sexist!
HMPH
Yaya worked on it, too! You have to praise Yaya, too!
She's being mean again...
CHATTER
CHATTER

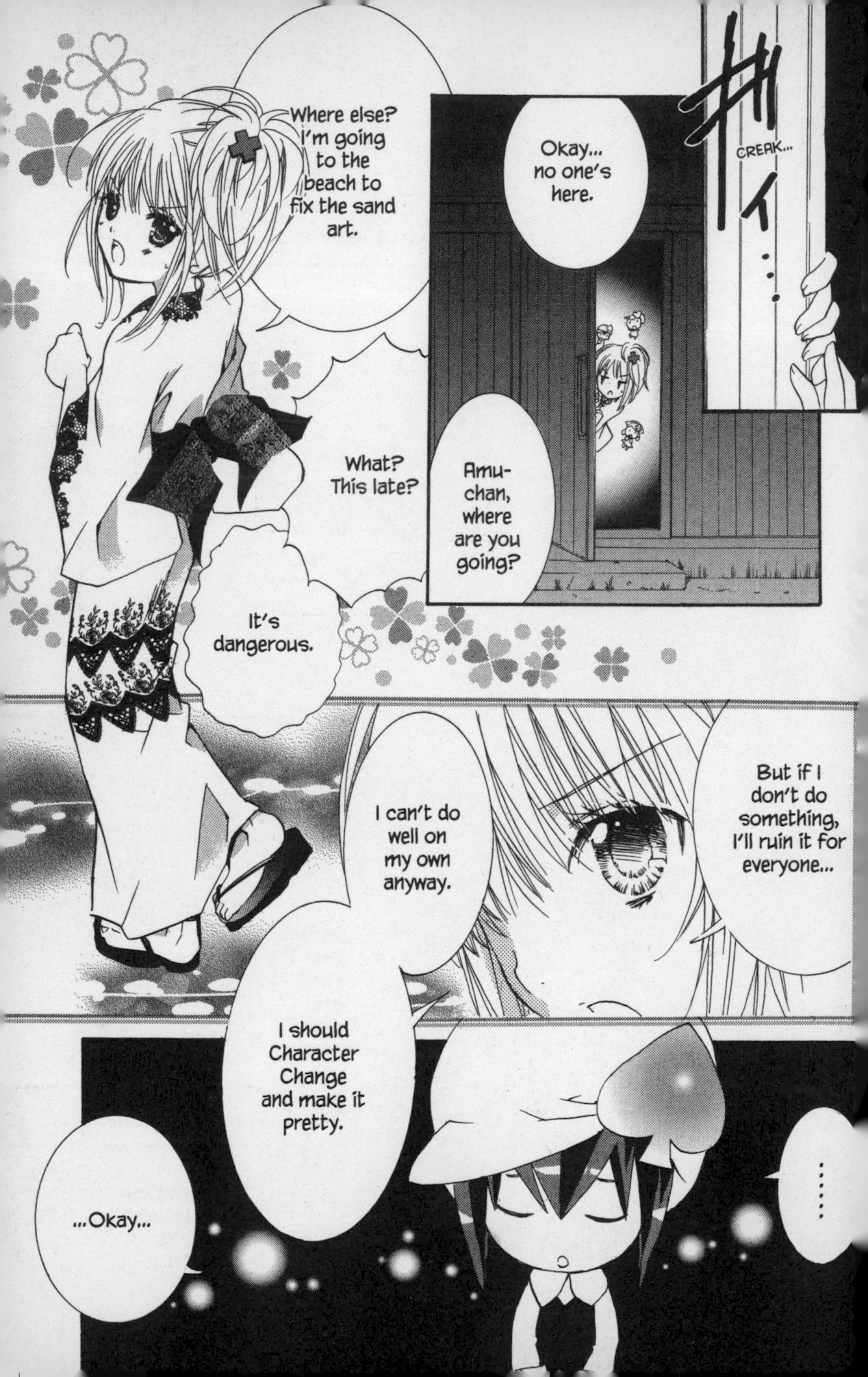
CREAK...
Okay... no one's here.
Amu-chan, where are you going?
Where else? I'm going to the beach to fix the sand art.
What? This late?
It's dangerous.
But if I don't do something, I'll ruin it for everyone...
I can't do well on my own anyway.
I should Character Change and make it pretty.
......
...Okay...

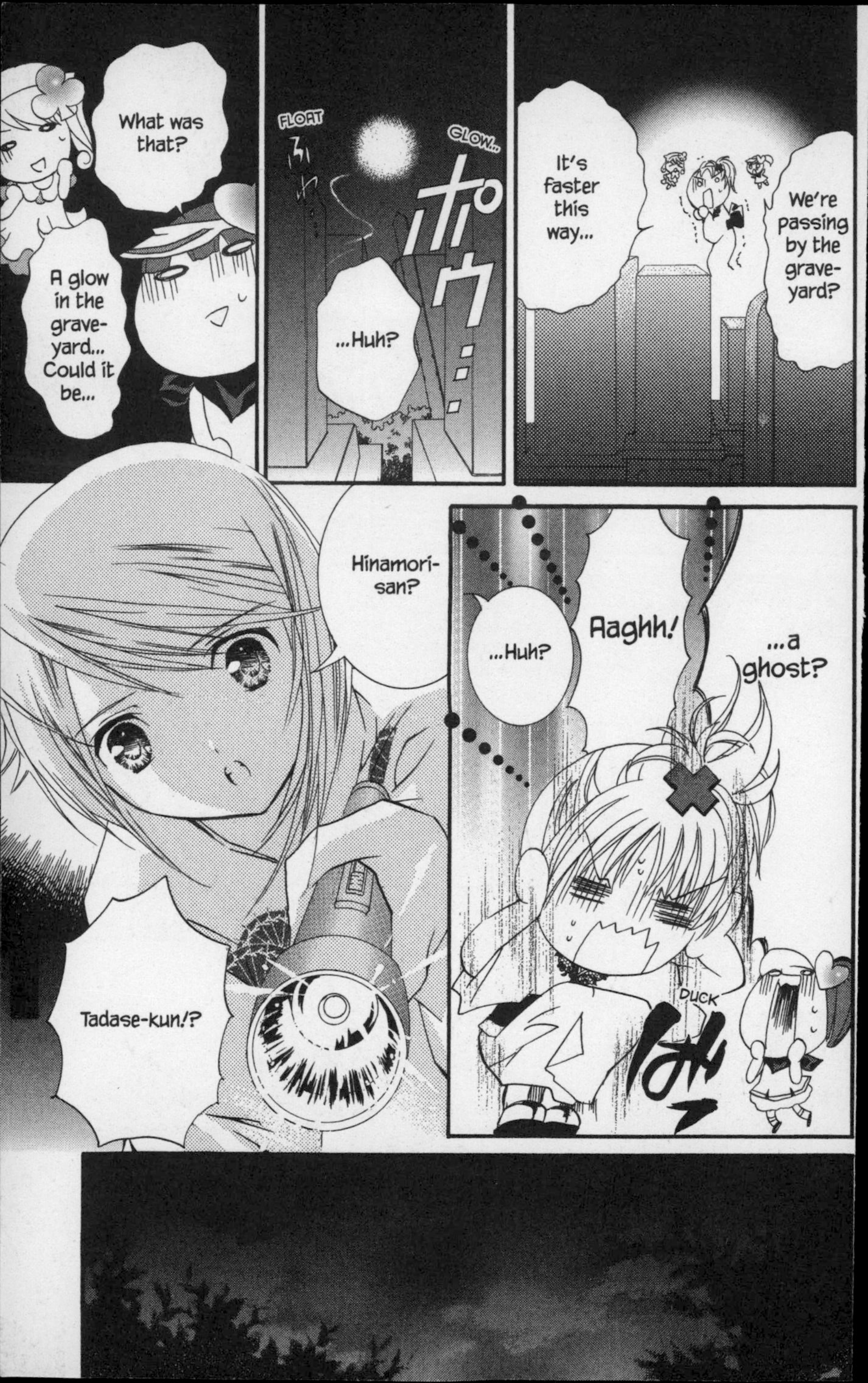
We're passing by the graveyard?
It's faster this way...
GLOW...
FLOAT
...Huh?
What was that?
A glow in the graveyard... Could it be...
...a ghost?
Aaghh!
...Huh?
DUCK
Hinamori-san?
Tadase-kun!?

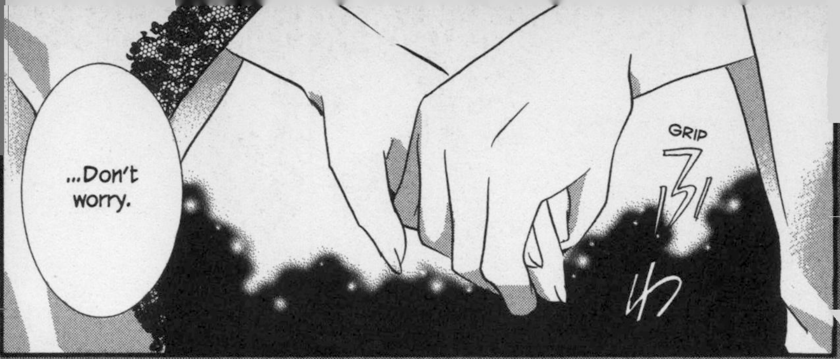
GRIP
...Don't worry.

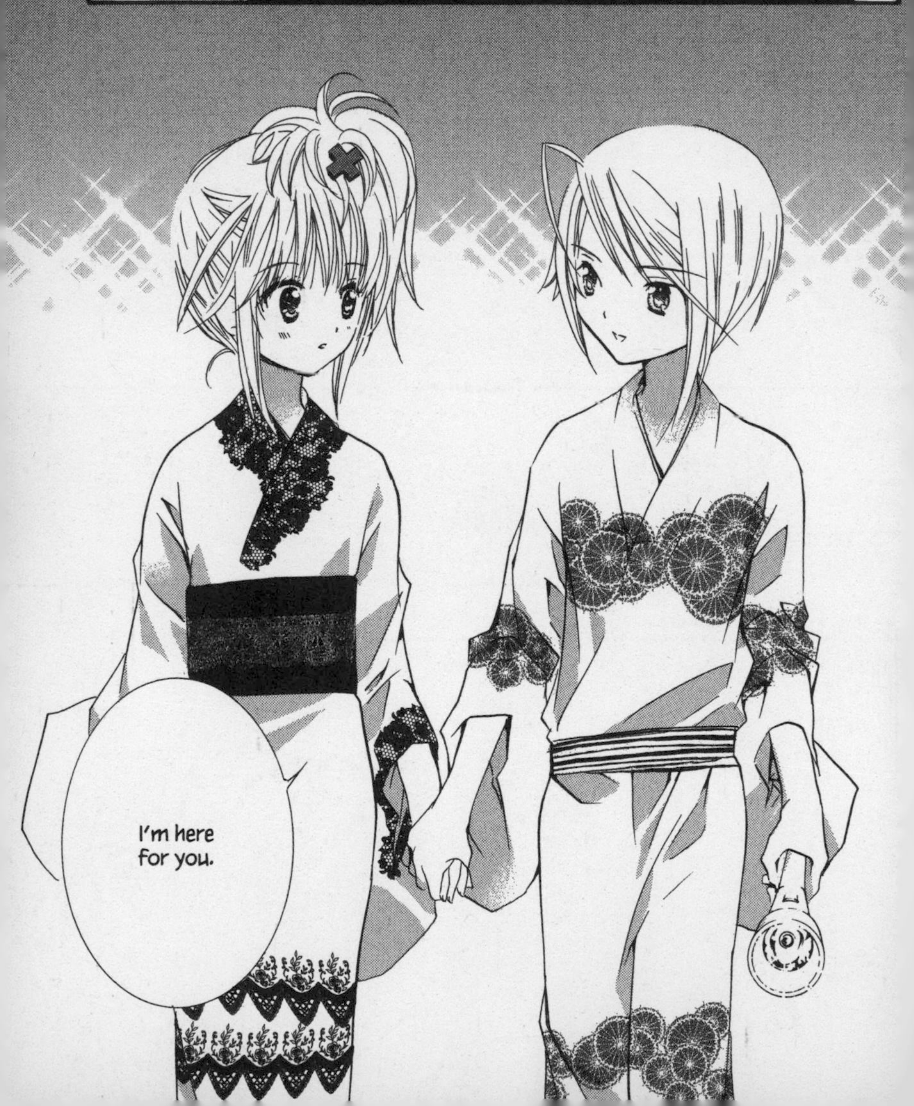
I'm here for you.

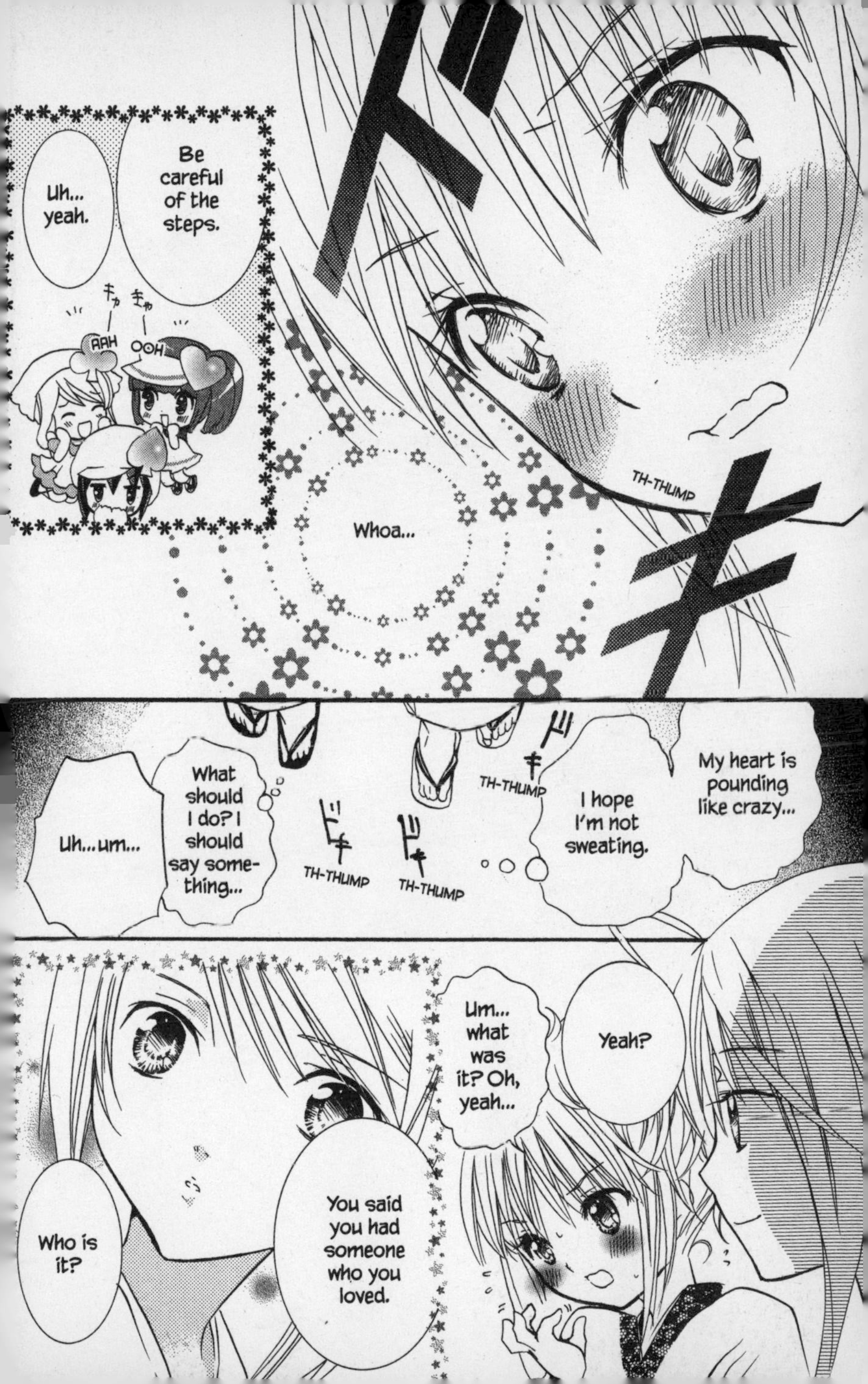
TH-THUMP
Whoa...
Be careful of the steps.
Uh... yeah.
OOH
AAH
My heart is pounding like crazy...
I hope I'm not sweating.
TH-THUMP
TH-THUMP
TH-THUMP
What should I do? I should say some-thing...
Uh...um...
Yeah?
Um... what was it? Oh, yeah...
You said you had someone who you loved.
Who is it?

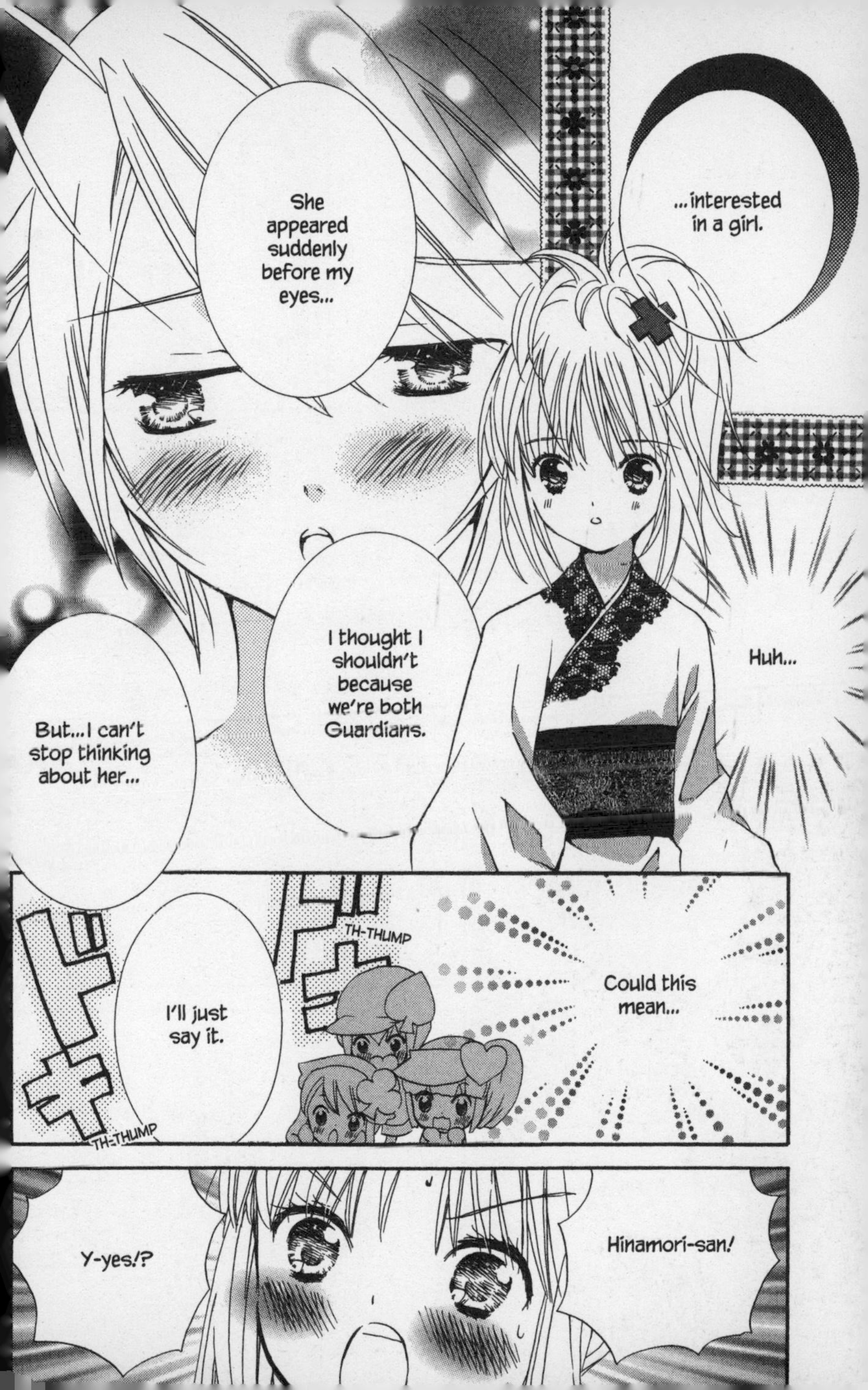
...interested in a girl.
She appeared suddenly before my eyes...
Huh...
I thought I shouldn't because we're both Guardians.
But...I can't stop thinking about her...
Could this mean...
TH-THUMP
I'll just say it.
TH-THUMP
Hinamori-san!
Y-yes!?

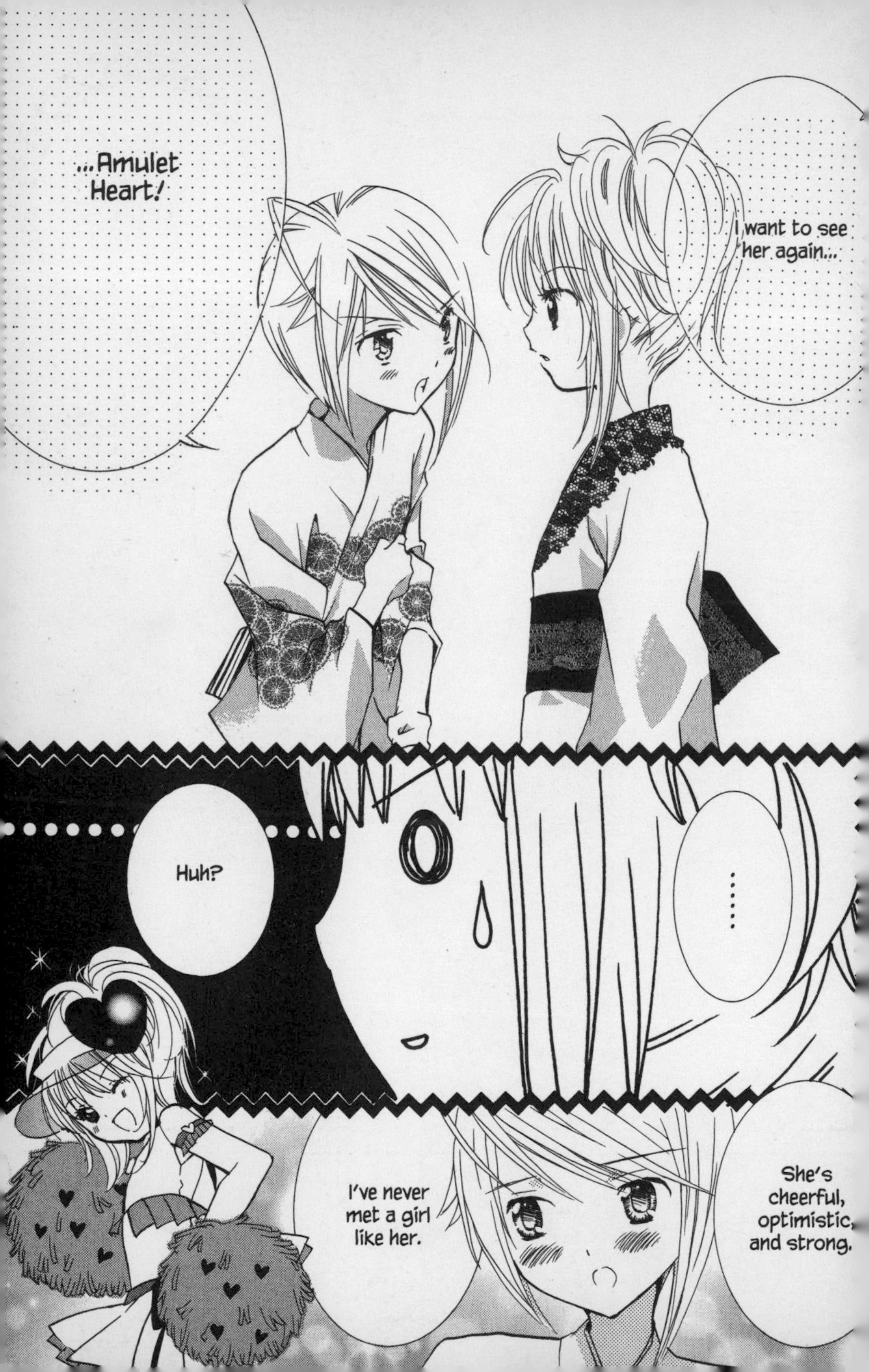
I want to see her again...
...Amulet Heart!
......
Huh?
She's cheerful, optimistic, and strong.
I've never met a girl like her.

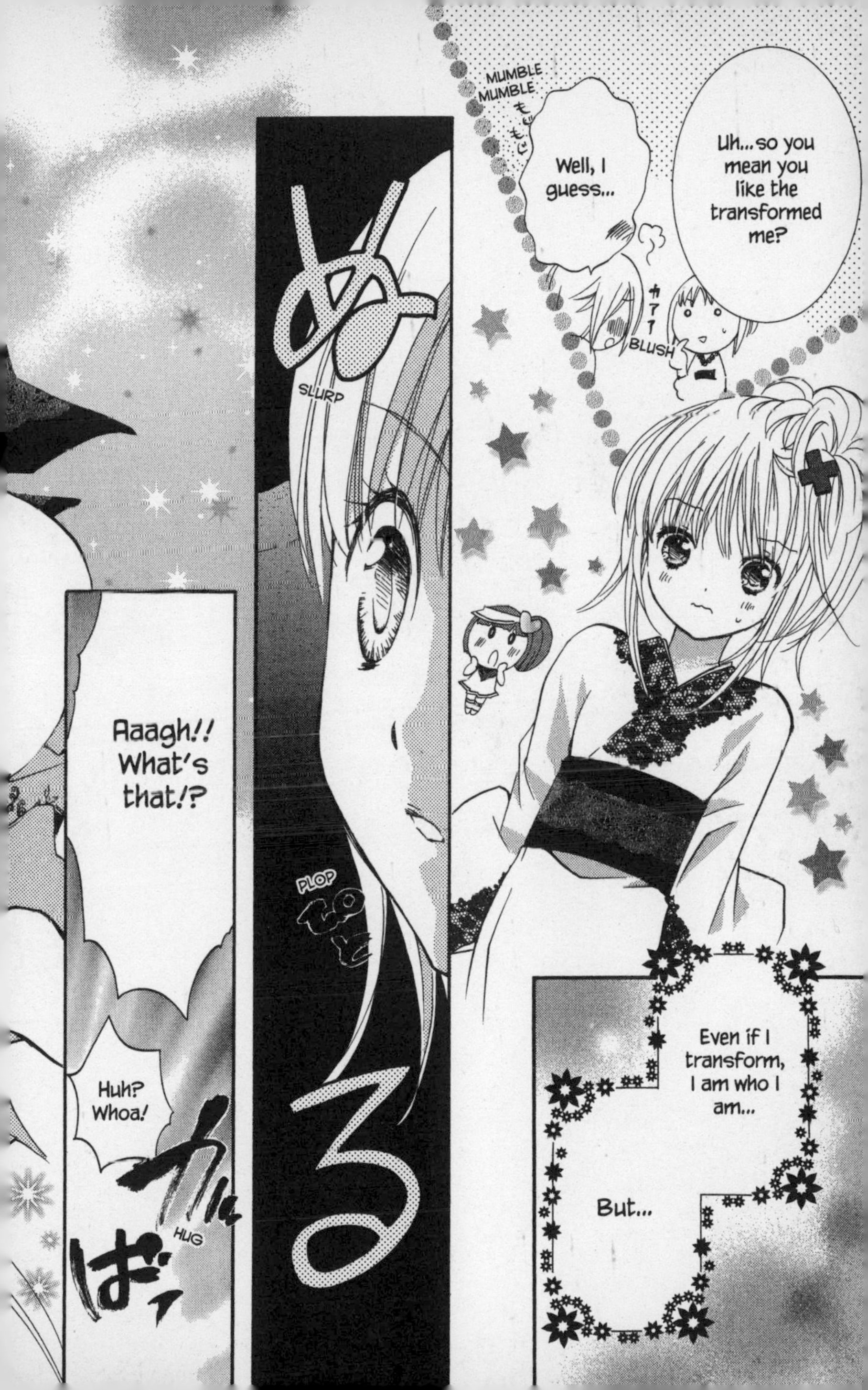
Uh...so you mean you like the transformed me?
MUMBLE MUMBLE
Well, I guess...
BLUSH
Even if I transform, I am who I am...
But...
SLURP
PLOP
Aaagh!! What's that!?
Huh? Whoa!
HUG

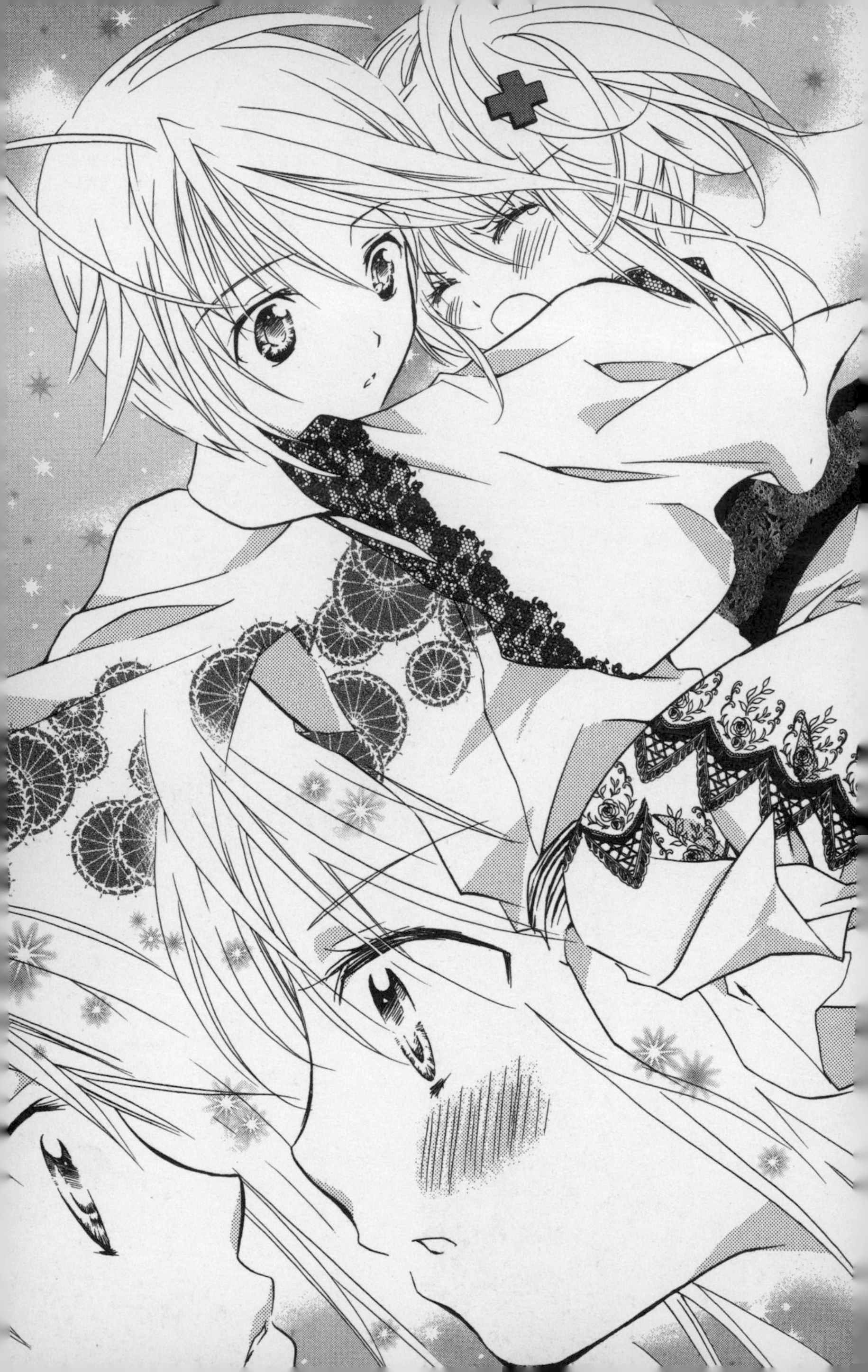

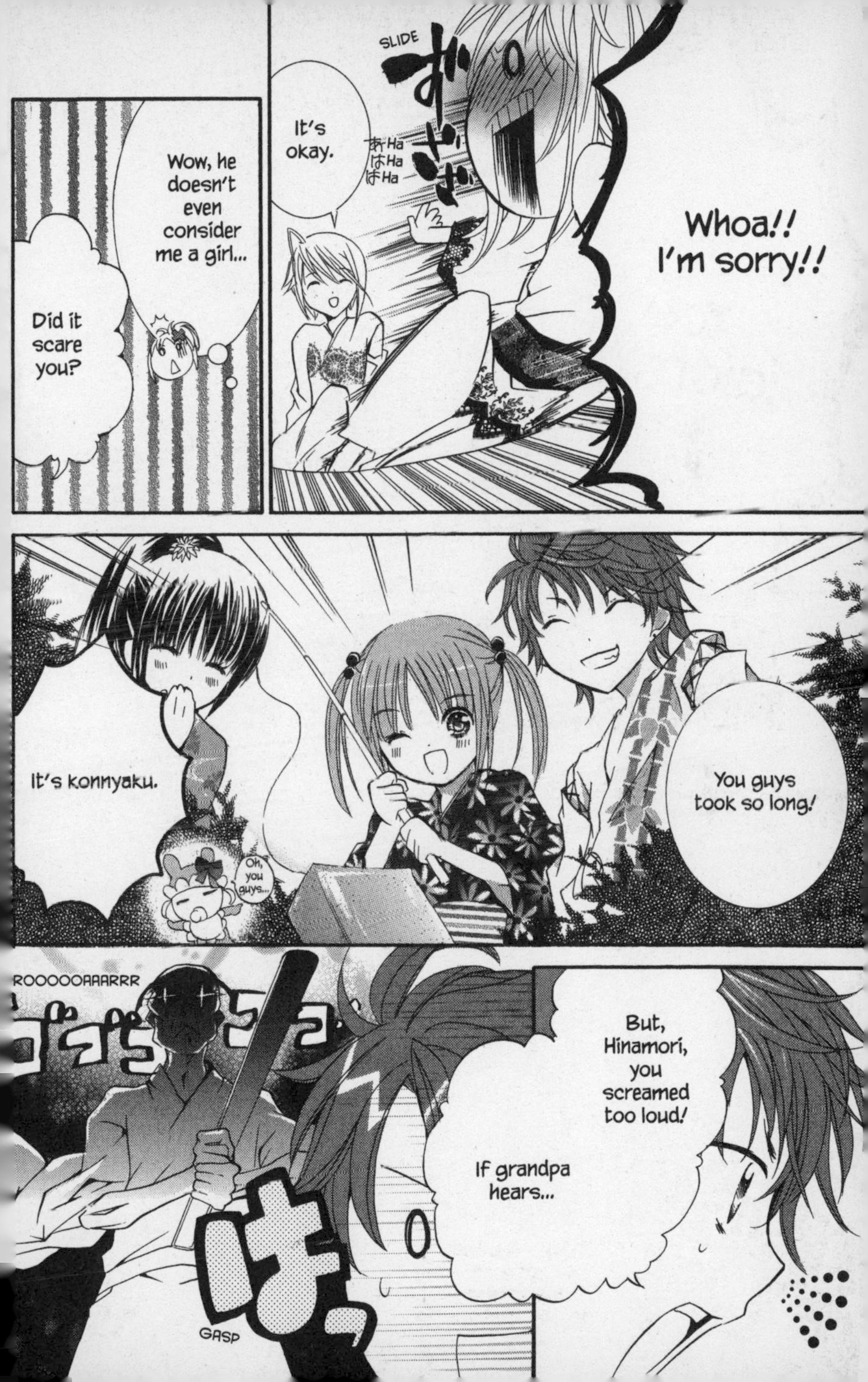
SLIDE
Whoa!! I'm sorry!!
Ha Ha Ha
It's okay.
Wow, he doesn't even consider me a girl...
Did it scare you?
You guys took so long!
It's konnyaku.
Oh, you guys...
But, Hinamori, you screamed too loud!
If grandpa hears...
GASP
ROOOOOAAARRR

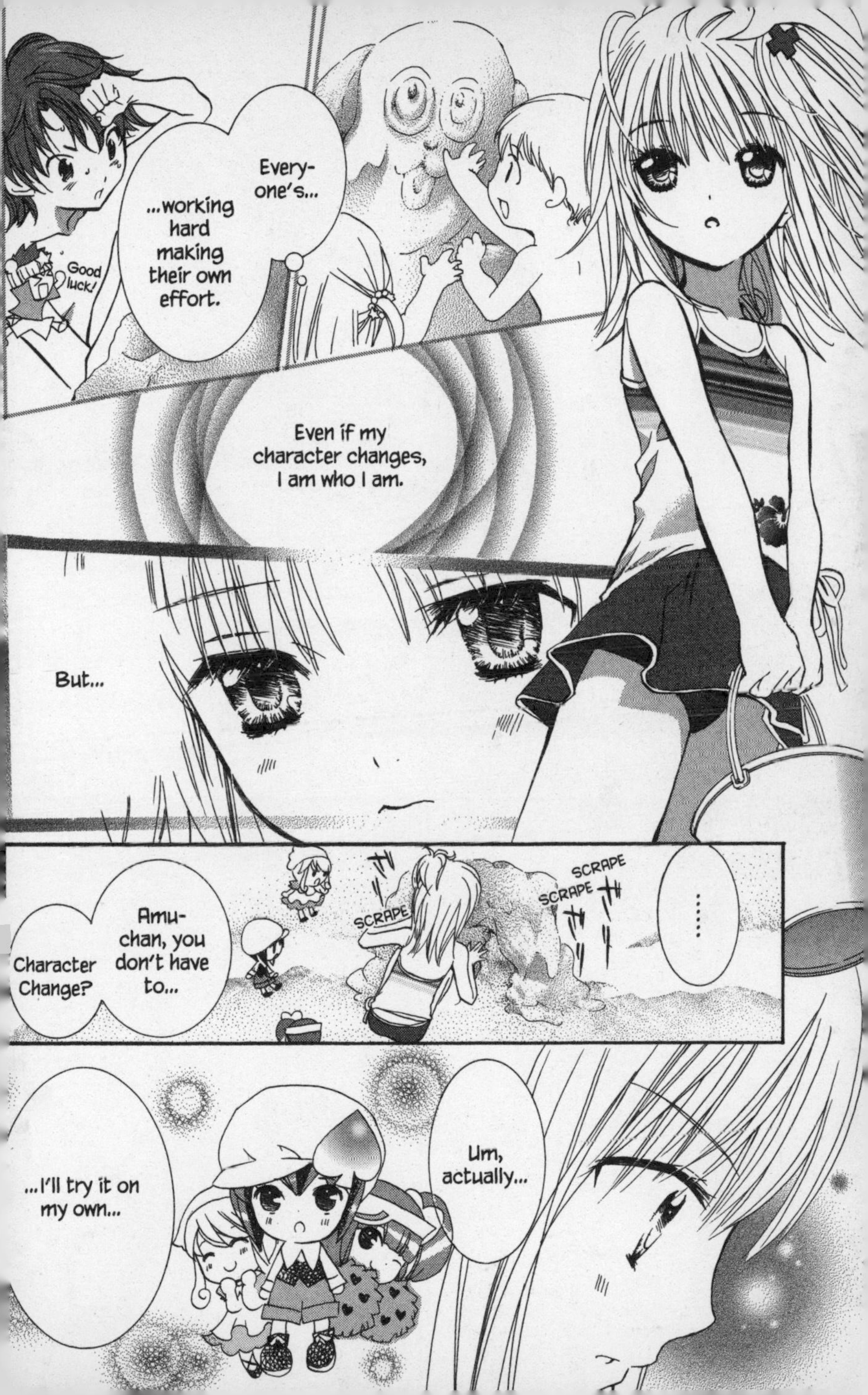

Every-one's...
...working hard making their own effort.
Good luck!
Even if my character changes, I am who I am.
But...
......
SCRAPE SCRAPE
SCRAPE
Amu-chan, you don't have to...
Character Change?
Um, actually...
...I'll try it on my own...

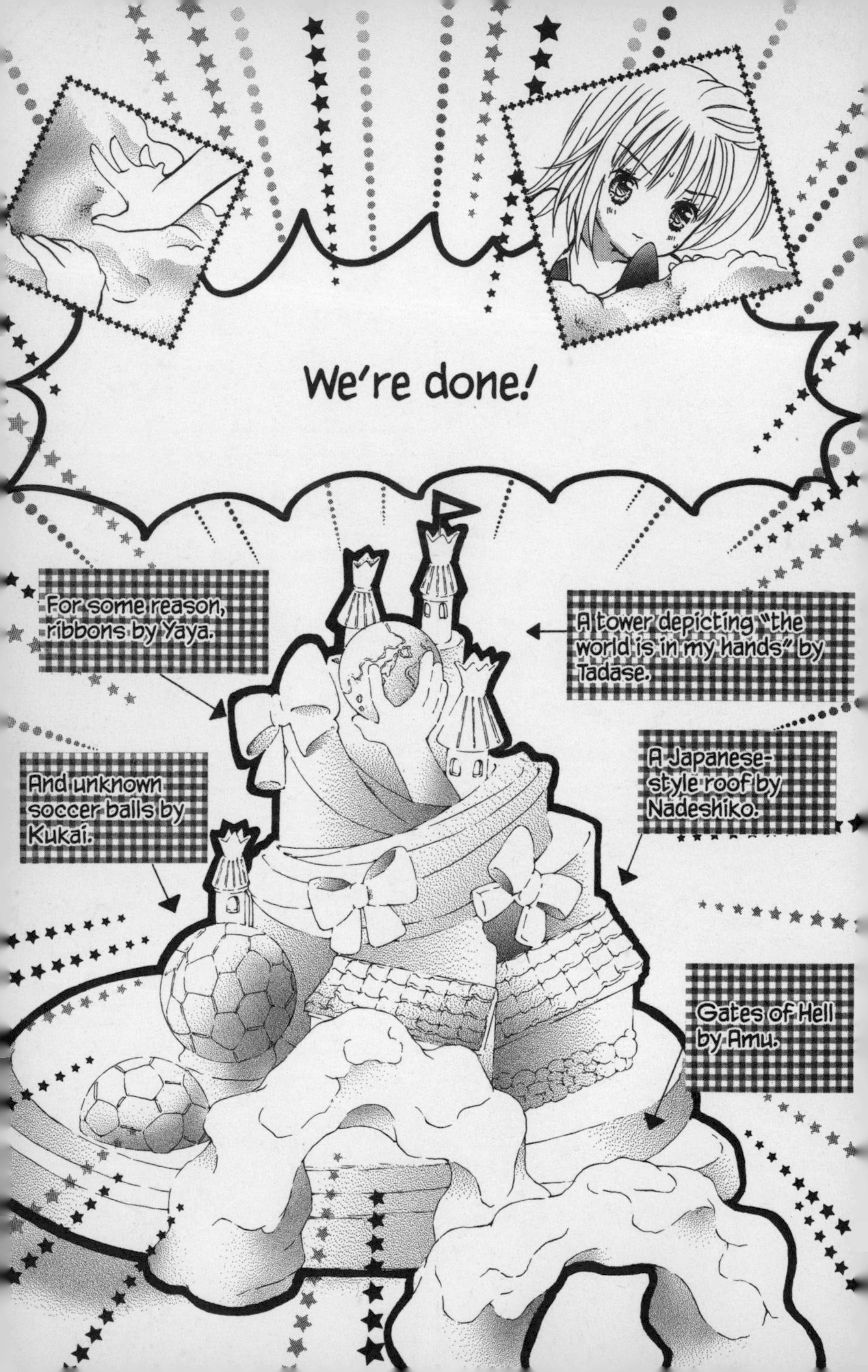
We're done!
A tower depicting "the world is in my hands" by Tadase.
For some reason, ribbons by Yaya.
A Japanese-style roof by Nadeshiko.
And unknown soccer balls by Kukai.
Gates of Hell by Amu.

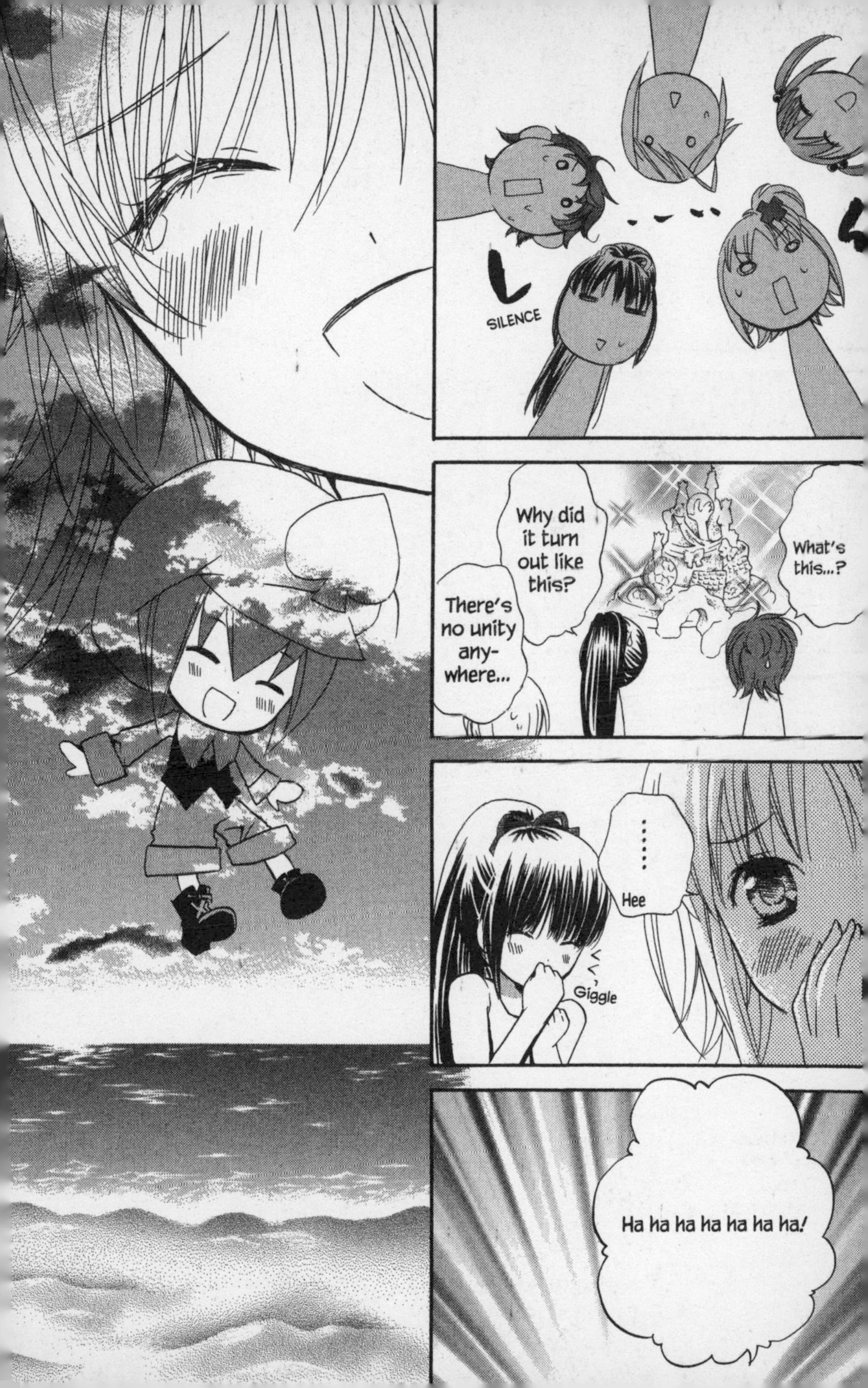
SILENCE
What's this...?
Why did it turn out like this?
There's no unity anywhere...
......
Hee
Giggle
Ha ha ha ha ha ha ha!

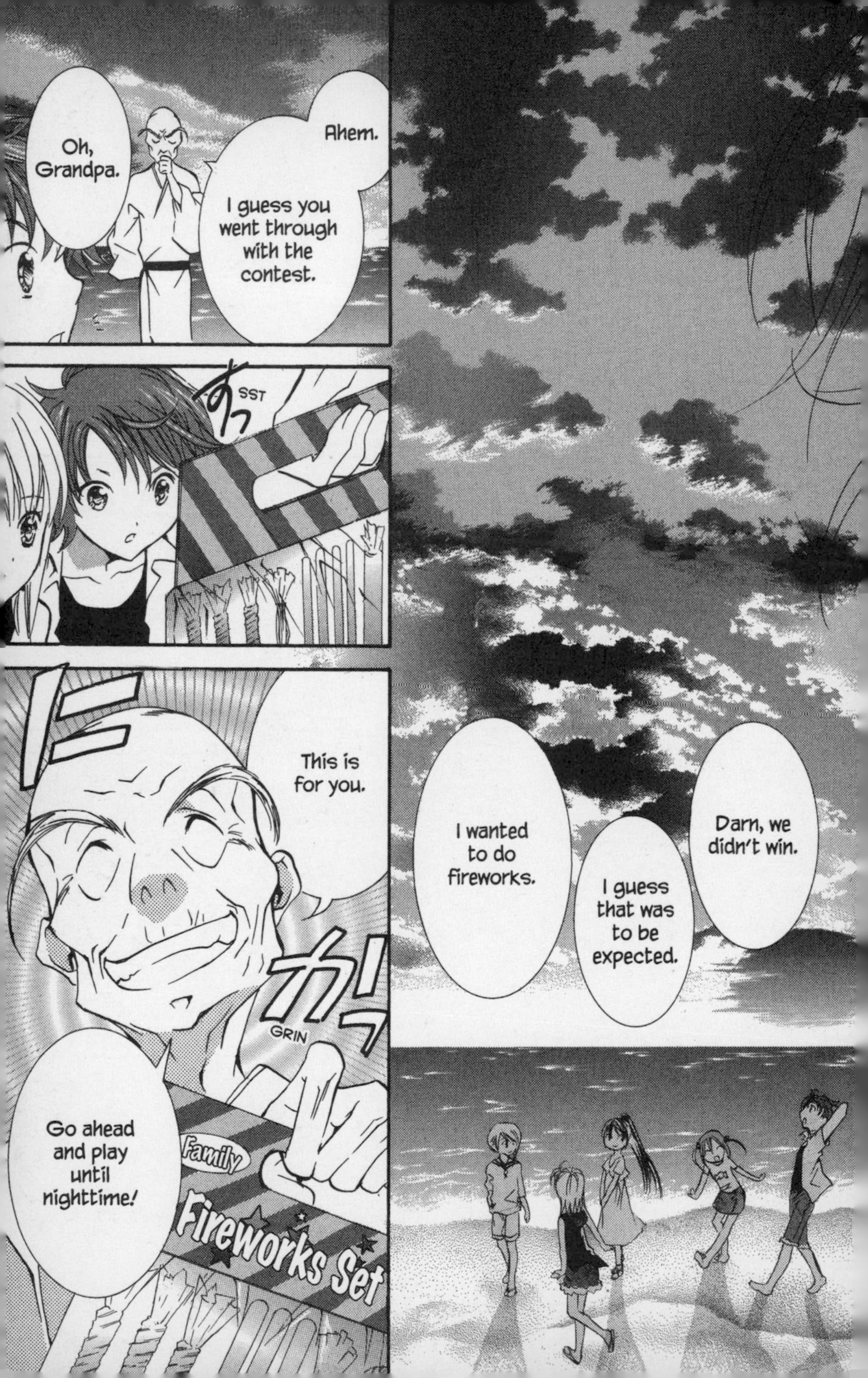
Darn, we didn't win.
I guess that was to be expected.
I wanted to do fireworks.
Ahem.
I guess you went through with the contest.
Oh, Grandpa.
SST
This is for you.
GRIN
Family Fireworks Set
Go ahead and play until nighttime!

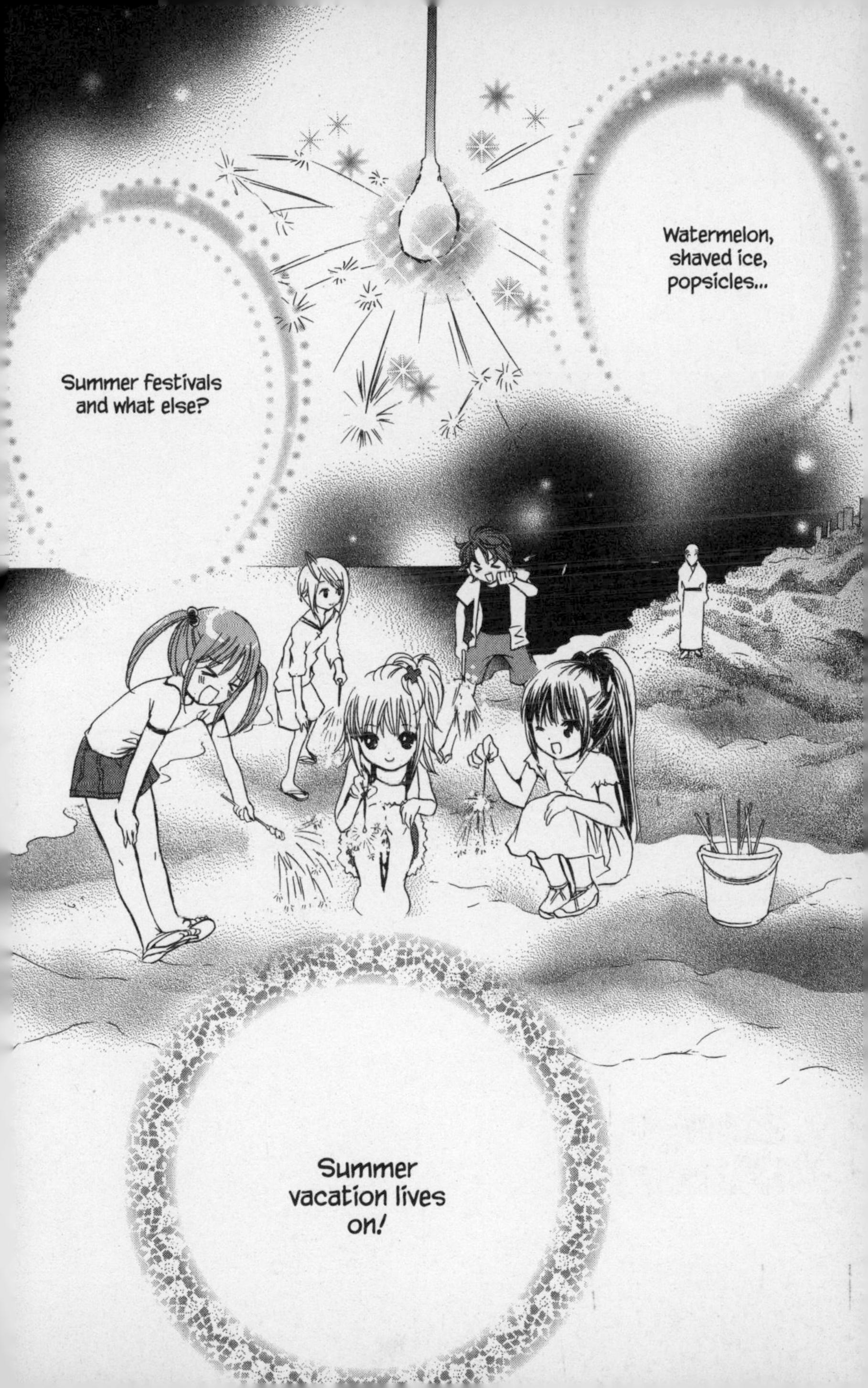
Watermelon, shaved ice, popsicles...
Summer festivals and what else?
Summer vacation lives on!

Shugo
Chara!

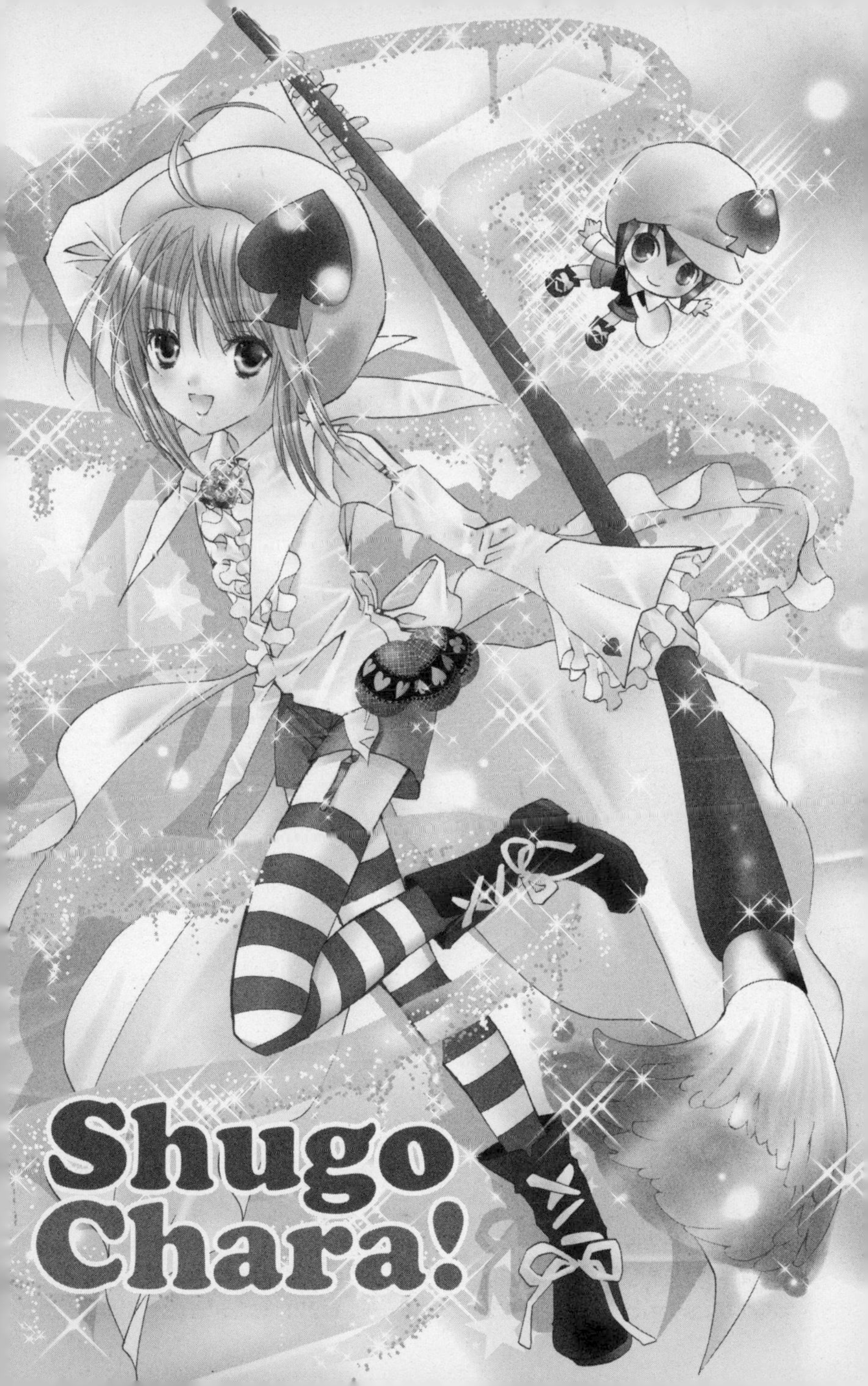
Shugo
Chara!

SMILE

Hello. Sorry I'm late.

The faculty meeting ran long...

Continued ⤵

The costumes for Character Transformation were decided on by first picking a theme. I thought it should be cheerleader-like.

We don't wear clothes like Amu-chan, but we like to see and draw them! When we see girls wearing them, we gawk.

Q3: Do you like Tadase or Ikuto?

A3: I like them both. I can't decide!

Thank you for all the letters! Sorry we can't answer all of the questions. We'll answer more questions in volume 3. We'll see you then!

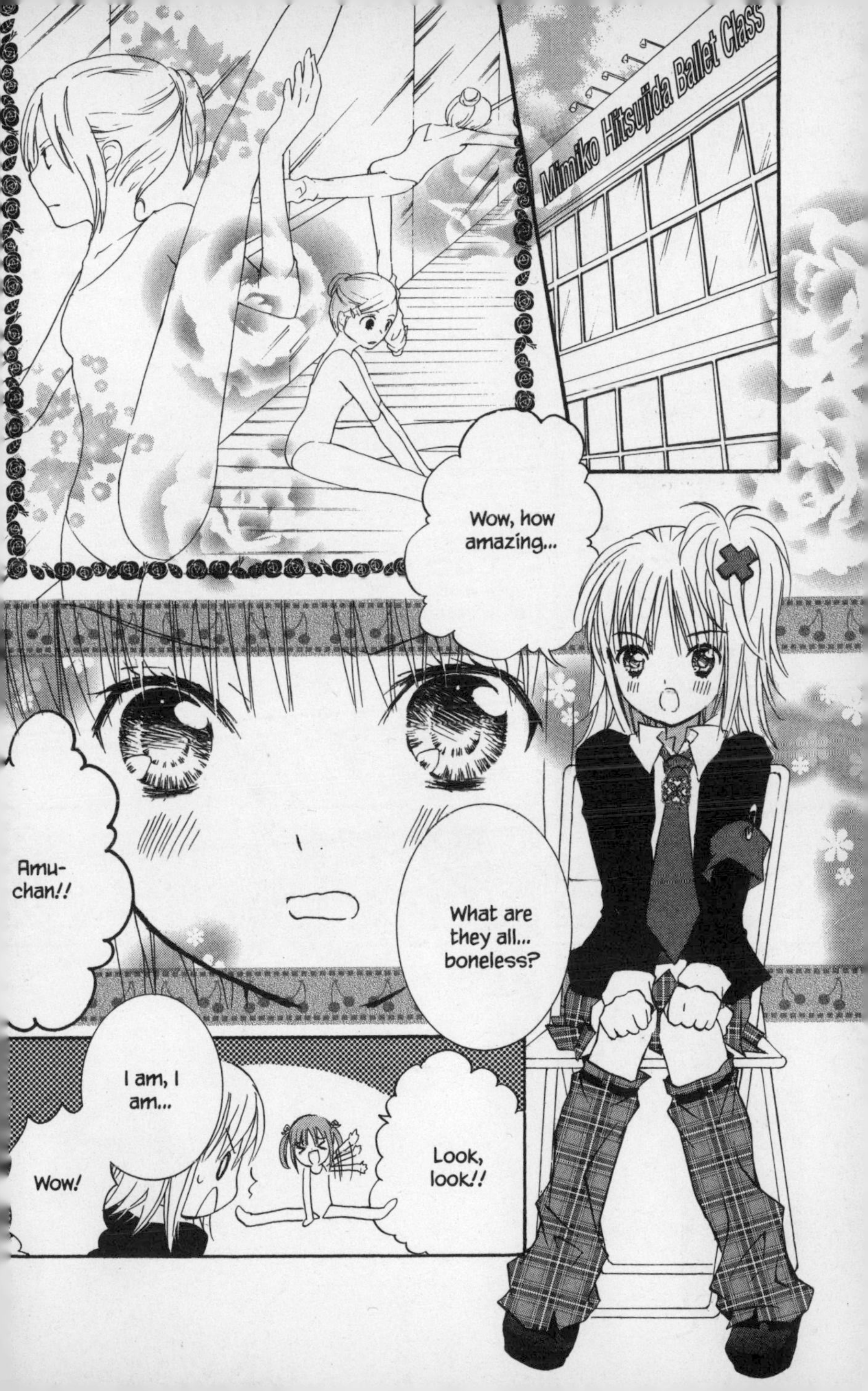
Mimiko Hitsujida Ballet Class
Wow, how amazing...
What are they all... boneless?
Amu-chan!!
Look, look!!
I am, I am...
Wow!

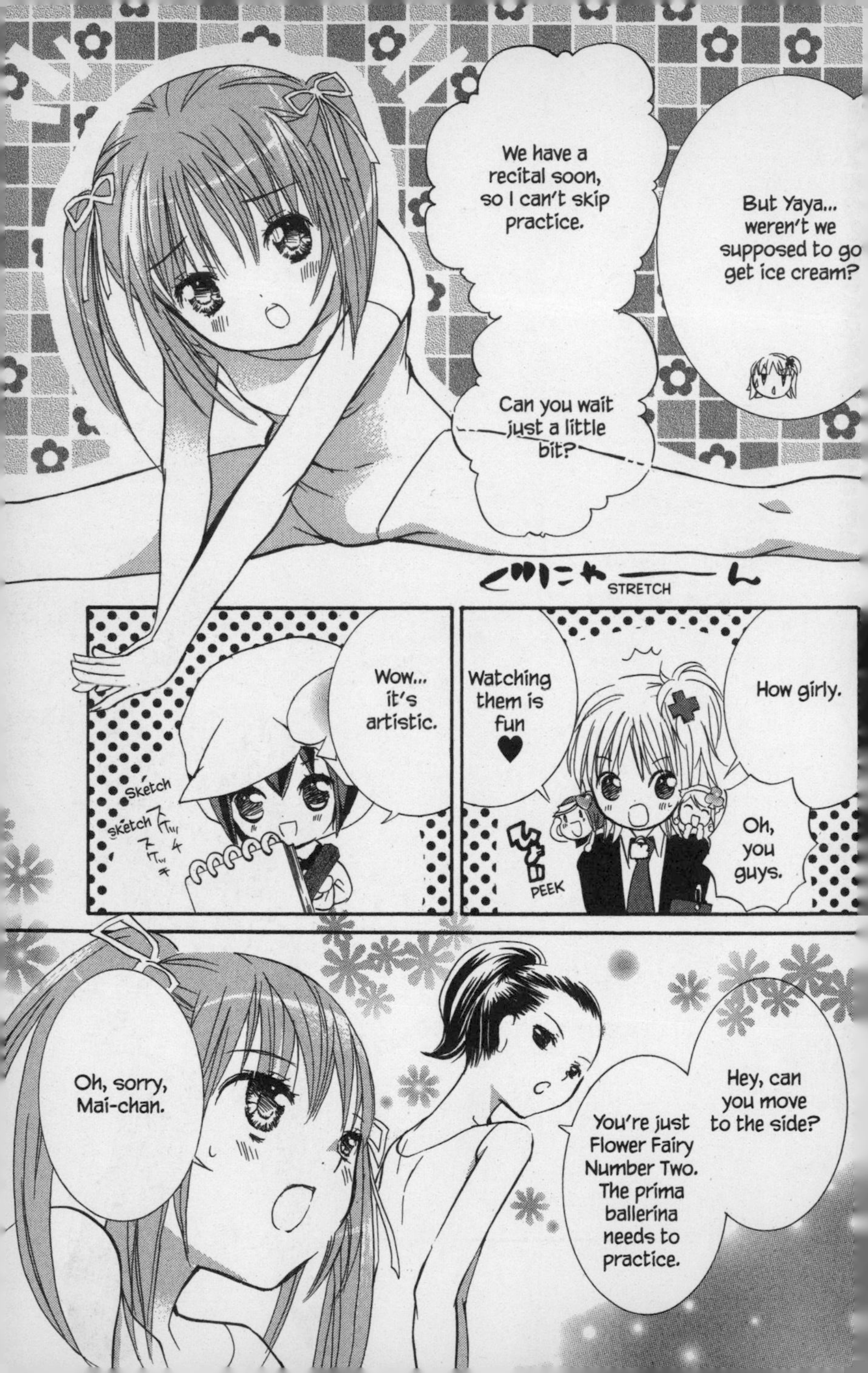
But Yaya... weren't we supposed to go get ice cream?
We have a recital soon, so I can't skip practice.
Can you wait just a little bit?
STRETCH
How girly.
Oh, you guys.
Watching them is fun ♥
PEEK
Wow... it's artistic.
Sketch
sketch
Hey, can you move to the side?
You're just Flower Fairy Number Two. The prima ballerina needs to practice.
Oh, sorry, Mai-chan.

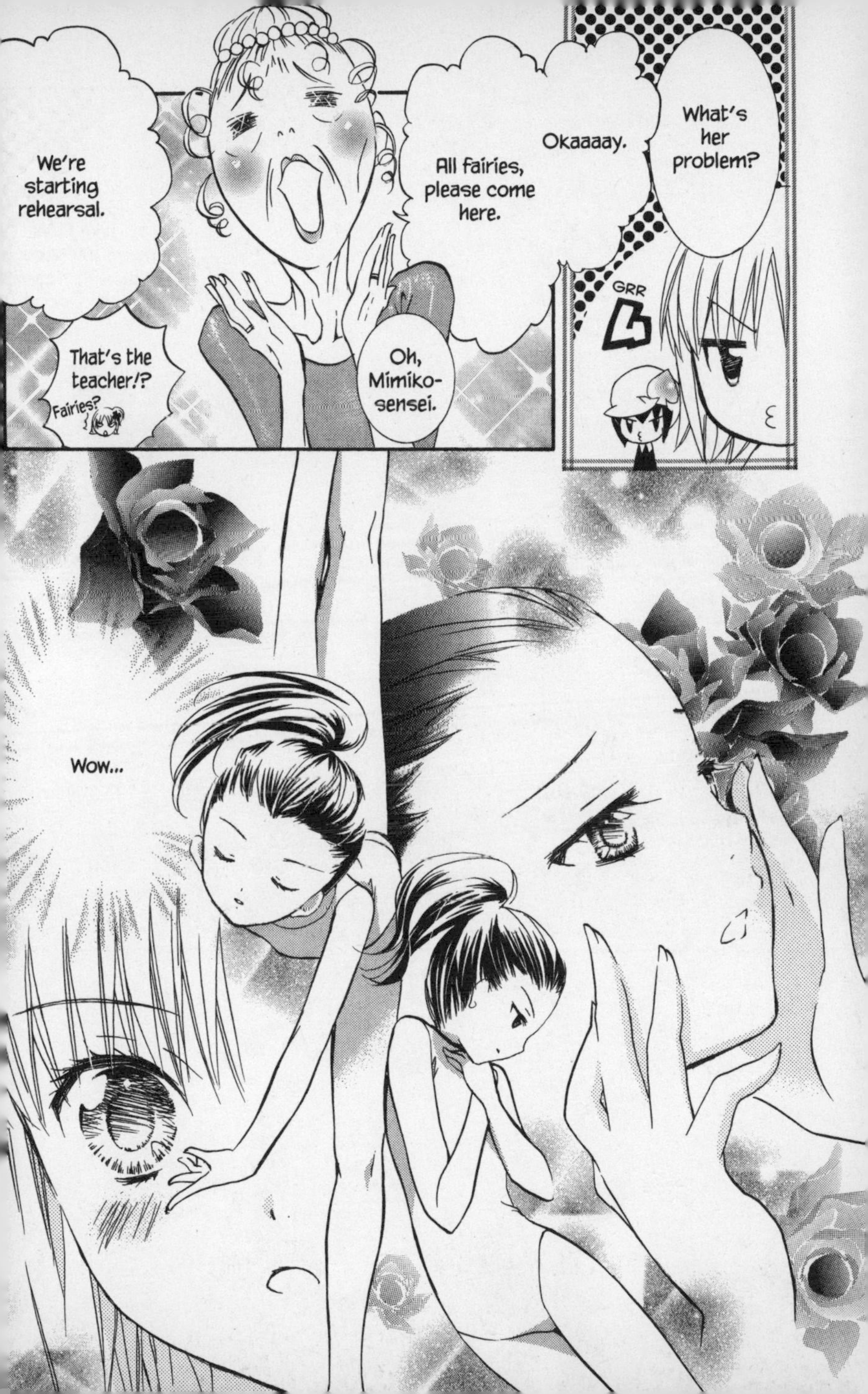
What's her problem?
GRR
Okaaaay.
All fairies, please come here.
Oh, Mimiko-sensei.
We're starting rehearsal.
That's the teacher!?
Fairies?
Wow...

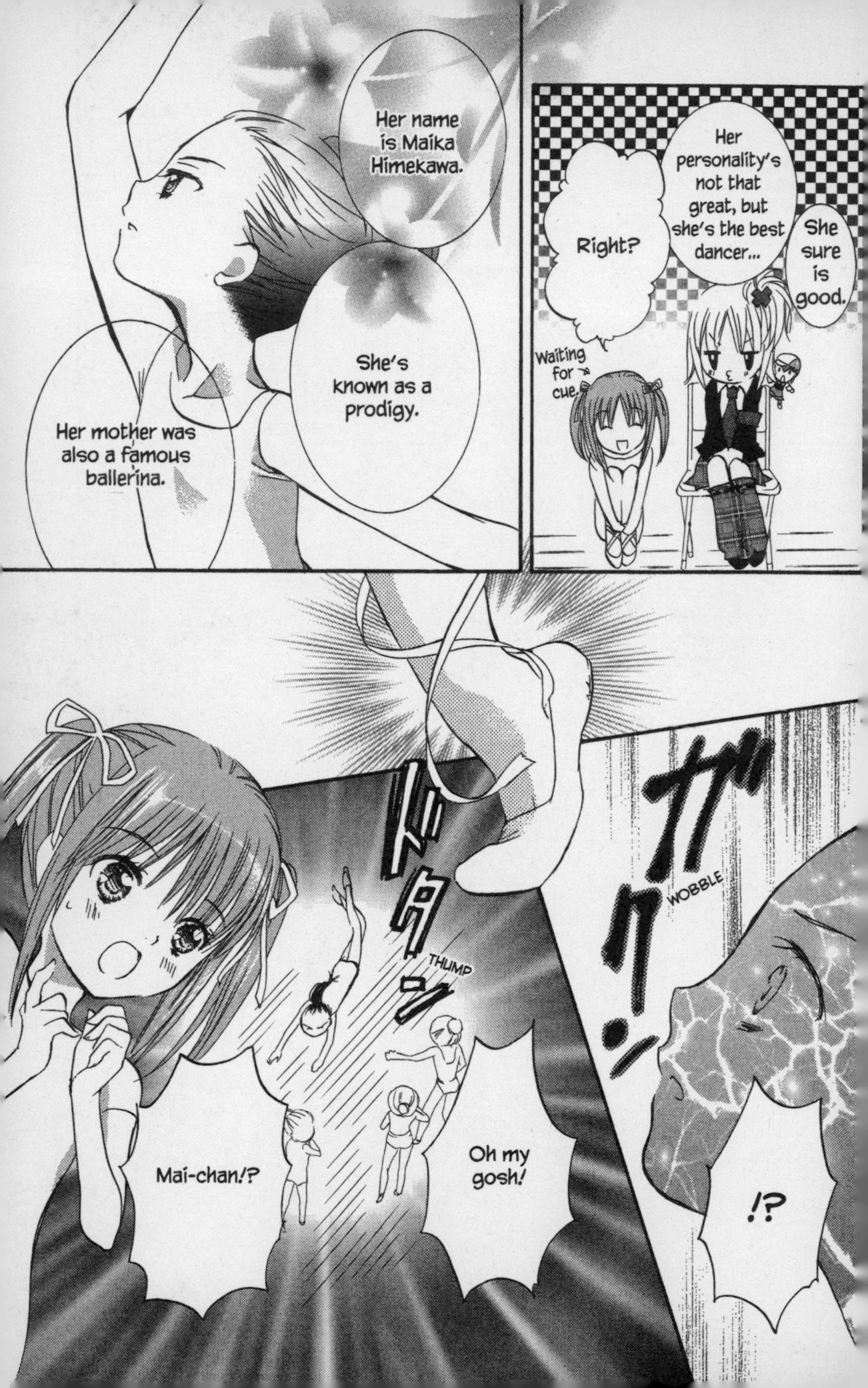
Her personality's not that great, but she's the best dancer...
Right?
She sure is good.
Waiting for cue.
Her name is Maika Himekawa.
She's known as a prodigy.
Her mother was also a famous ballerina.
WOBBLE
!?
THUMP
Oh my gosh!
Mai-chan!?

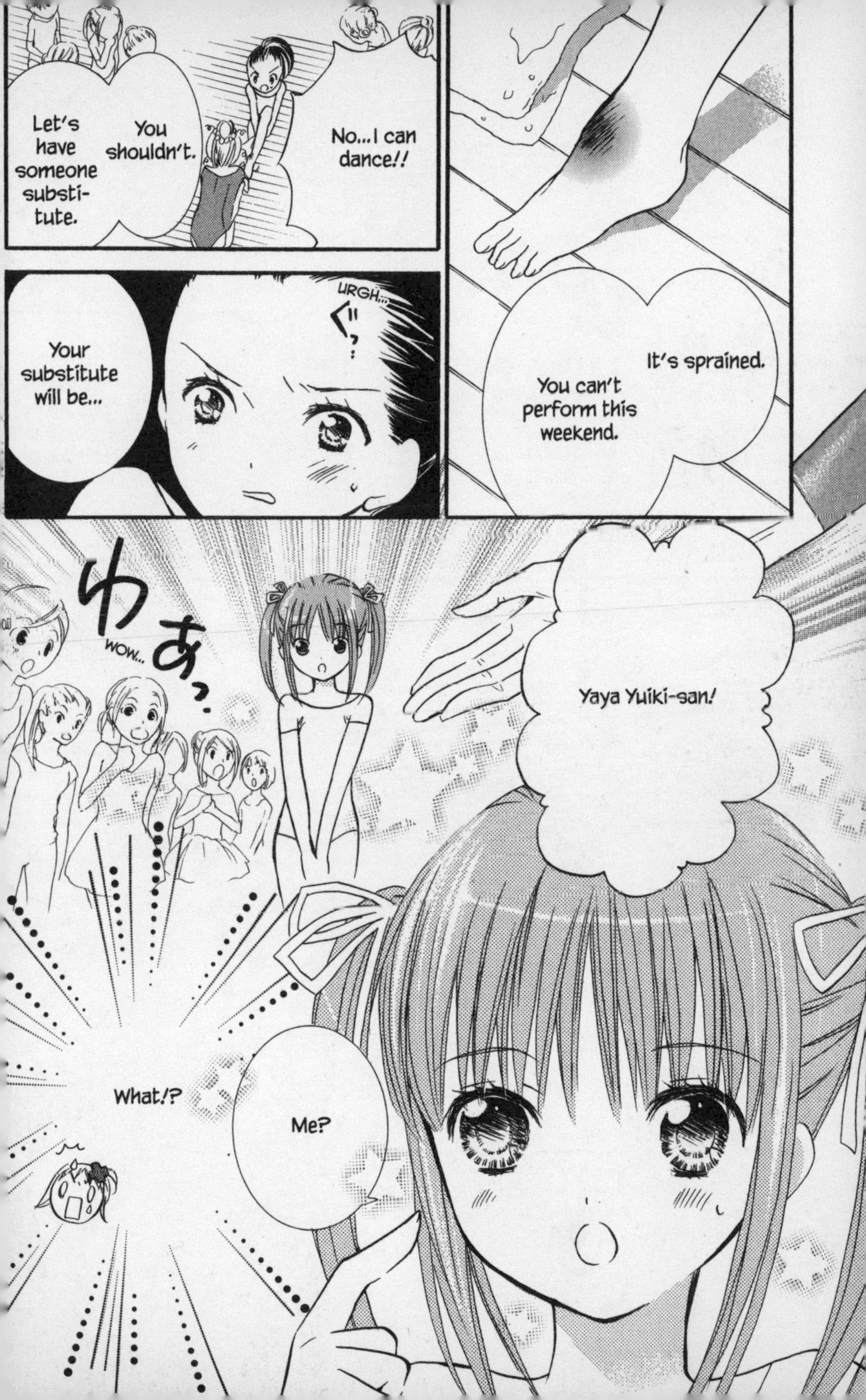
It's sprained.
You can't perform this weekend.
No...I can dance!!
You shouldn't.
Let's have someone substi-tute.
URGH...
Your substitute will be...
Yaya Yuiki-san!
WOW...
Me?
What!?

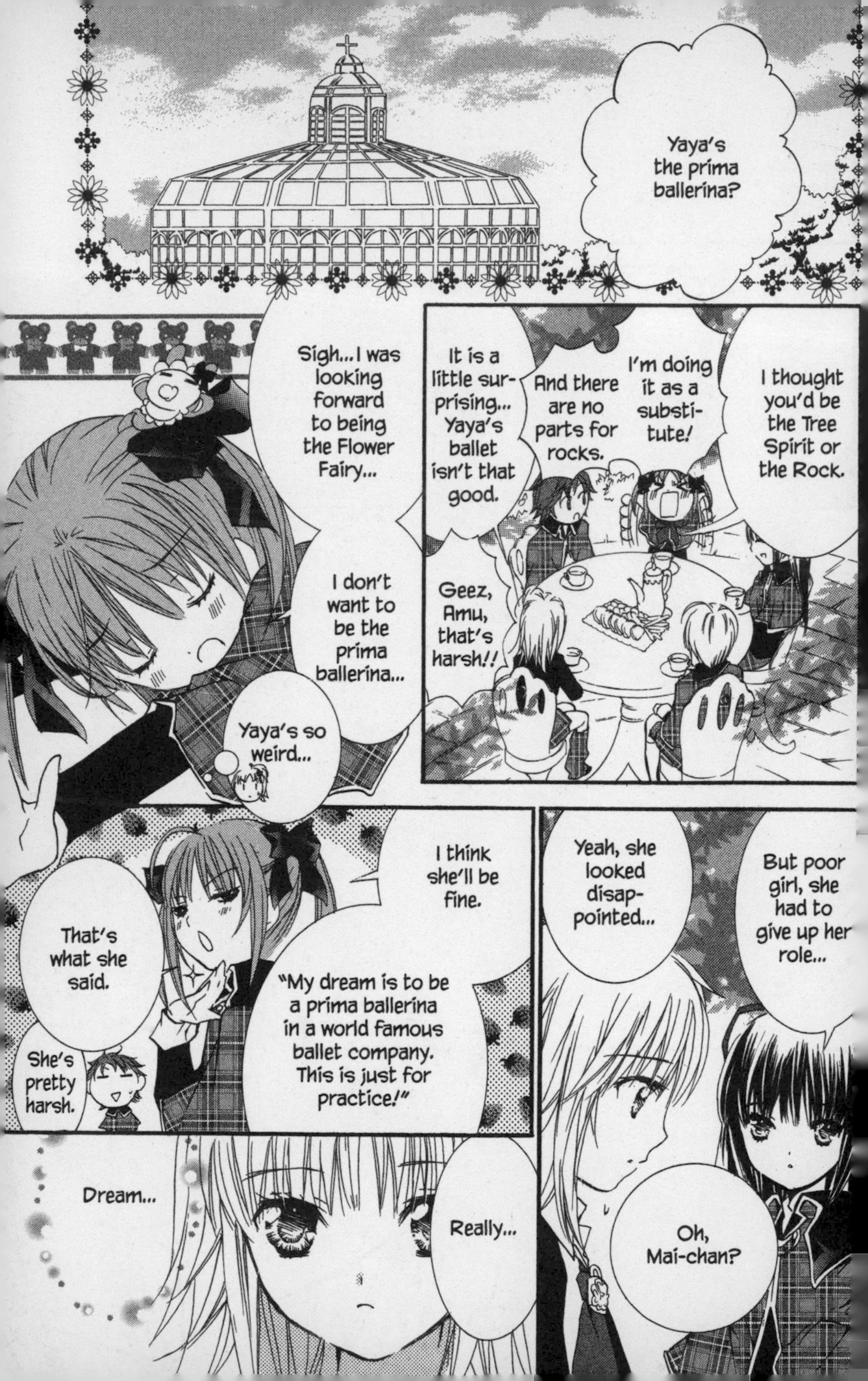

Yaya's the prima ballerina?
I thought you'd be the Tree Spirit or the Rock.
I'm doing it as a substitute!
And there are no parts for rocks.
It is a little surprising... Yaya's ballet isn't that good.
Geez, Amu, that's harsh!!
Sigh...I was looking forward to being the Flower Fairy...
I don't want to be the prima ballerina...
Yaya's so weird...
But poor girl, she had to give up her role...
Yeah, she looked disappointed...
Oh, Mai-chan?
I think she'll be fine.
That's what she said.
"My dream is to be a prima ballerina in a world famous ballet company. This is just for practice!"
She's pretty harsh.
Really...
Dream...

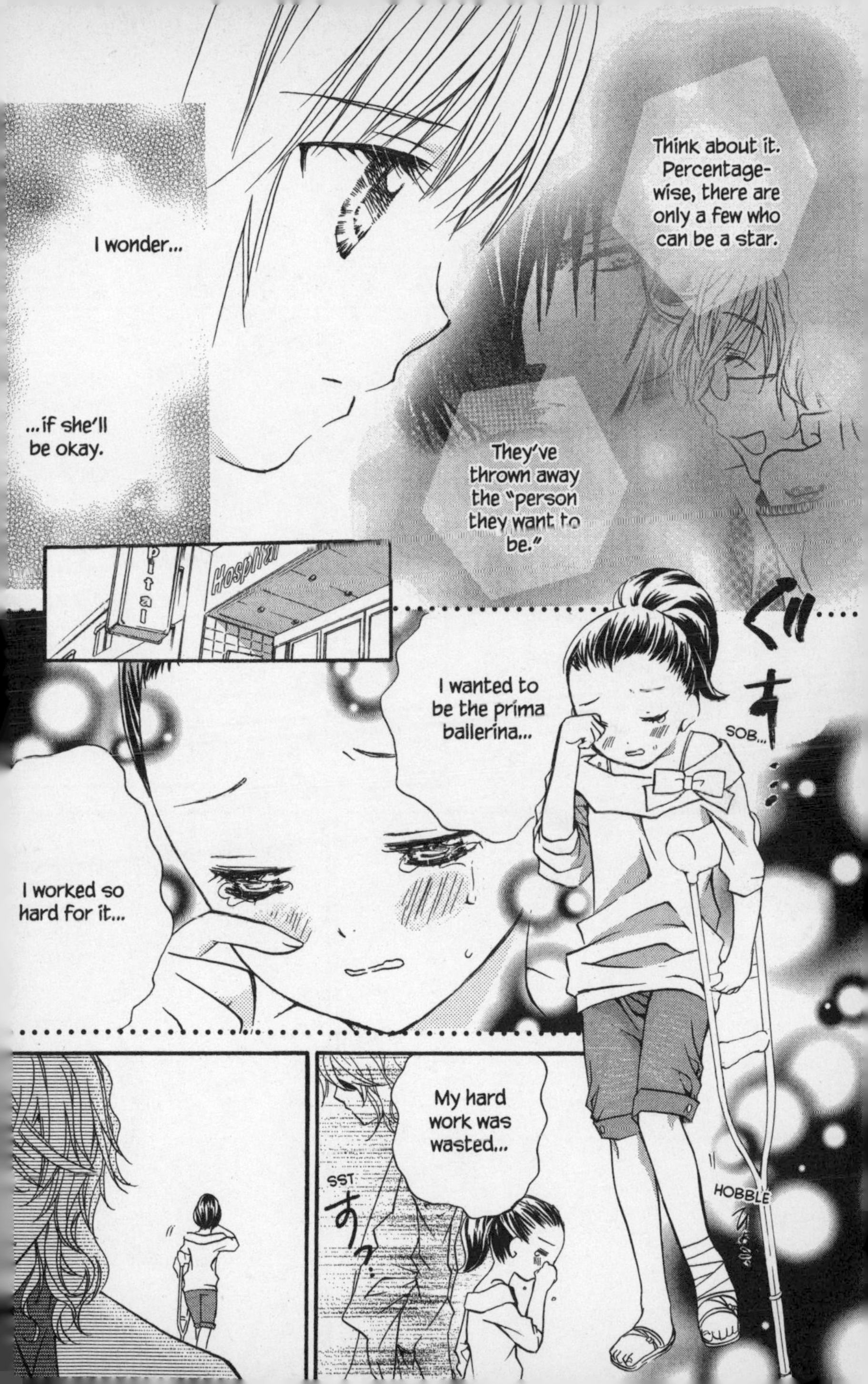
Think about it. Percentage-wise, there are only a few who can be a star.
They've thrown away the "person they want to be."
I wonder...
...if she'll be okay.
I wanted to be the prima ballerina...
SOB...
I worked so hard for it...
My hard work was wasted...
SST
HOBBLE

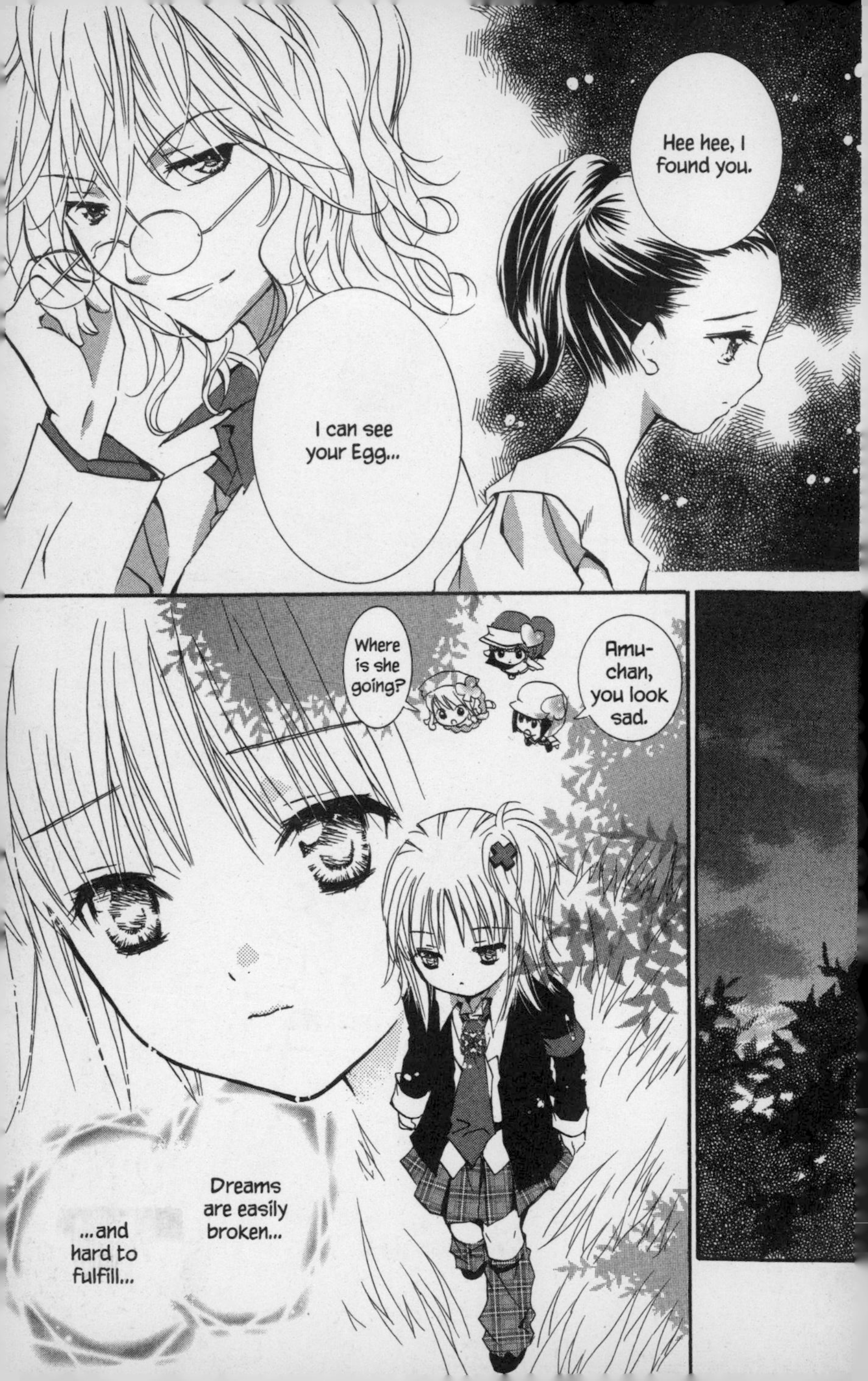
Hee hee, I found you.
I can see your Egg...
Amu-chan, you look sad.
Where is she going?
Dreams are easily broken...
...and hard to fulfill...

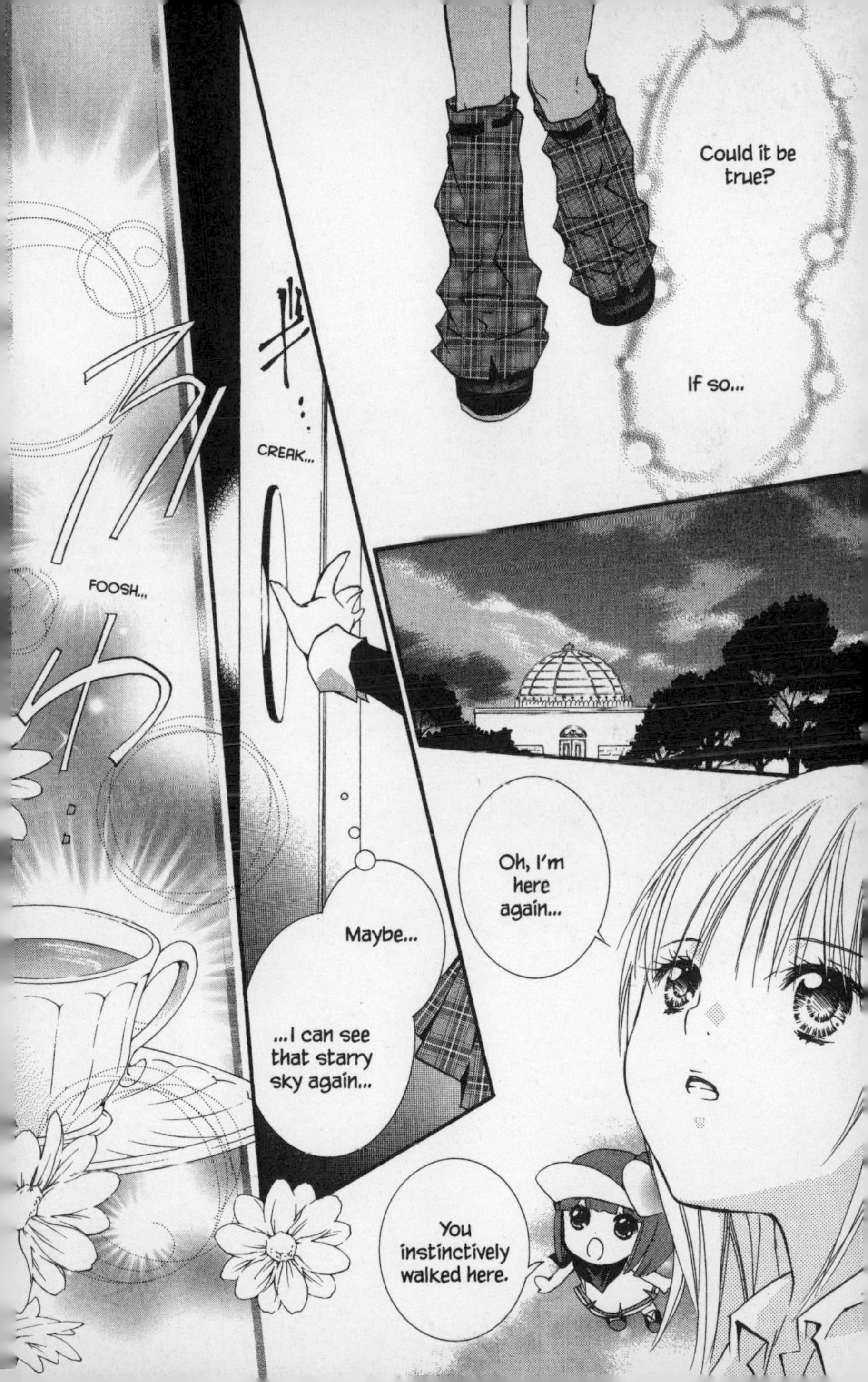
Could it be true?
If so...
Oh, I'm here again...
You instinctively walked here.
CREAK...
Maybe...
...I can see that starry sky again...
FOOSH...

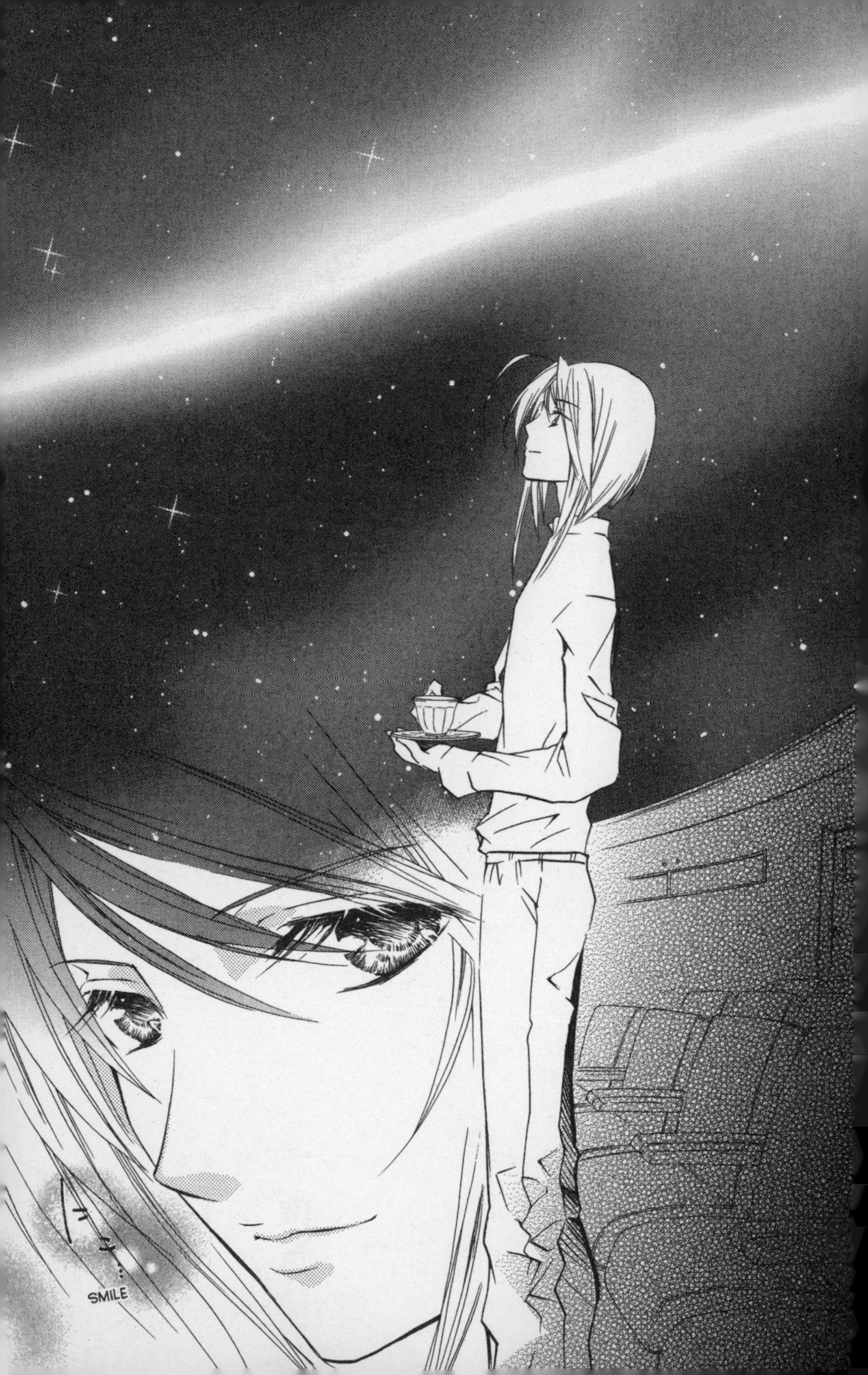
SMILE

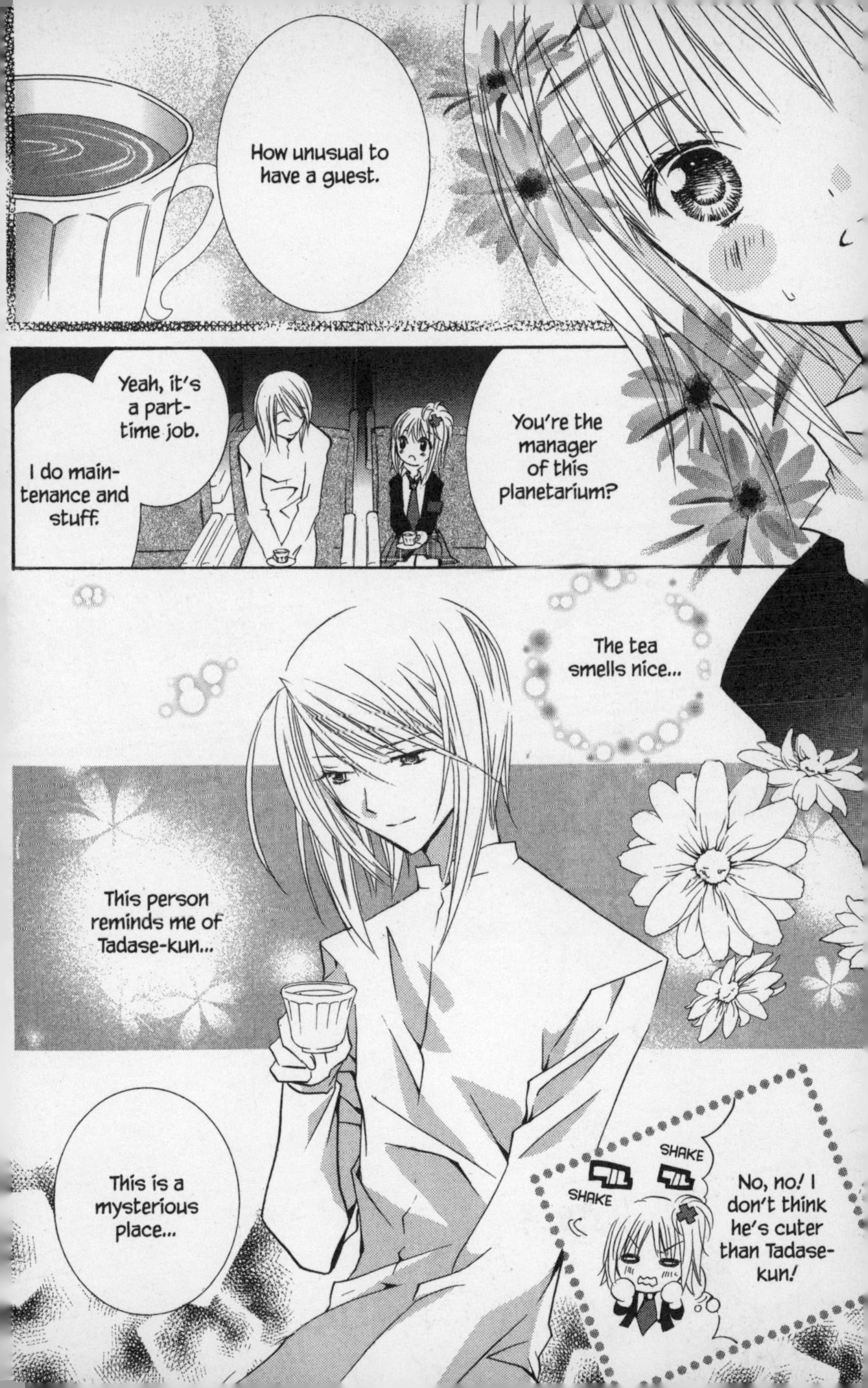
How unusual to have a guest.
You're the manager of this planetarium?
Yeah, it's a part-time job.
I do maintenance and stuff.
The tea smells nice...
This person reminds me of Tadase-kun...
SHAKE
SHAKE
No, no! I don't think he's cuter than Tadase-kun!
This is a mysterious place...

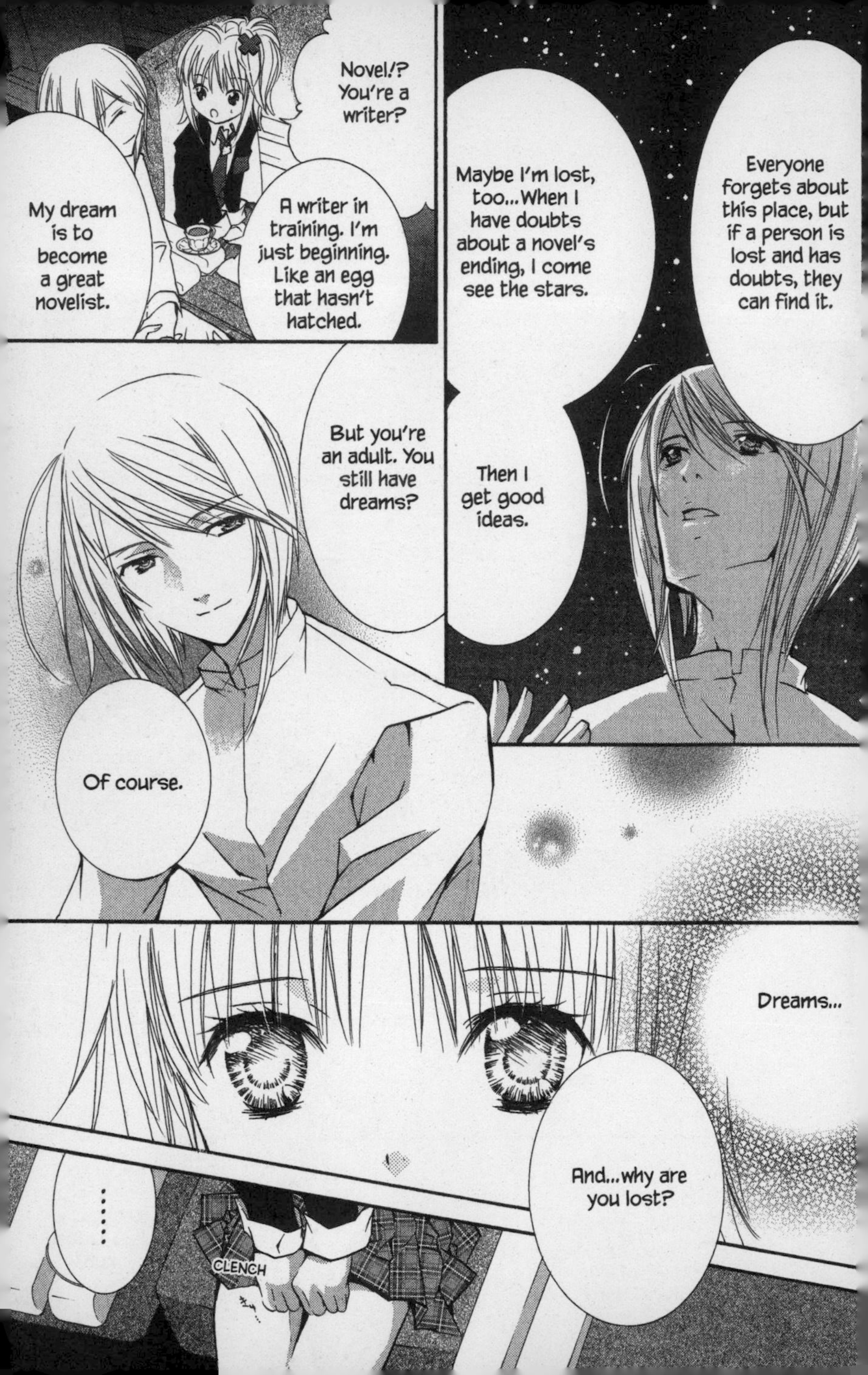
Everyone forgets about this place, but if a person is lost and has doubts, they can find it.
Maybe I'm lost, too...When I have doubts about a novel's ending, I come see the stars.
Then I get good ideas.
Novel!? You're a writer?
A writer in training. I'm just beginning. Like an egg that hasn't hatched.
My dream is to become a great novelist.
But you're an adult. You still have dreams?
Of course.
Dreams...
And...why are you lost?
......
CLENCH

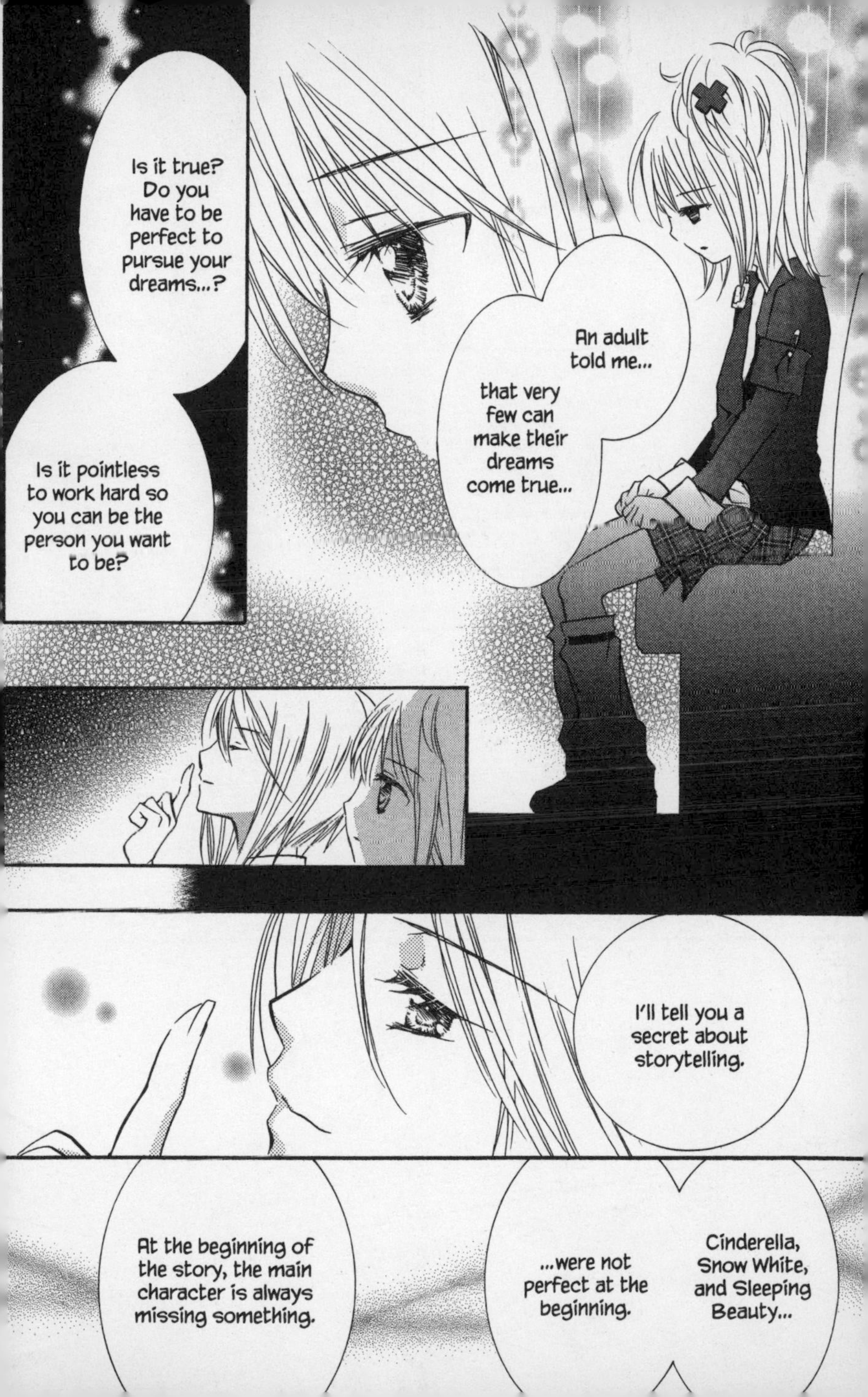
An adult told me...
that very few can make their dreams come true...
Is it true? Do you have to be perfect to pursue your dreams...?
Is it pointless to work hard so you can be the person you want to be?
I'll tell you a secret about storytelling.
Cinderella, Snow White, and Sleeping Beauty...
...were not perfect at the beginning.
At the beginning of the story, the main character is always missing something.

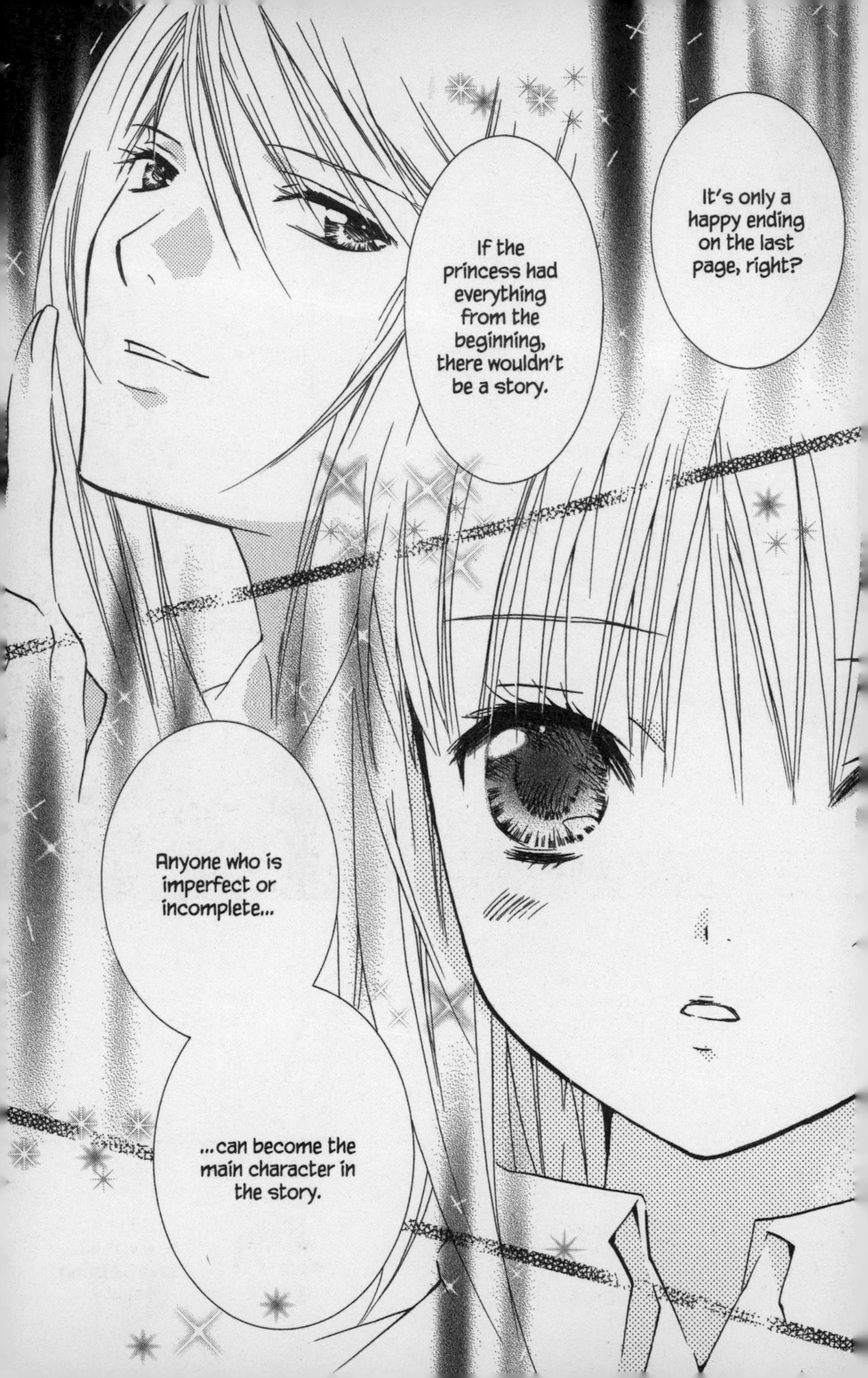
It's only a happy ending on the last page, right?
If the princess had everything from the beginning, there wouldn't be a story.
Anyone who is imperfect or incomplete...
...can become the main character in the story.

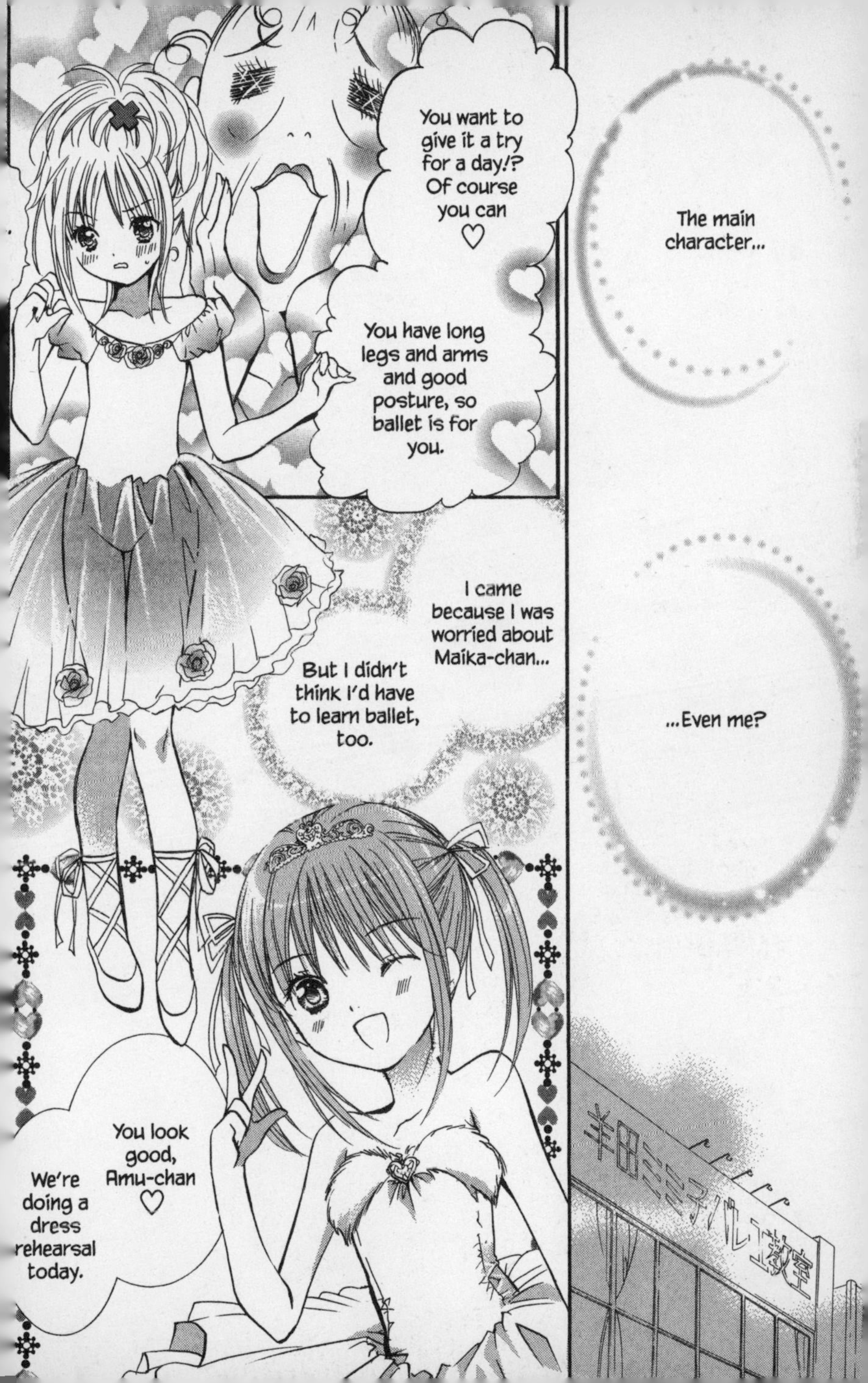
The main character...
...Even me?
You want to give it a try for a day!? Of course you can ♡
You have long legs and arms and good posture, so ballet is for you.
I came because I was worried about Maika-chan...
But I didn't think I'd have to learn ballet, too.
You look good, Amu-chan ♡
We're doing a dress rehearsal today.

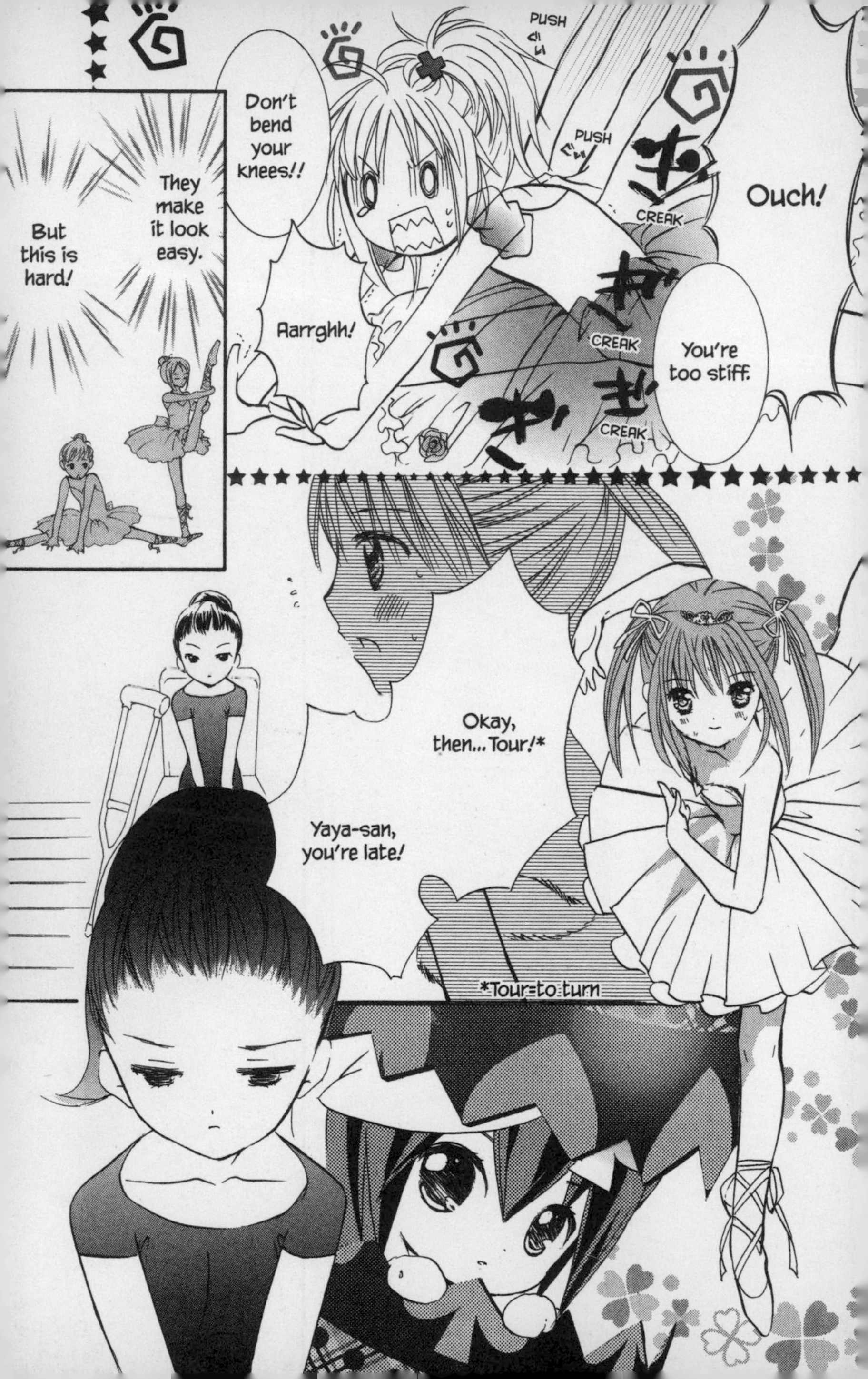
Ouch!
PUSH
PUSH
CREAK
Don't bend your knees!!
You're too stiff.
CREAK
CREAK
Aarrghh!
They make it look easy.
But this is hard!
Okay, then... Tour!*
Yaya-san, you're late!
*Tour=to turn

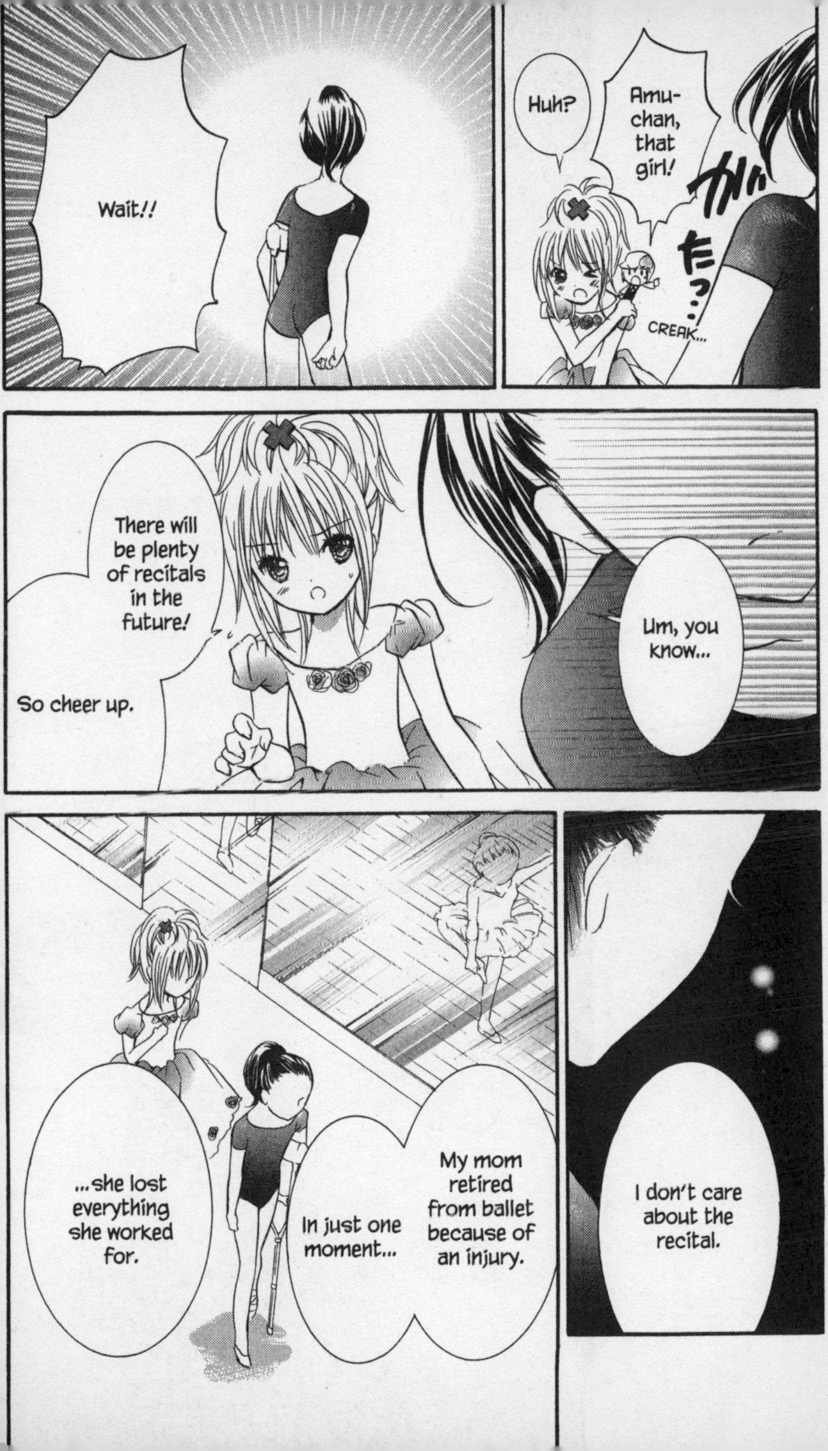
Amu-chan, that girl!
Huh?
CREAK...
Wait!!
Um, you know...
There will be plenty of recitals in the future!
So cheer up.
I don't care about the recital.
My mom retired from ballet because of an injury.
In just one moment...
...she lost everything she worked for.

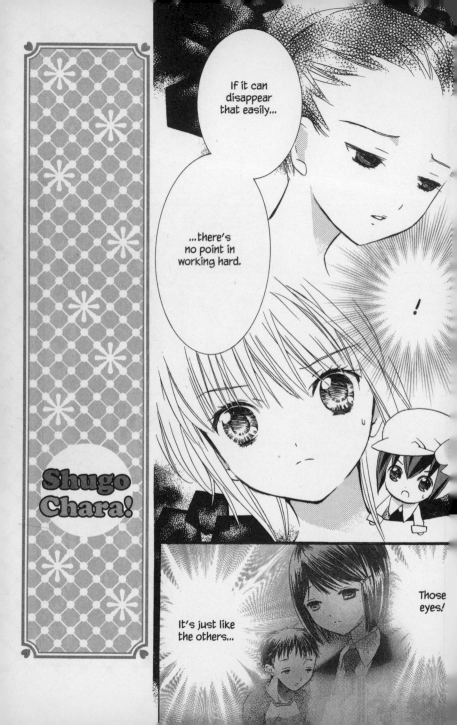

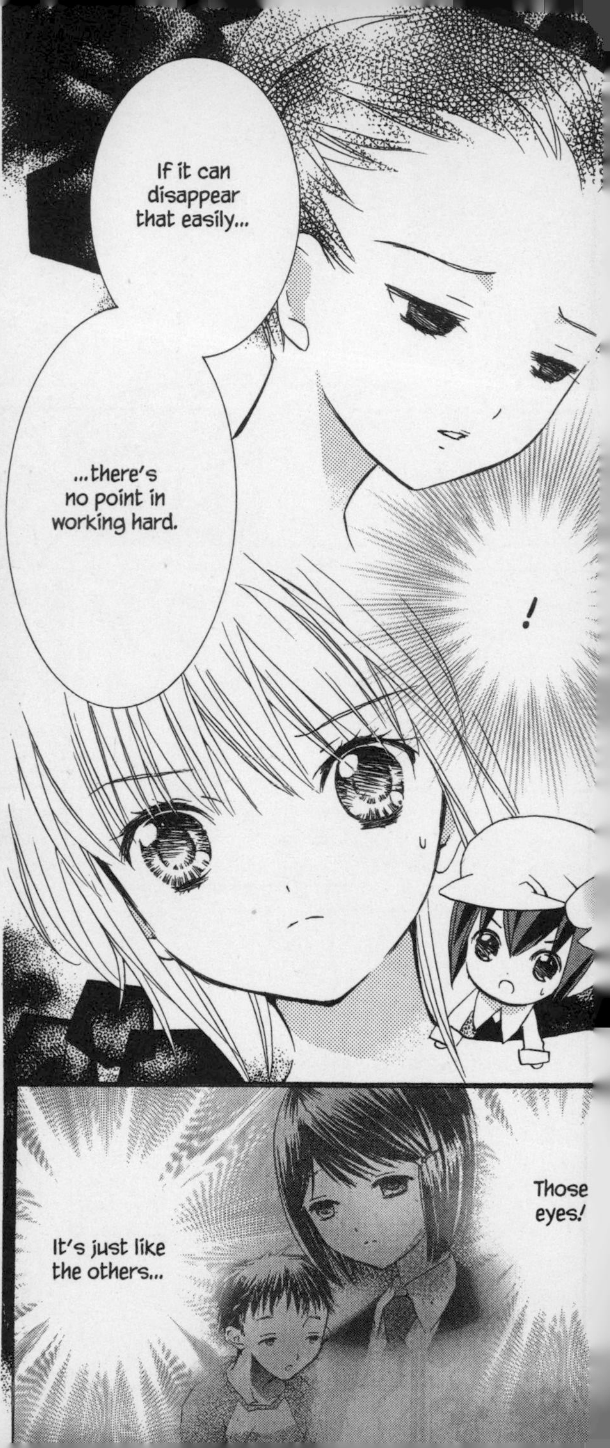
If it can disappear that easily...
...there's no point in working hard.
!
Those eyes!
It's just like the others...

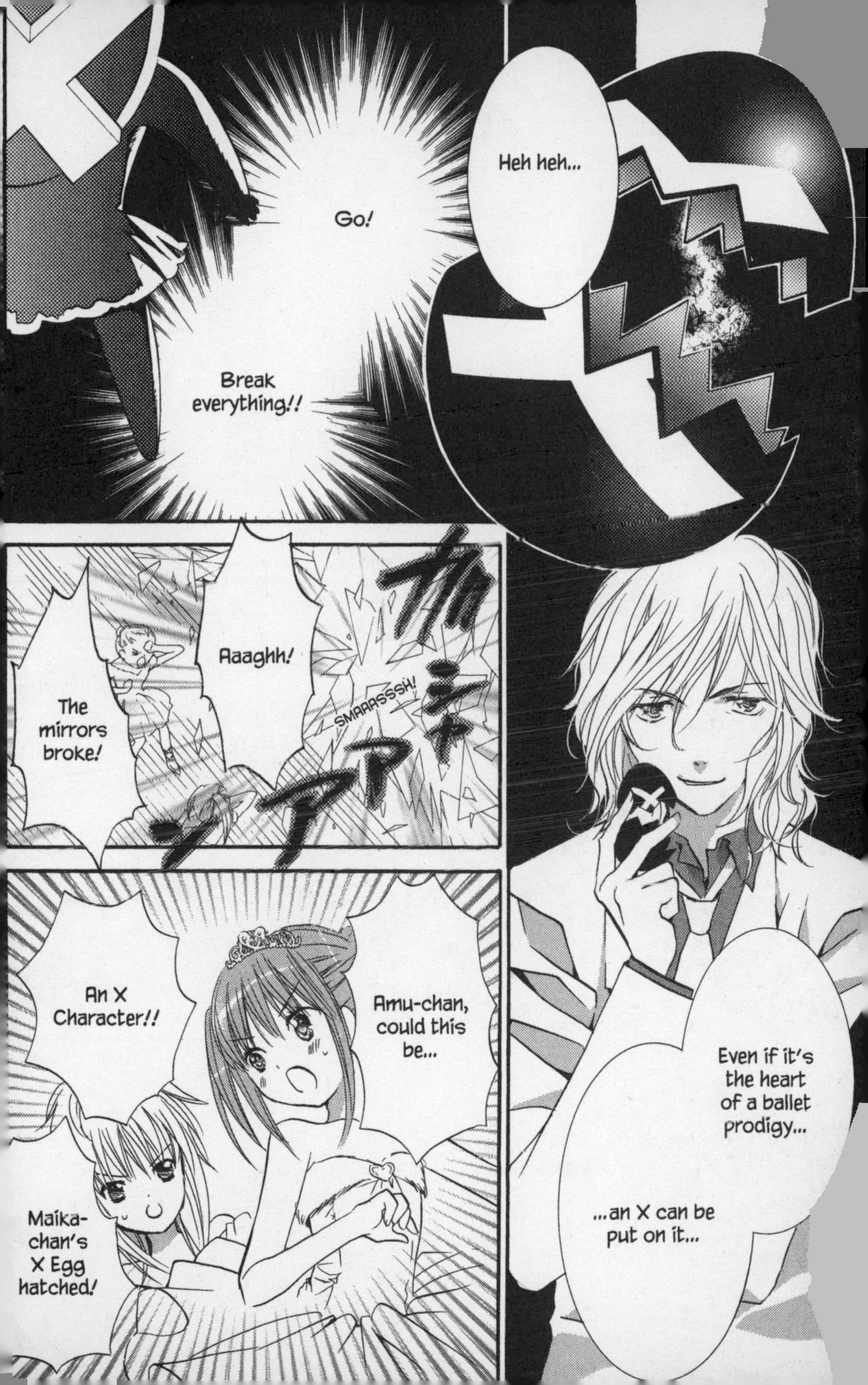
Heh heh...
Even if it's the heart of a ballet prodigy...
...an X can be put on it...
Go!
Break everything!!
SMAAASSSH!
Aaaghh!
The mirrors broke!
Amu-chan, could this be...
An X Character!!
Maika-chan's X Egg hatched!

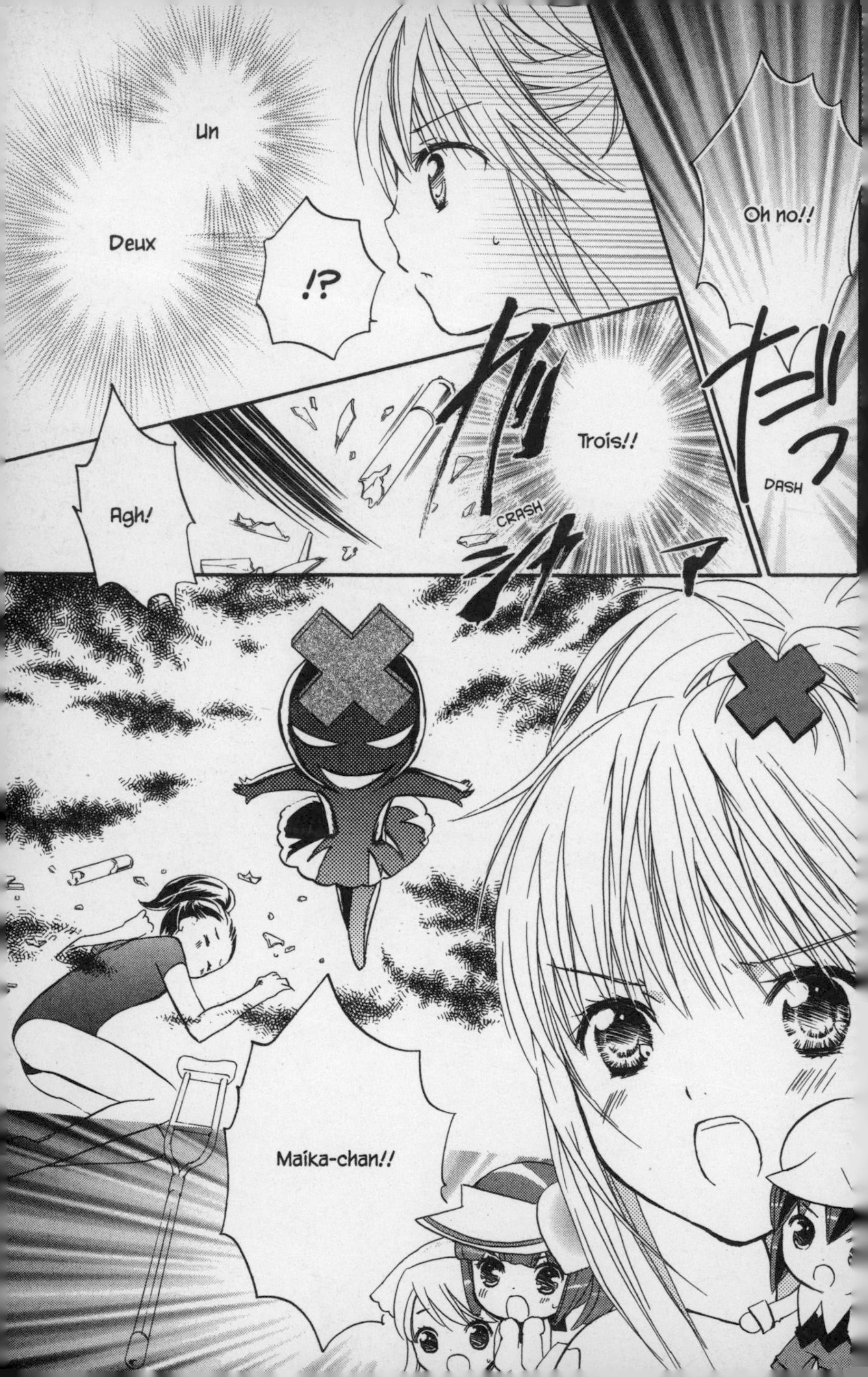
Oh no!!
DASH
Un
Deux
!?
Trois!!
CRASH
Agh!
Maika-chan!!

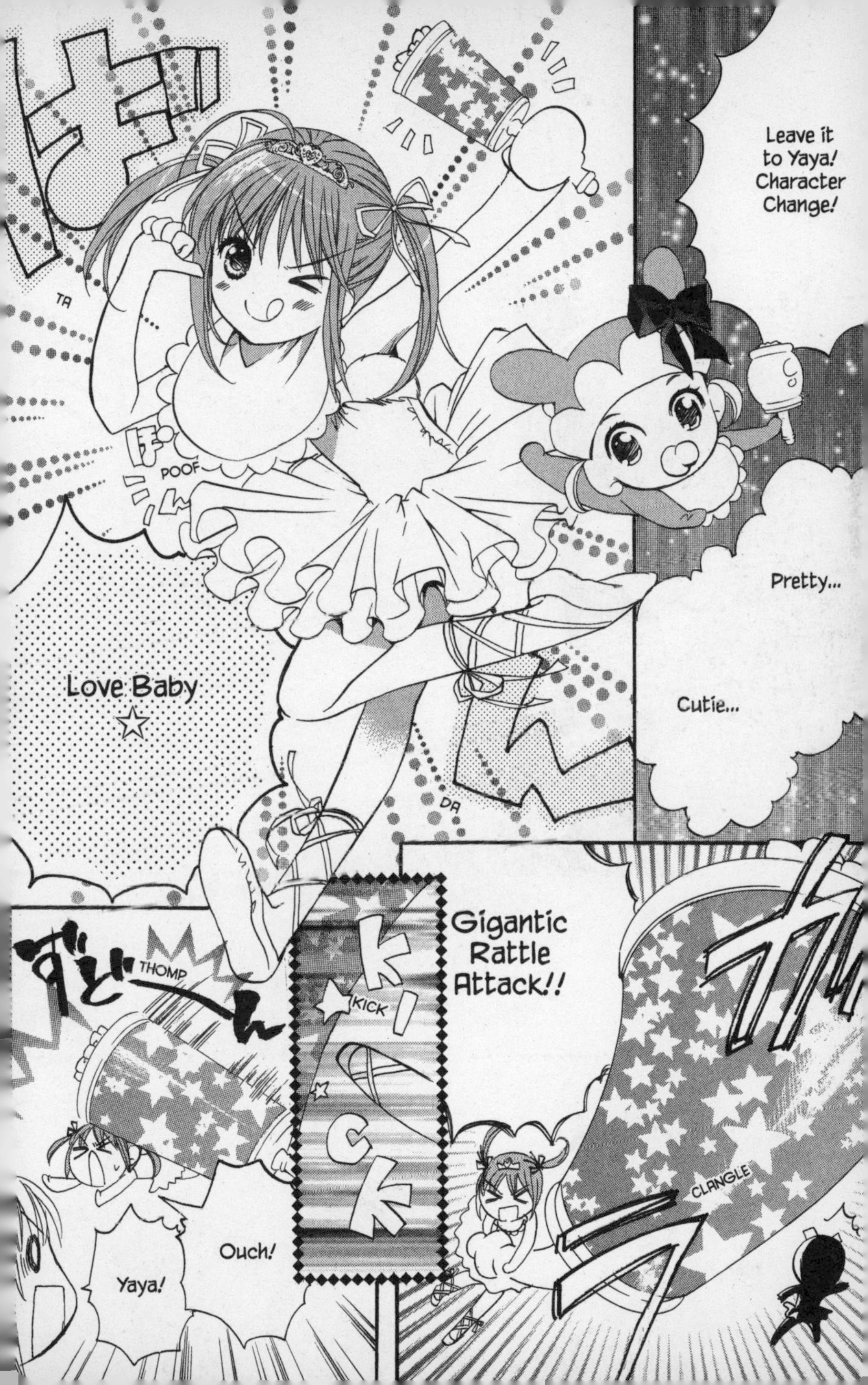
Leave it to Yaya! Character Change!
Pretty...
Cutie...
TA
POOF
Love Baby ☆
DA
Gigantic Rattle Attack!!
CLANGLE
KICK
THOMP
Ouch!
Yaya!

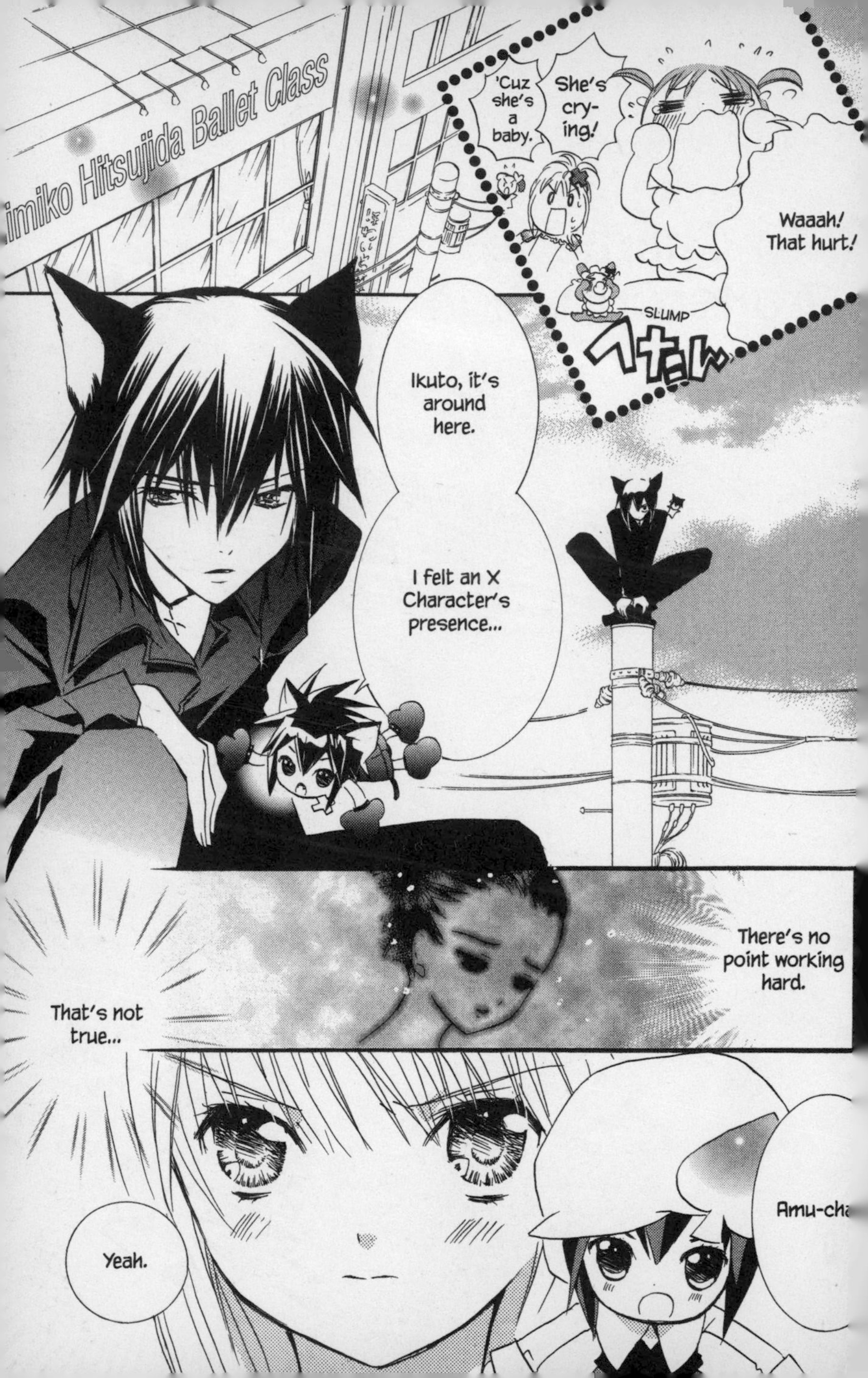
Waaah! That hurt!
She's cry-ing!
'Cuz she's a baby.
SLUMP
imiko Hitsujida Ballet Class
Ikuto, it's around here.
I felt an X Character's presence...
There's no point working hard.
That's not true...
Amu-cha
Yeah.

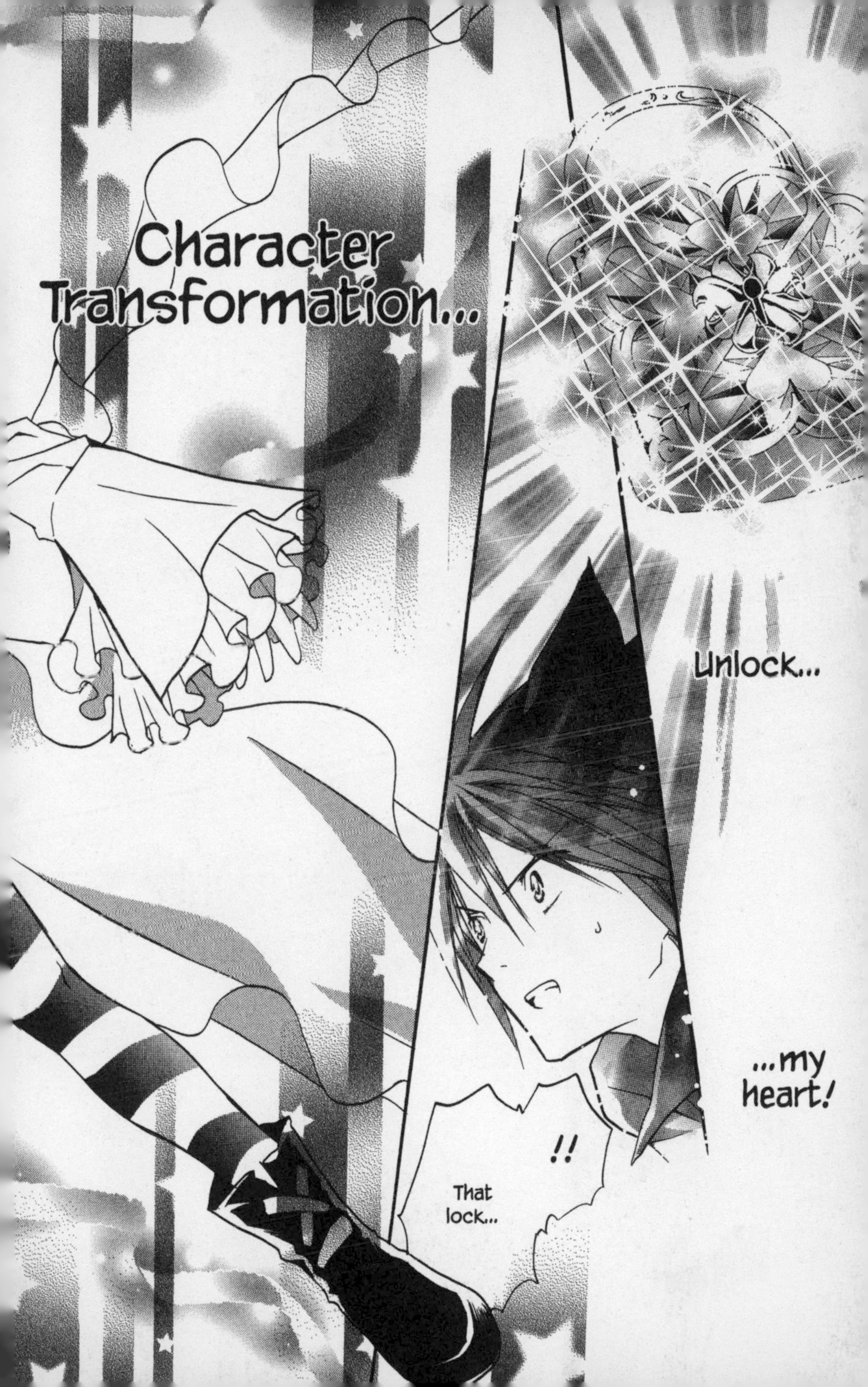
Unlock...
...my heart!
!!
That lock...
Character Transformation...

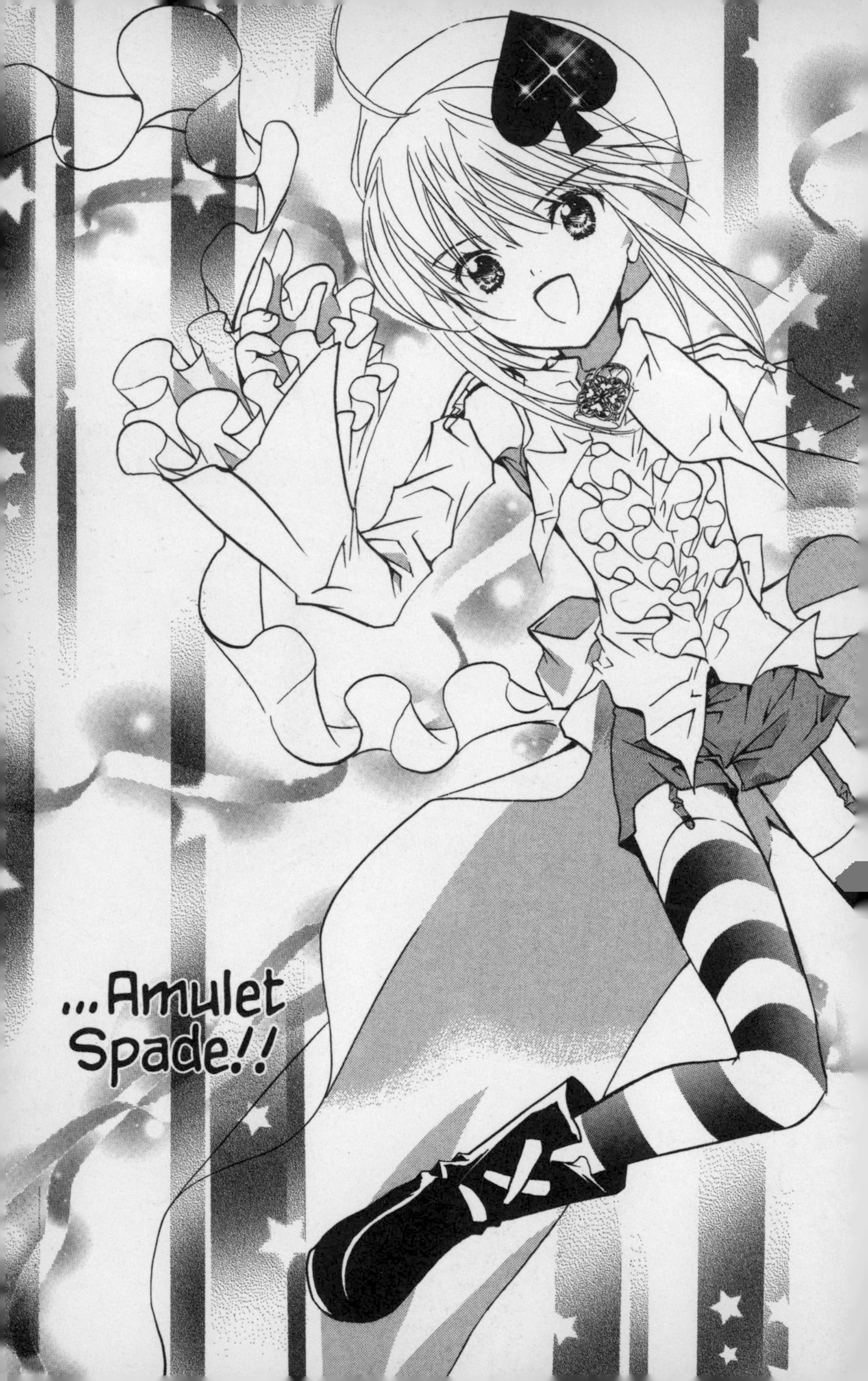
...Amulet Spade!!

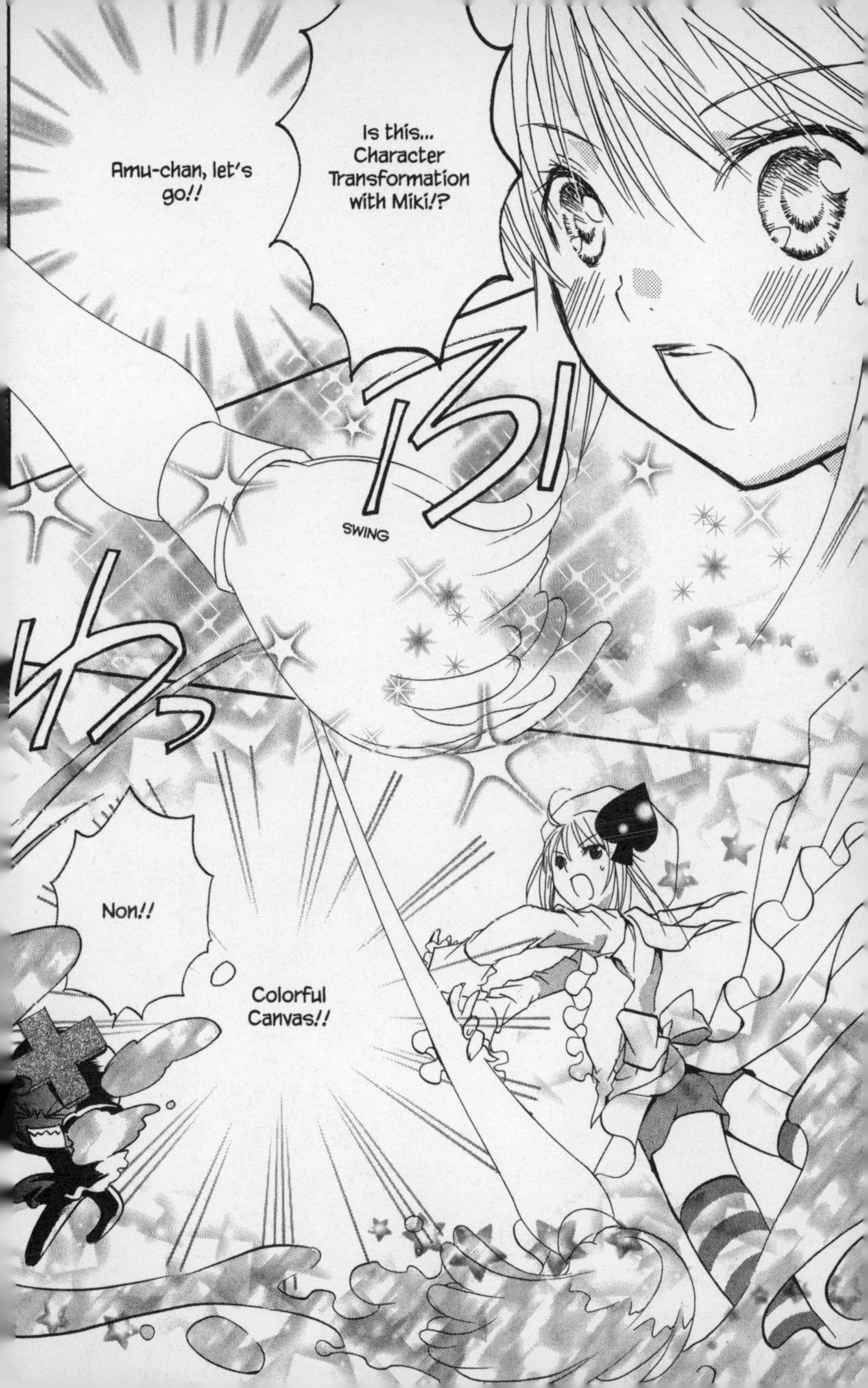
Is this... Character Transformation with Miki!?
Amu-chan, let's go!!
SWING
Non!!
Colorful Canvas!!

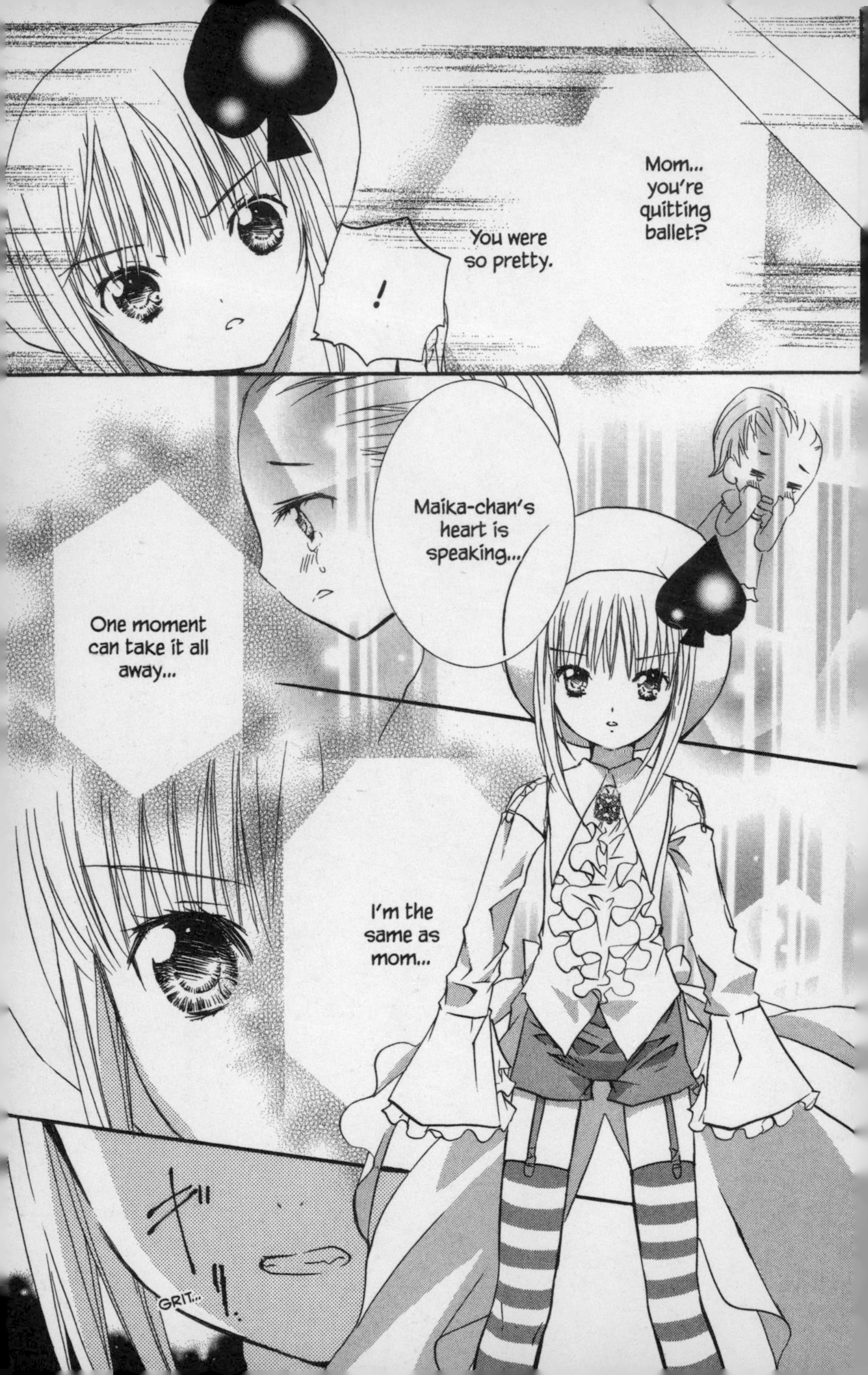
Mom... you're quitting ballet?
You were so pretty.
!
Maika-chan's heart is speaking...
One moment can take it all away...
I'm the same as mom...
GRIT...

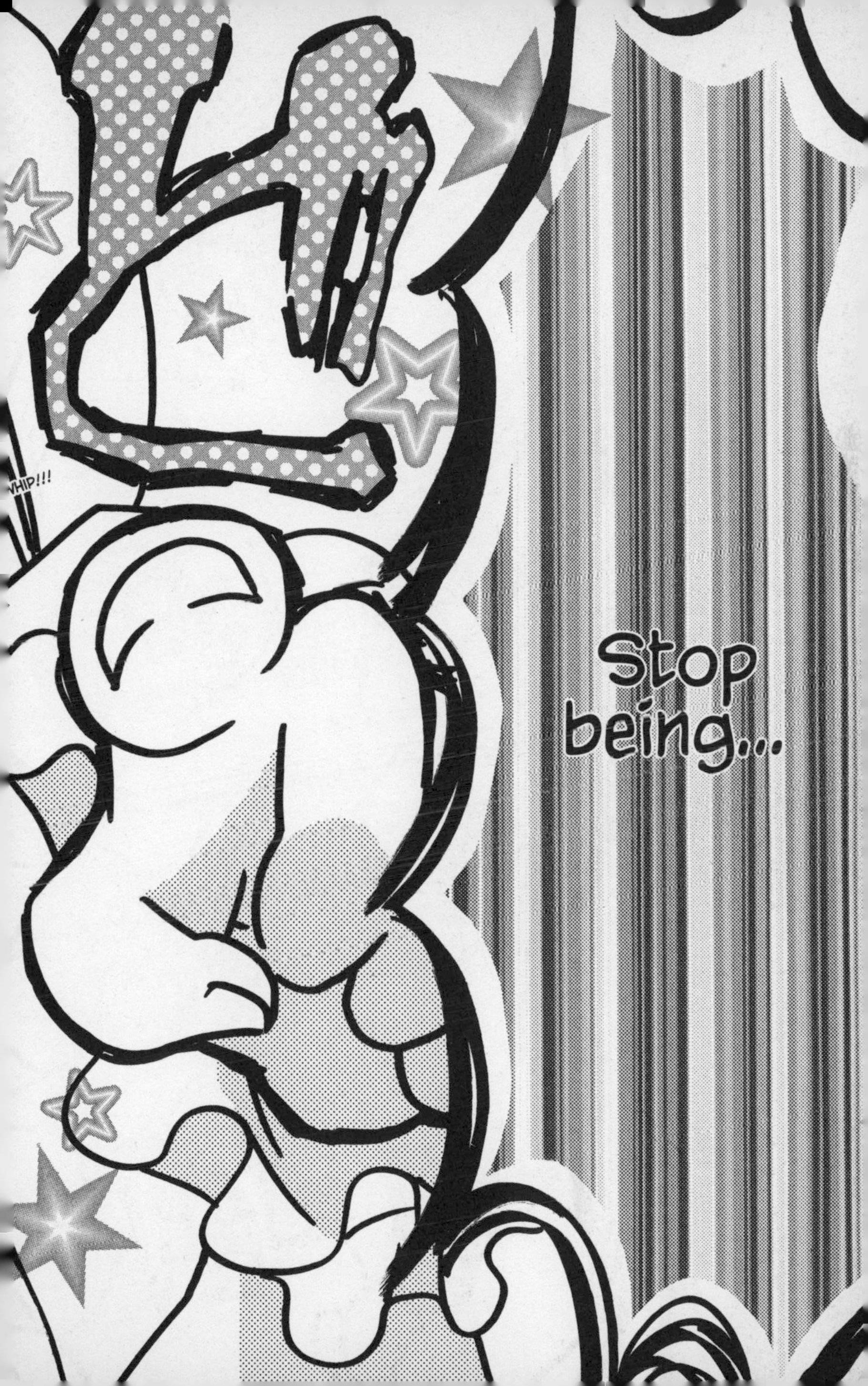
Stop being...
WHIP!!!

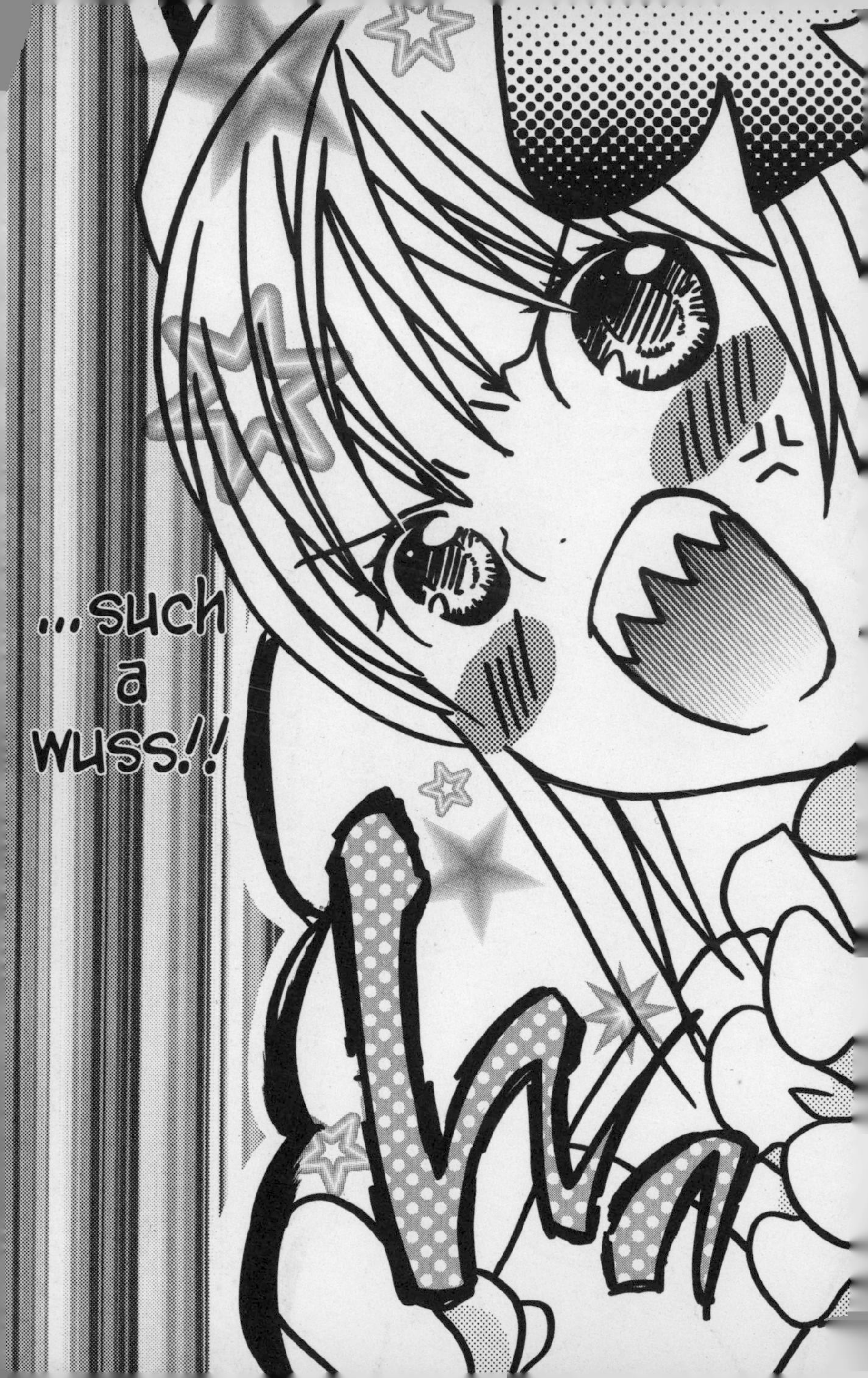
...such a wuss!!

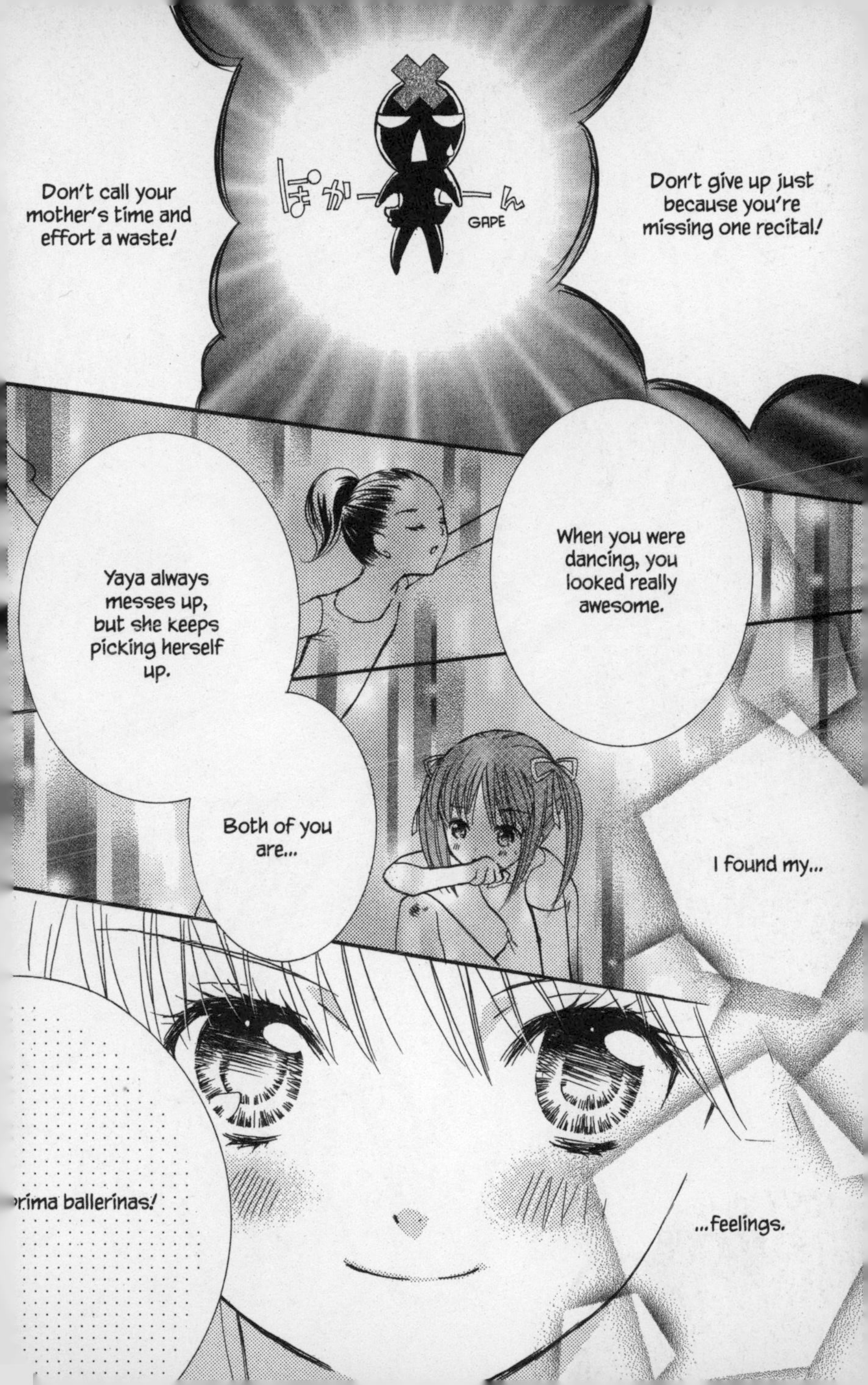
Don't give up just because you're missing one recital!
ぽかーーん
GAPE
Don't call your mother's time and effort a waste!
When you were dancing, you looked really awesome.
Yaya always messes up, but she keeps picking herself up.
I found my...
Both of you are...
...feelings.
prima ballerinas!

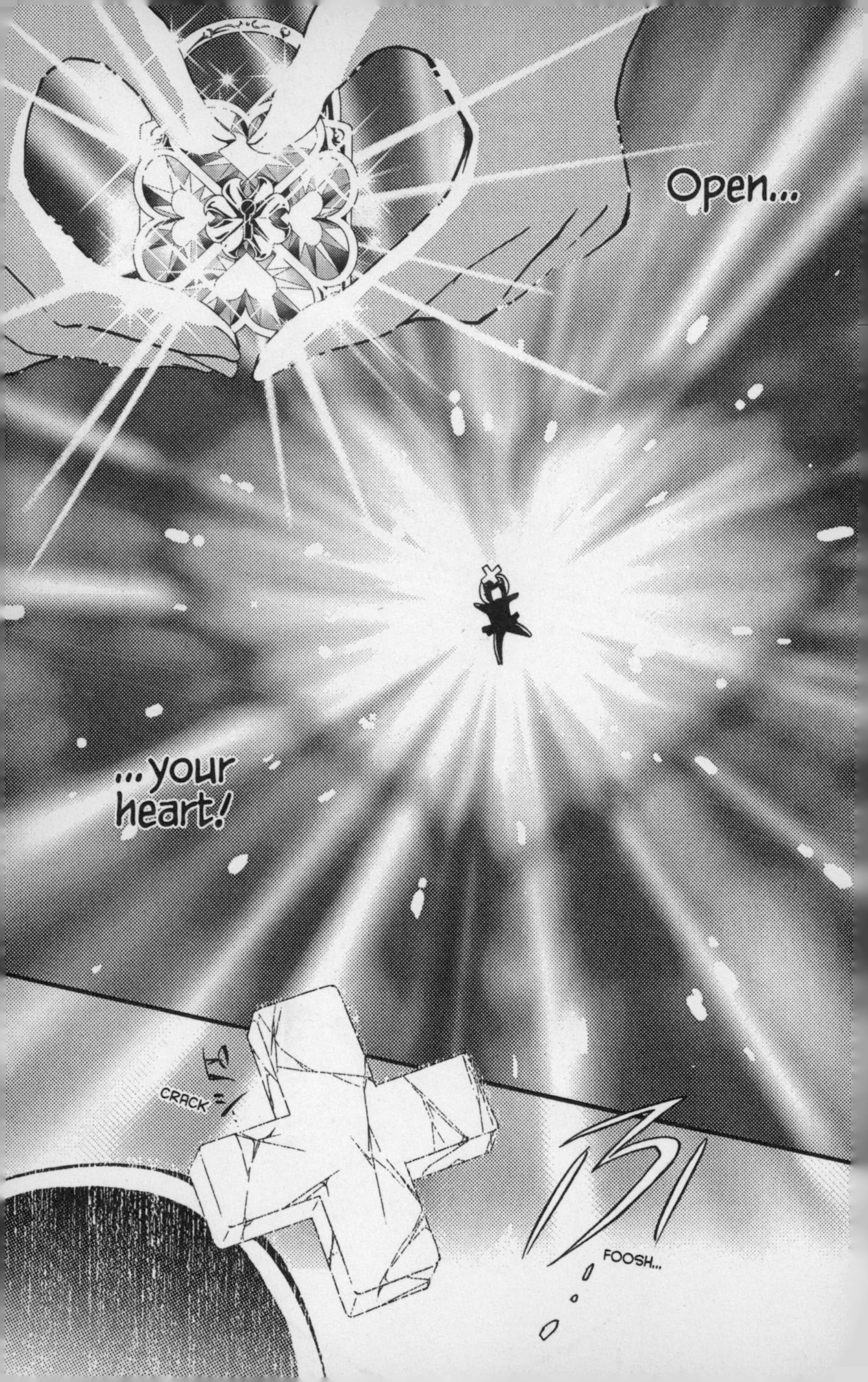
Open...
...your heart!
CRACK
FOOSH...

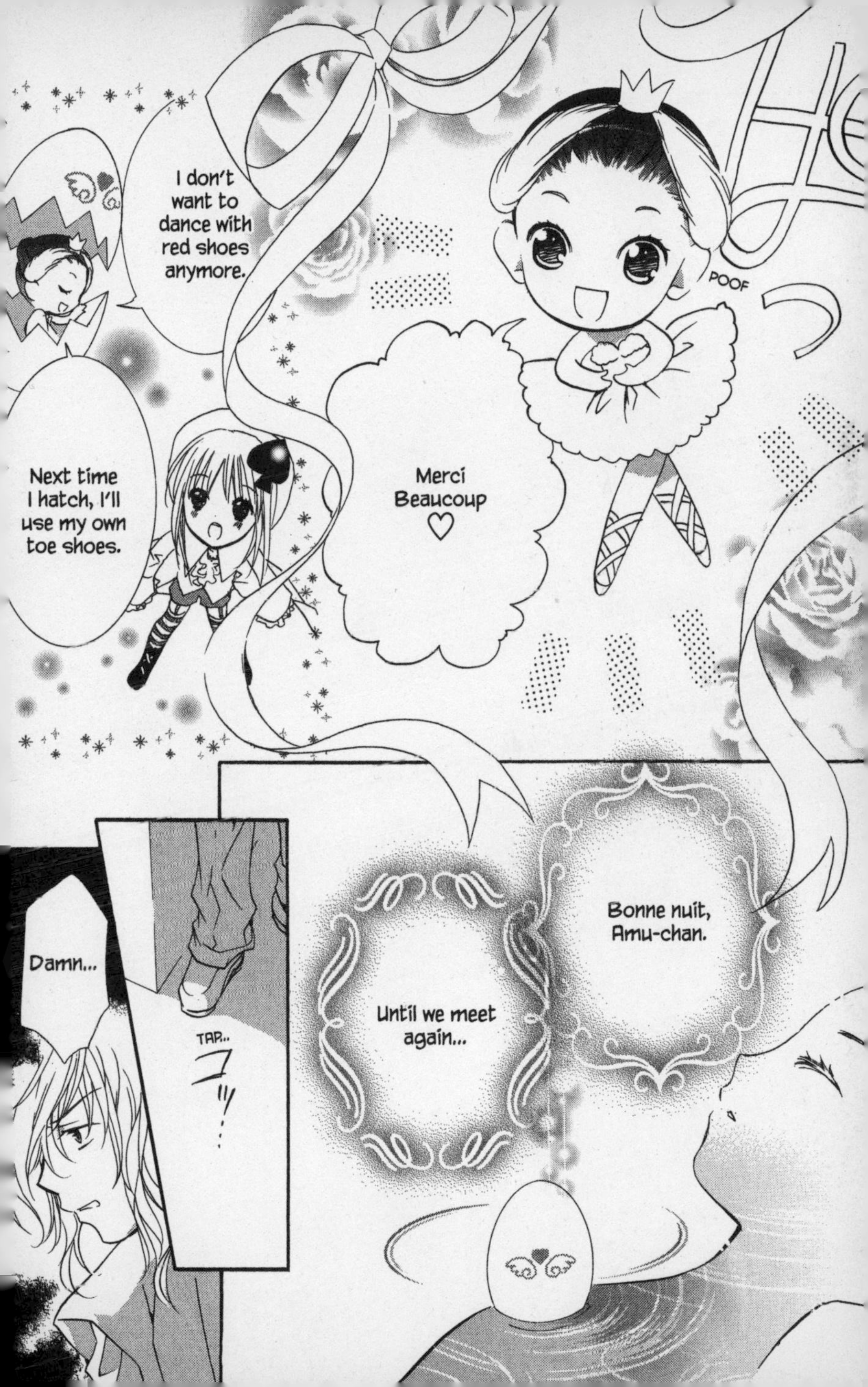
POOF
Merci Beaucoup ♡
I don't want to dance with red shoes anymore.
Next time I hatch, I'll use my own toe shoes.
Bonne nuit, Amu-chan.
Until we meet again...
TAP..
Damn...

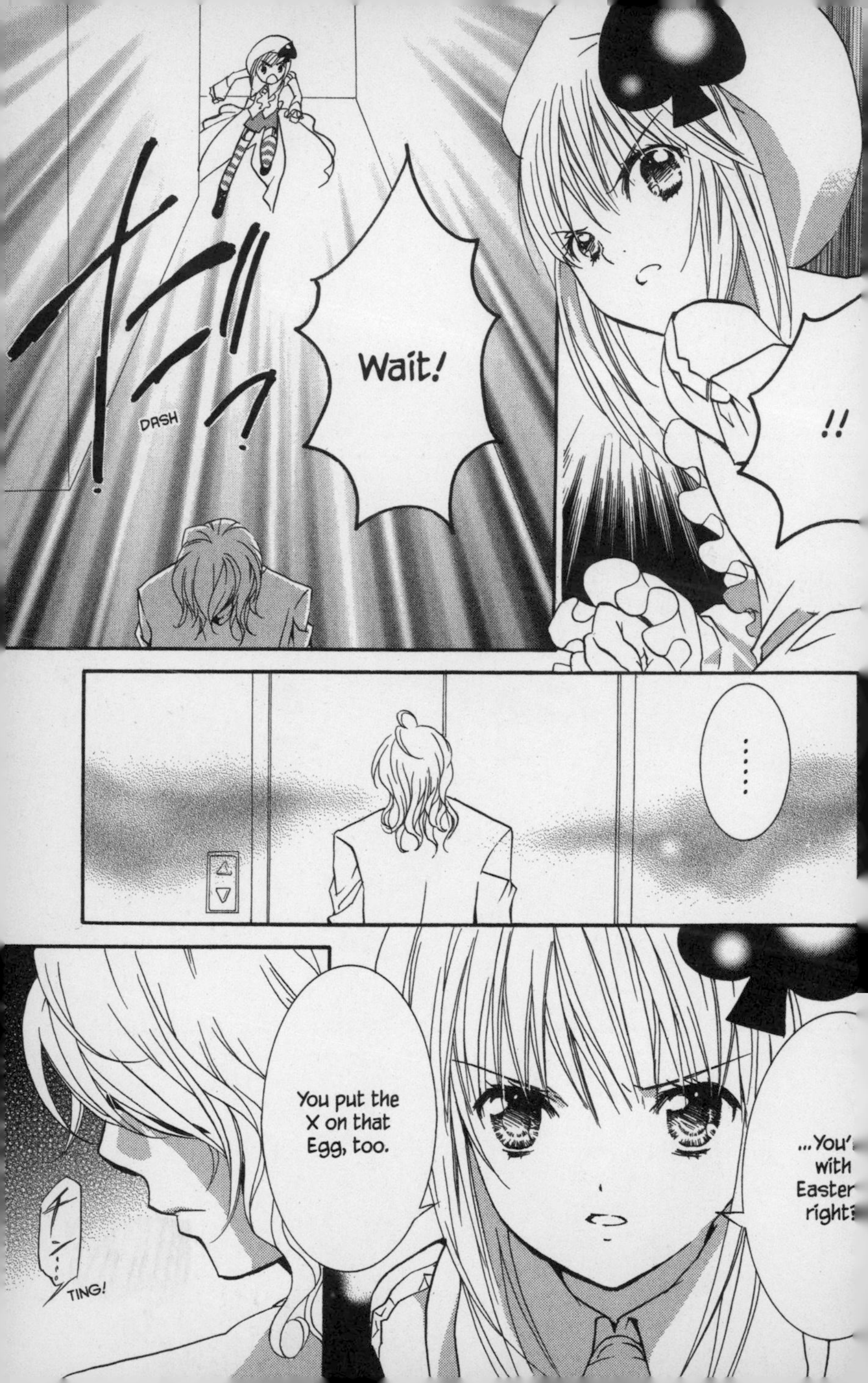
!!
Wait!
DASH
......
...You'
with
Easter
right?
You put the X on that Egg, too.
TING!

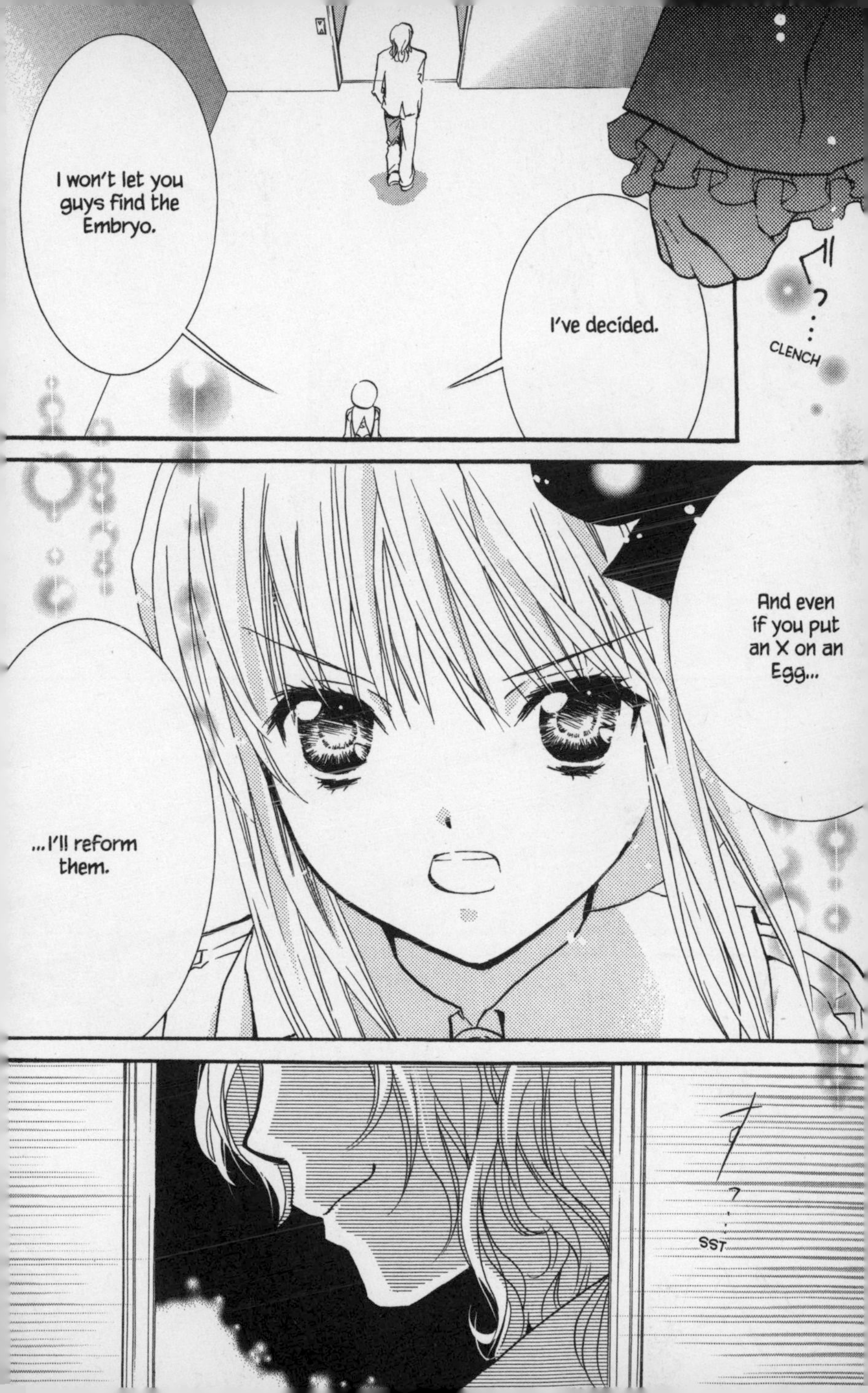
CLENCH
I've decided.
I won't let you guys find the Embryo.
And even if you put an X on an Egg...
...I'll reform them.
SST

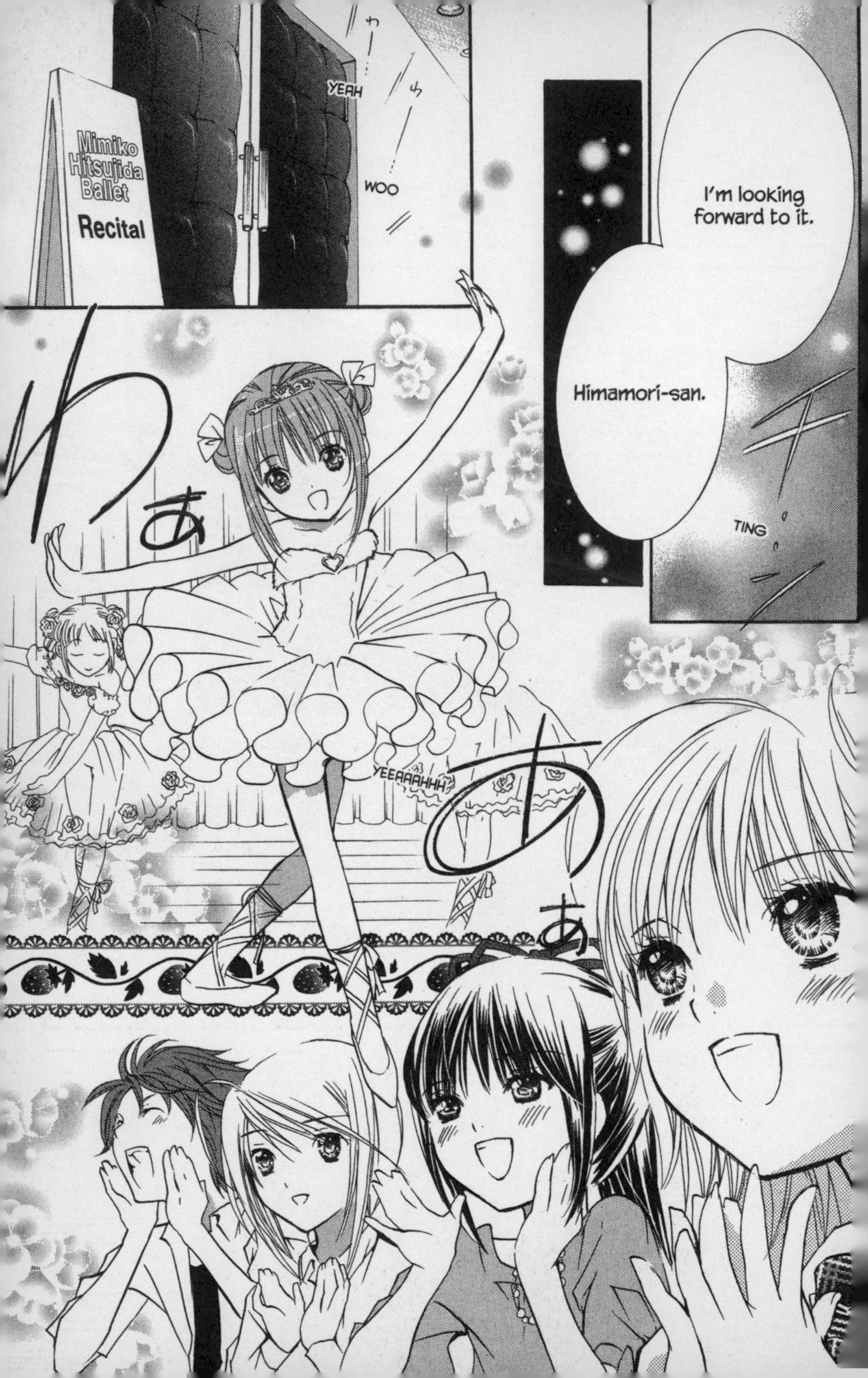
I'm looking forward to it.
Himamori-san.
TING
Mimiko Hitsujida Ballet Recital
YEAH
WOO
YEEAAAHHH

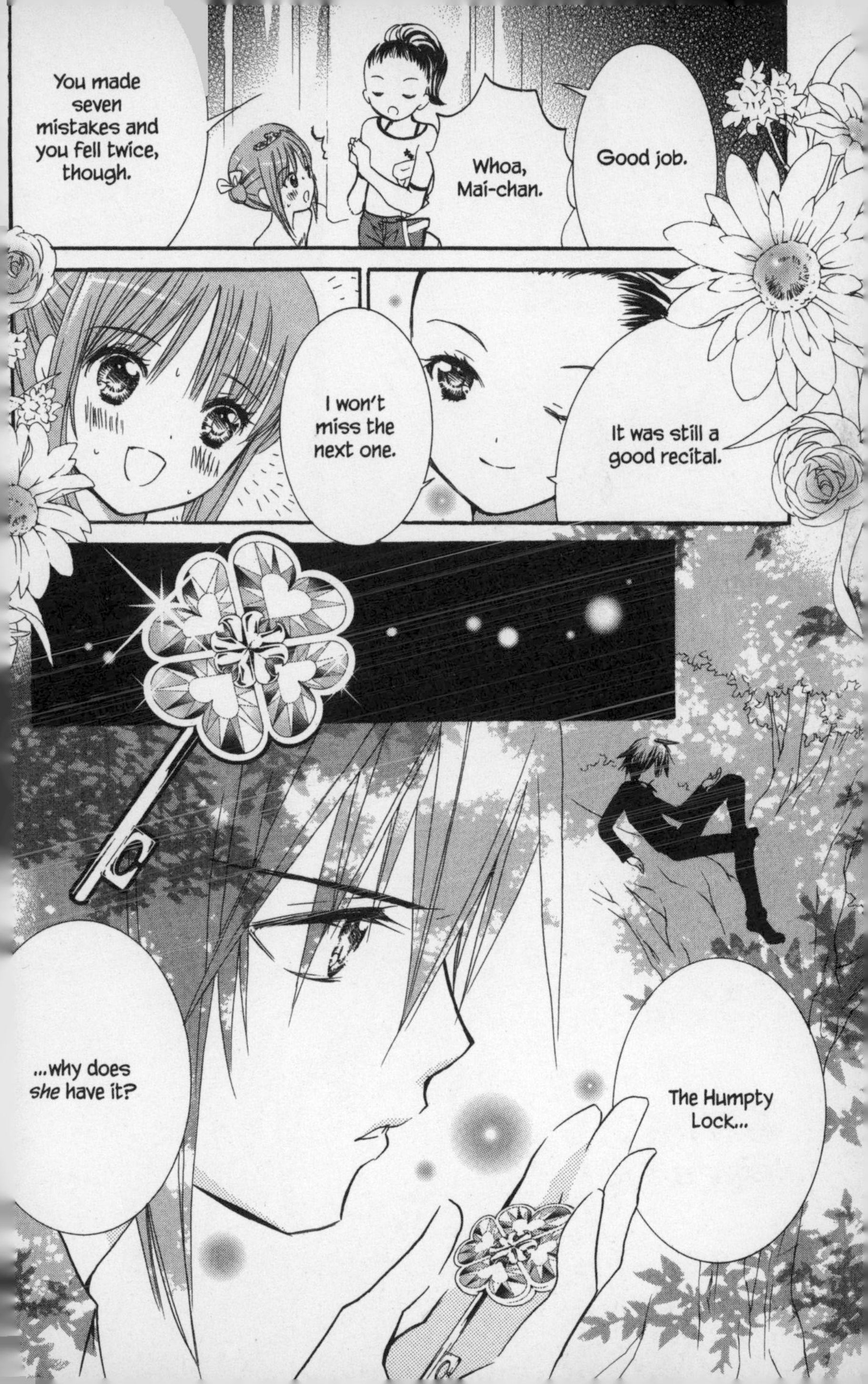
Good job.
Whoa, Mai-chan.
You made seven mistakes and you fell twice, though.
It was still a good recital.
I won't miss the next one.
The Humpty Lock...
...why does *she* have it?

Shugo Chara!

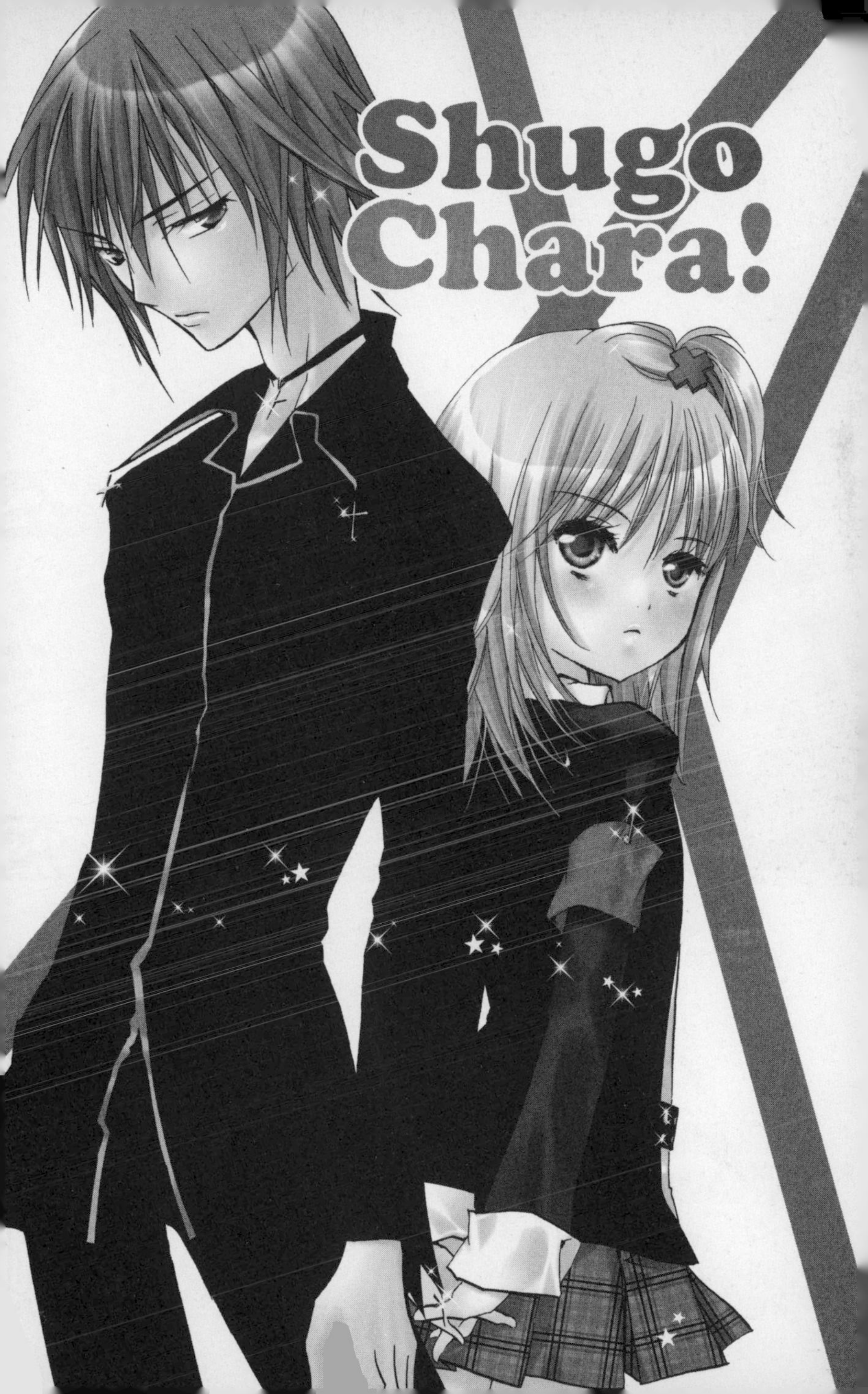
Shugo
Chara!

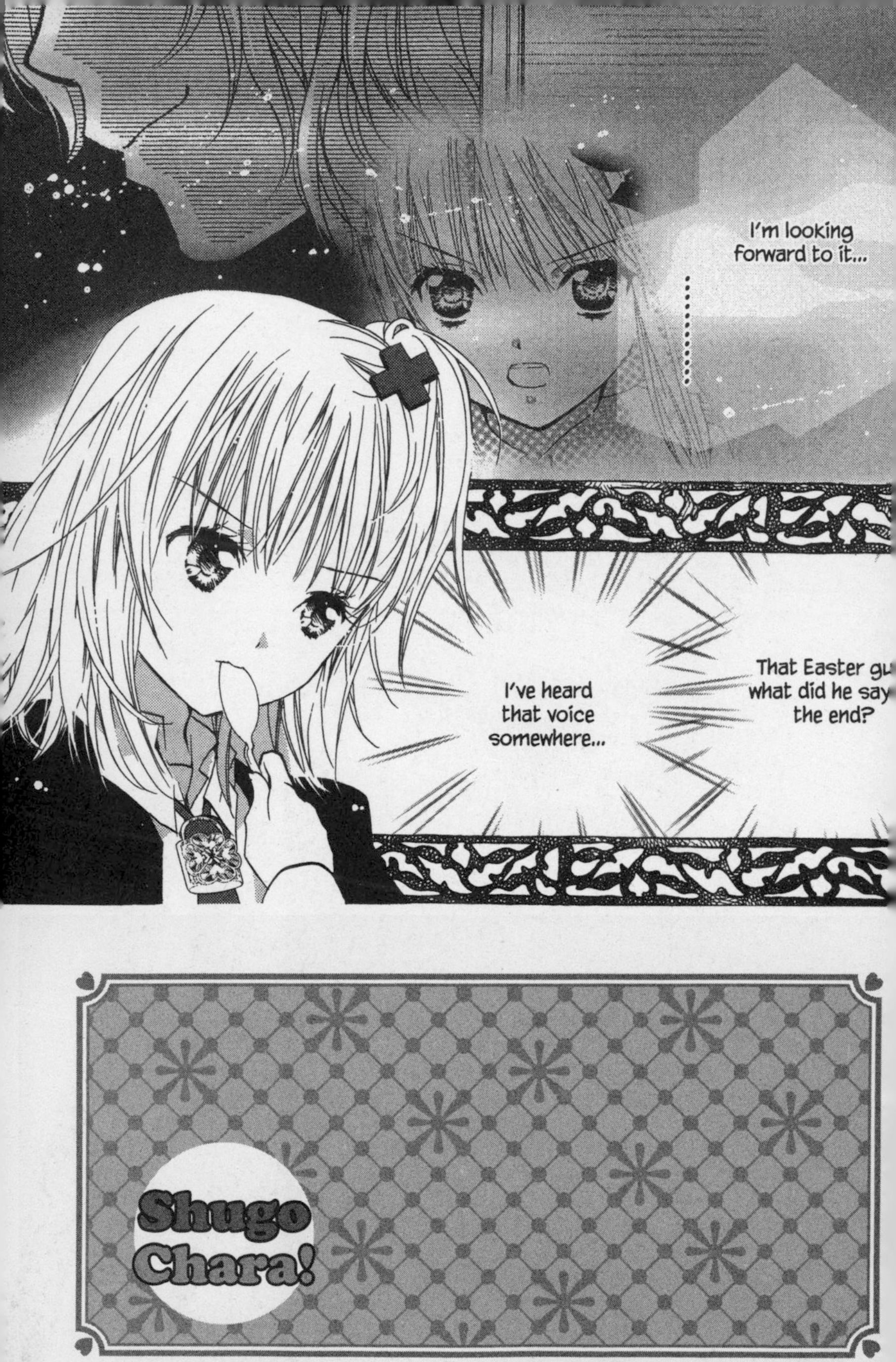
I'm looking forward to it...
......
That Easter gu what did he say the end?
I've heard that voice somewhere...

Shugo Chara!

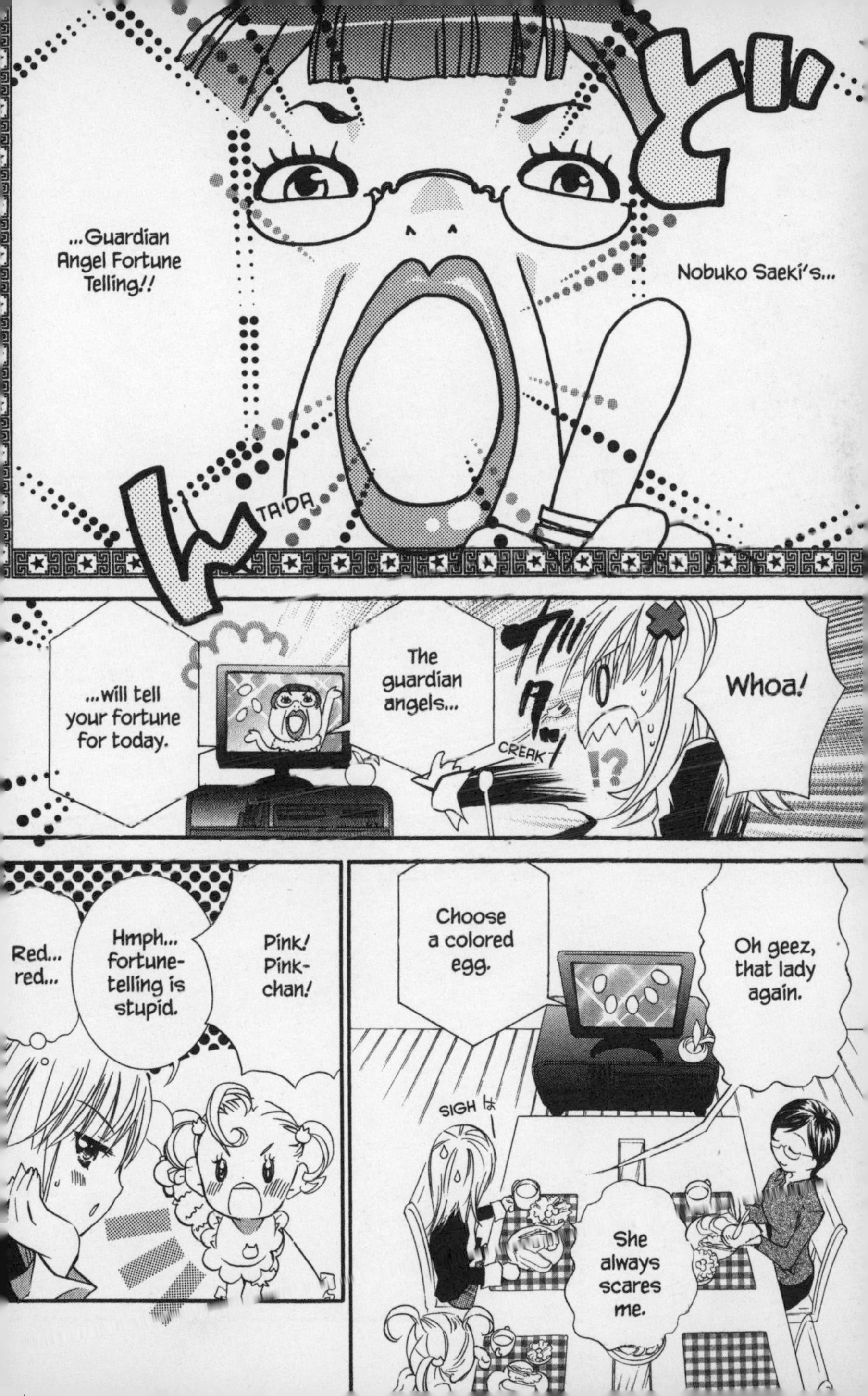
Nobuko Saeki's...
...Guardian Angel Fortune Telling!!
TA-DA
Whoa!
!?
CREAK
The guardian angels...
...will tell your fortune for today.
Oh geez, that lady again.
Choose a colored egg.
SIGH
She always scares me.
Pink! Pink-chan!
Hmph... fortune-telling is stupid.
Red... red...

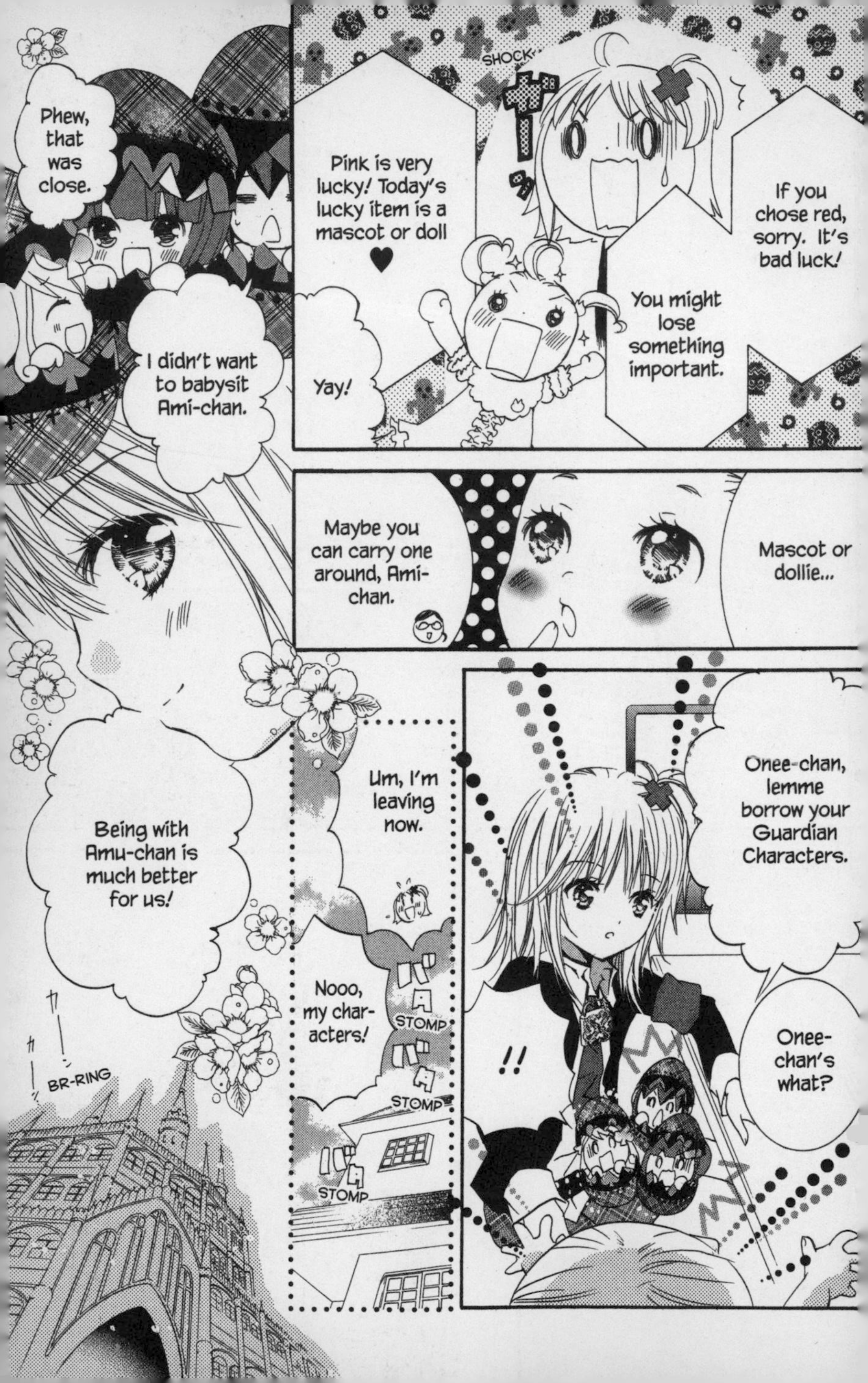

If you chose red, sorry. It's bad luck!
You might lose something important.
SHOCK
Pink is very lucky! Today's lucky item is a mascot or doll ♥
Yay!
Mascot or dollie...
Maybe you can carry one around, Ami-chan.
Onee-chan, lemme borrow your Guardian Characters.
Onee-chan's what?
!!
Um, I'm leaving now.
Nooo, my characters!
STOMP
STOMP
STOMP
Phew, that was close.
I didn't want to babysit Ami-chan.
Being with Amu-chan is much better for us!
BR-RING

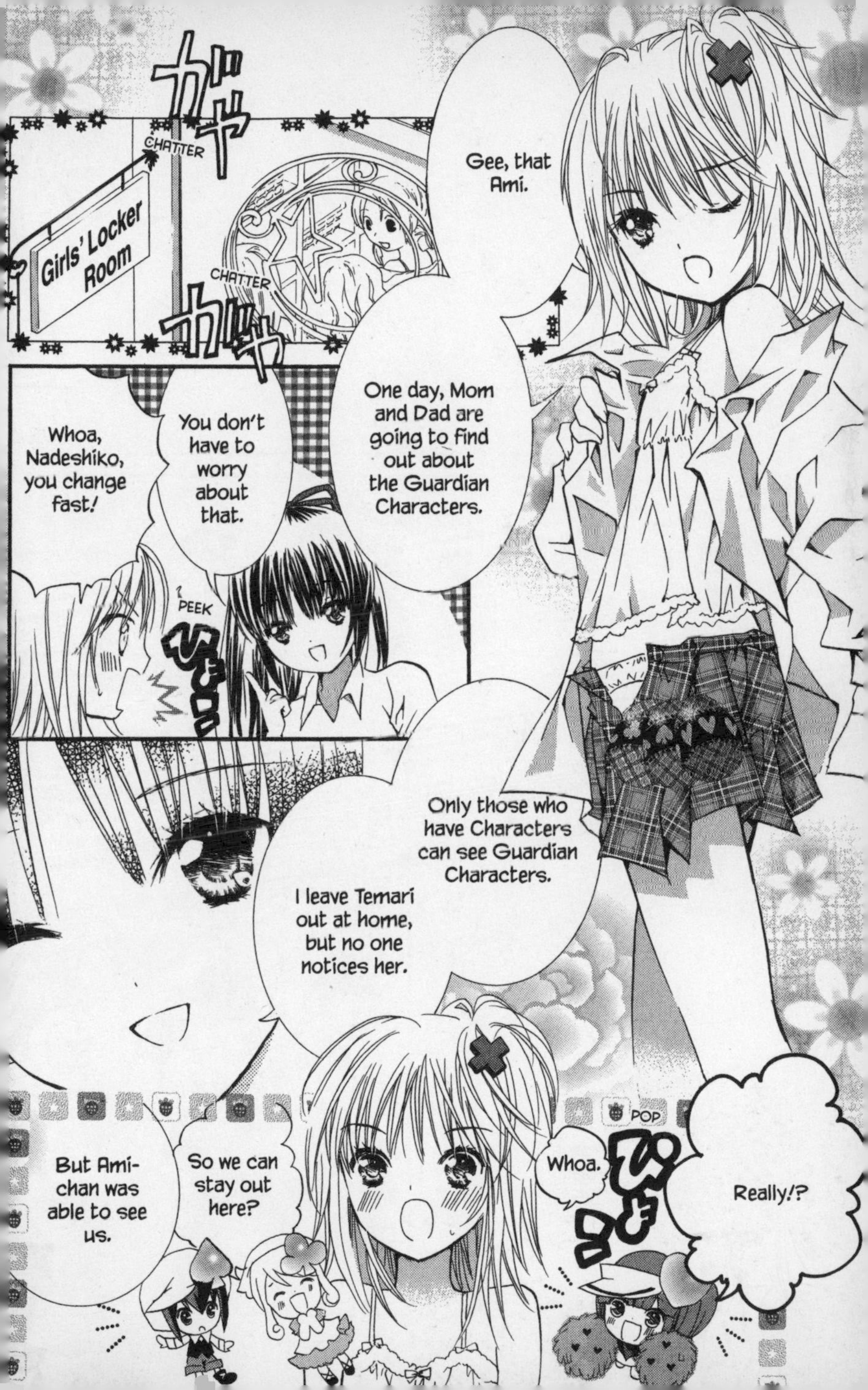
Gee, that Ami.
One day, Mom and Dad are going to find out about the Guardian Characters.
CHATTER
Girls' Locker Room
CHATTER
You don't have to worry about that.
Whoa, Nadeshiko, you change fast!
PEEK
Only those who have Characters can see Guardian Characters.
I leave Temari out at home, but no one notices her.
Really!?
POP
Whoa.
So we can stay out here?
But Ami-chan was able to see us.

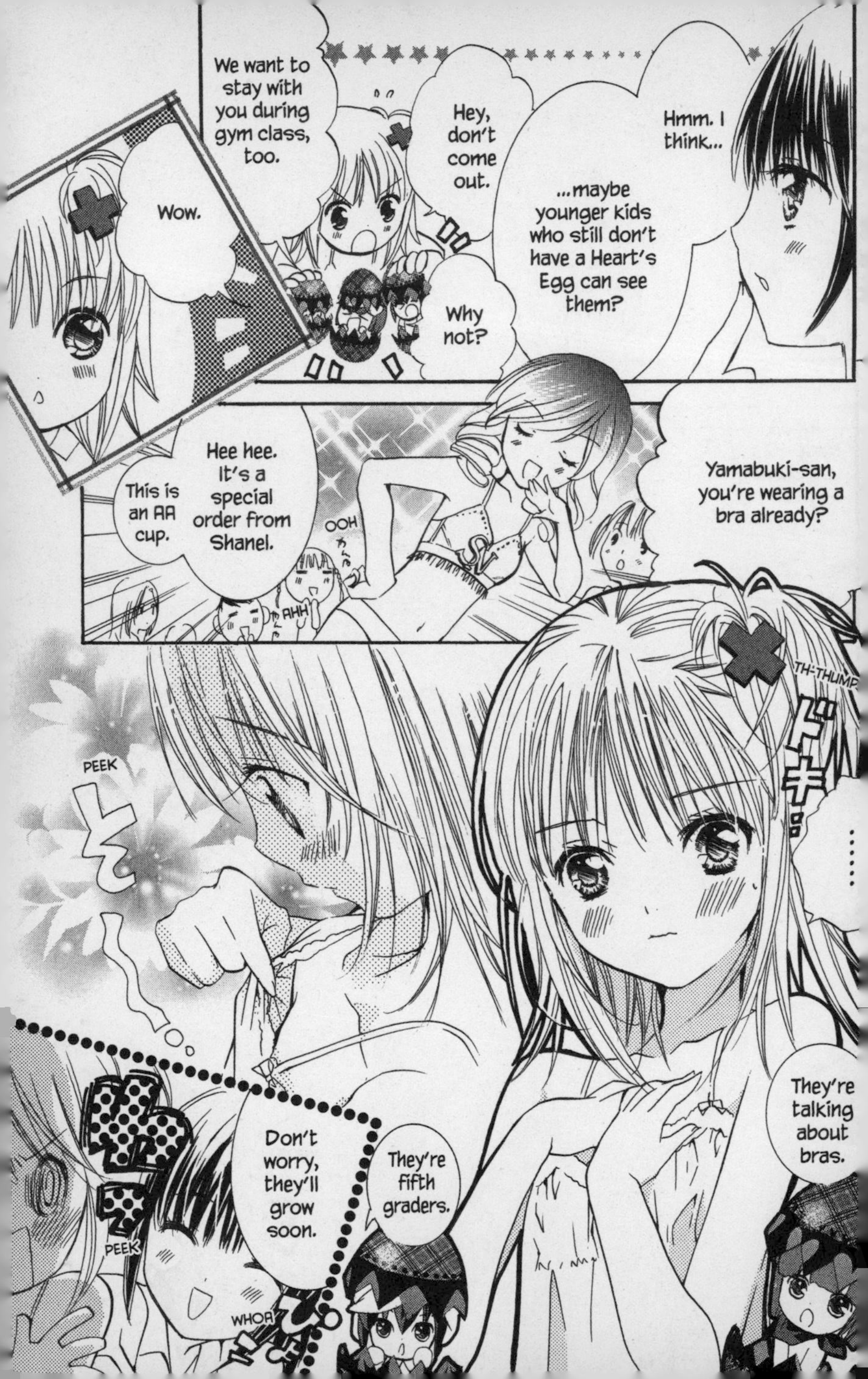

Hmm. I think...
...maybe younger kids who still don't have a Heart's Egg can see them?
Hey, don't come out.
Why not?
We want to stay with you during gym class, too.
Wow.
Yamabuki-san, you're wearing a bra already?
Hee hee. It's a special order from Shanel.
This is an AA cup.
OOH
AHH
TH-THUMP
PEEK
They're talking about bras.
They're fifth graders.
Don't worry, they'll grow soon.
PEEK
WHOA

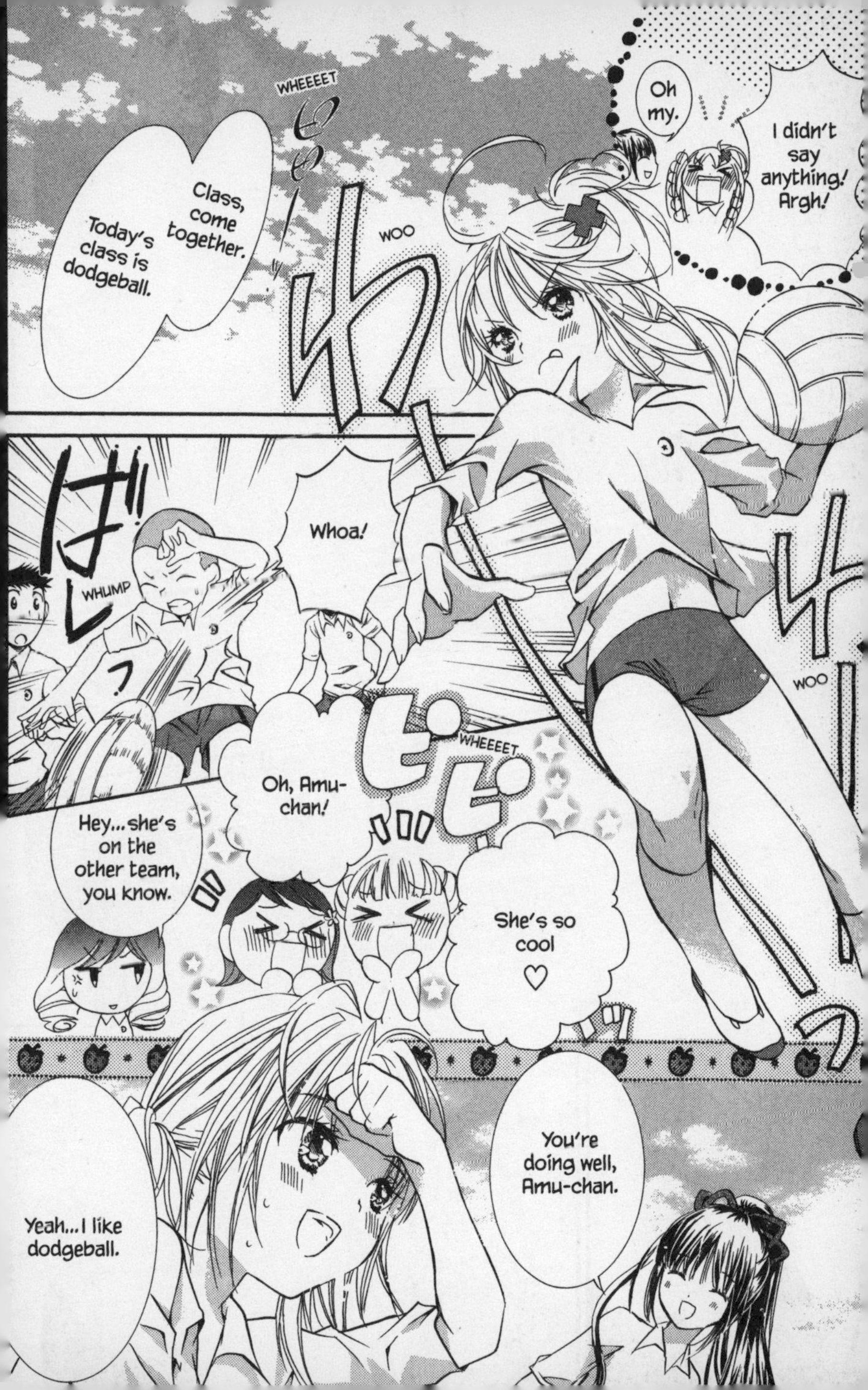
Oh my.
I didn't say anything! Argh!
WHEEEET
Class, come together. Today's class is dodgeball.
WOO
WOO
Whoa!
WHUMP
WHEEEET
She's so cool ♡
Oh, Amu-chan!
Hey...she's on the other team, you know.
You're doing well, Amu-chan.
Yeah...I like dodgeball.

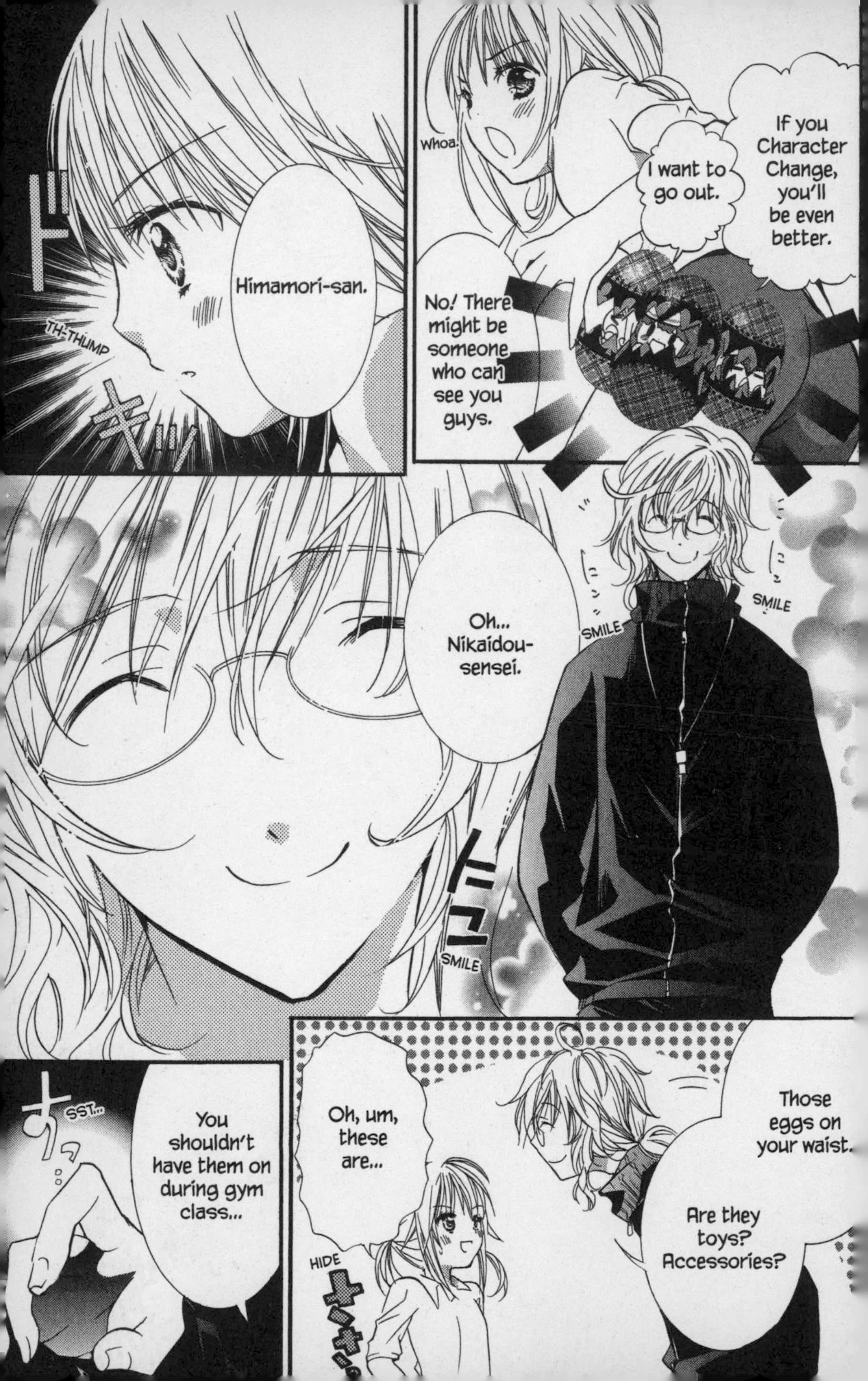
If you Character Change, you'll be even better.
I want to go out.
Whoa.
No! There might be someone who can see you guys.
Himamori-san.
TH-THUMP
SMILE
SMILE
Oh... Nikaidou-sensei.
SMILE
Those eggs on your waist.
Are they toys? Accessories?
Oh, um, these are...
HIDE
SST...
You shouldn't have them on during gym class...

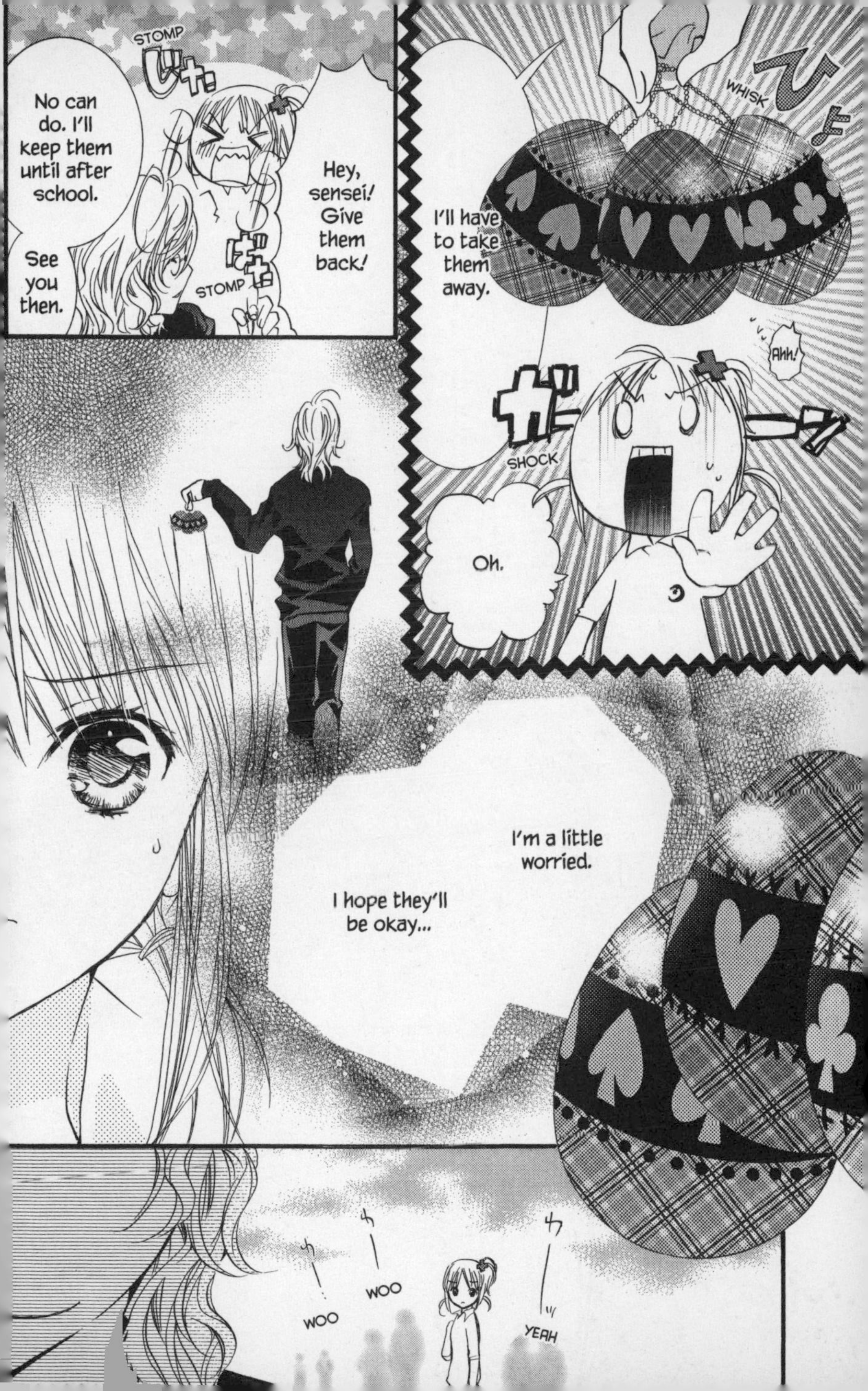
WHISK
I'll have to take them away.
Ahh!
SHOCK
Oh.
STOMP
Hey, sensei! Give them back!
No can do. I'll keep them until after school.
STOMP
See you then.
I'm a little worried.
I hope they'll be okay...
YEAH
WOO
WOO

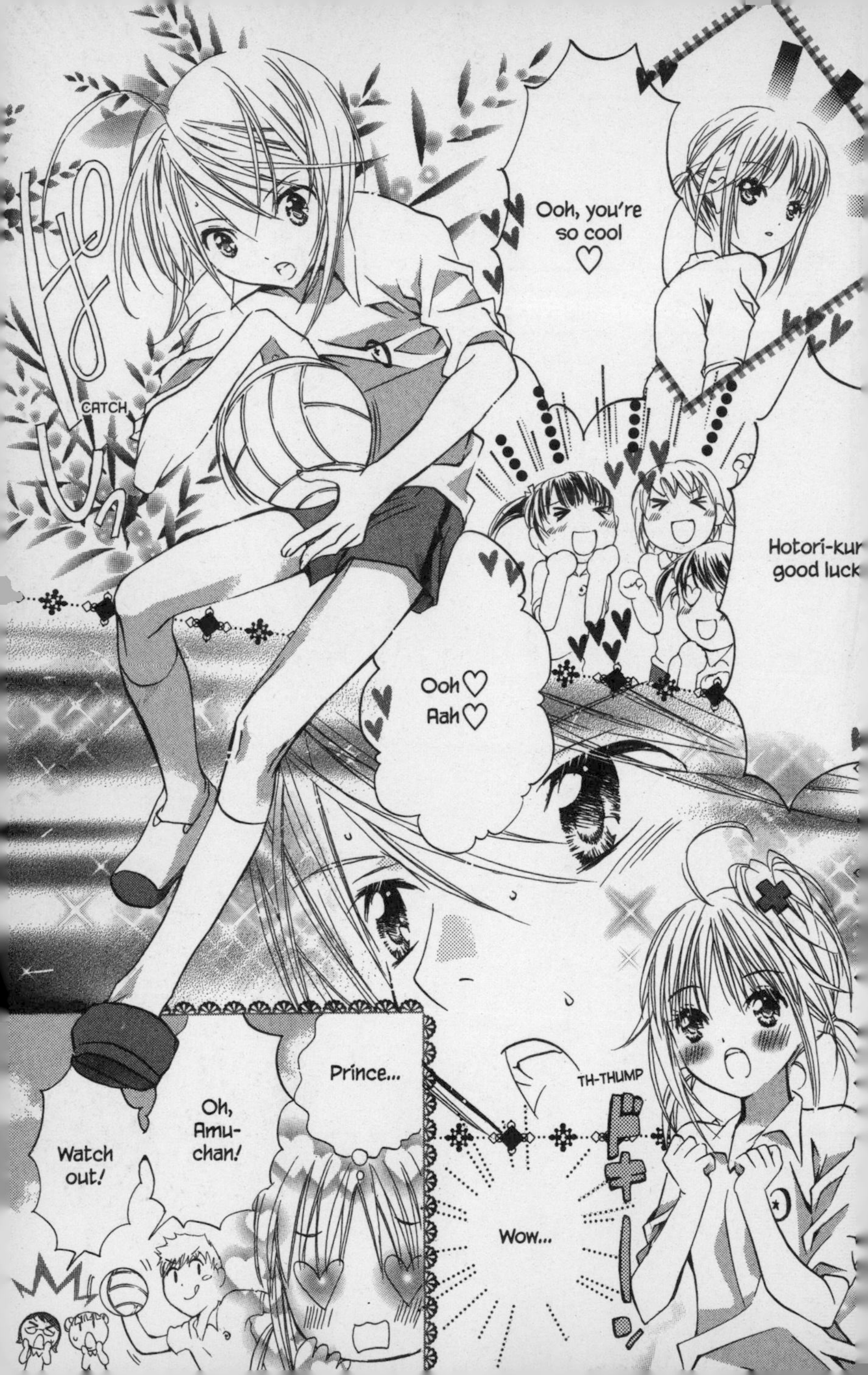
Ooh, you're so cool ♡
Hotori-ku good luck
Ooh ♡ Aah ♡
CATCH
TH-THUMP
Wow...
Prince...
Oh, Amu-chan!
Watch out!

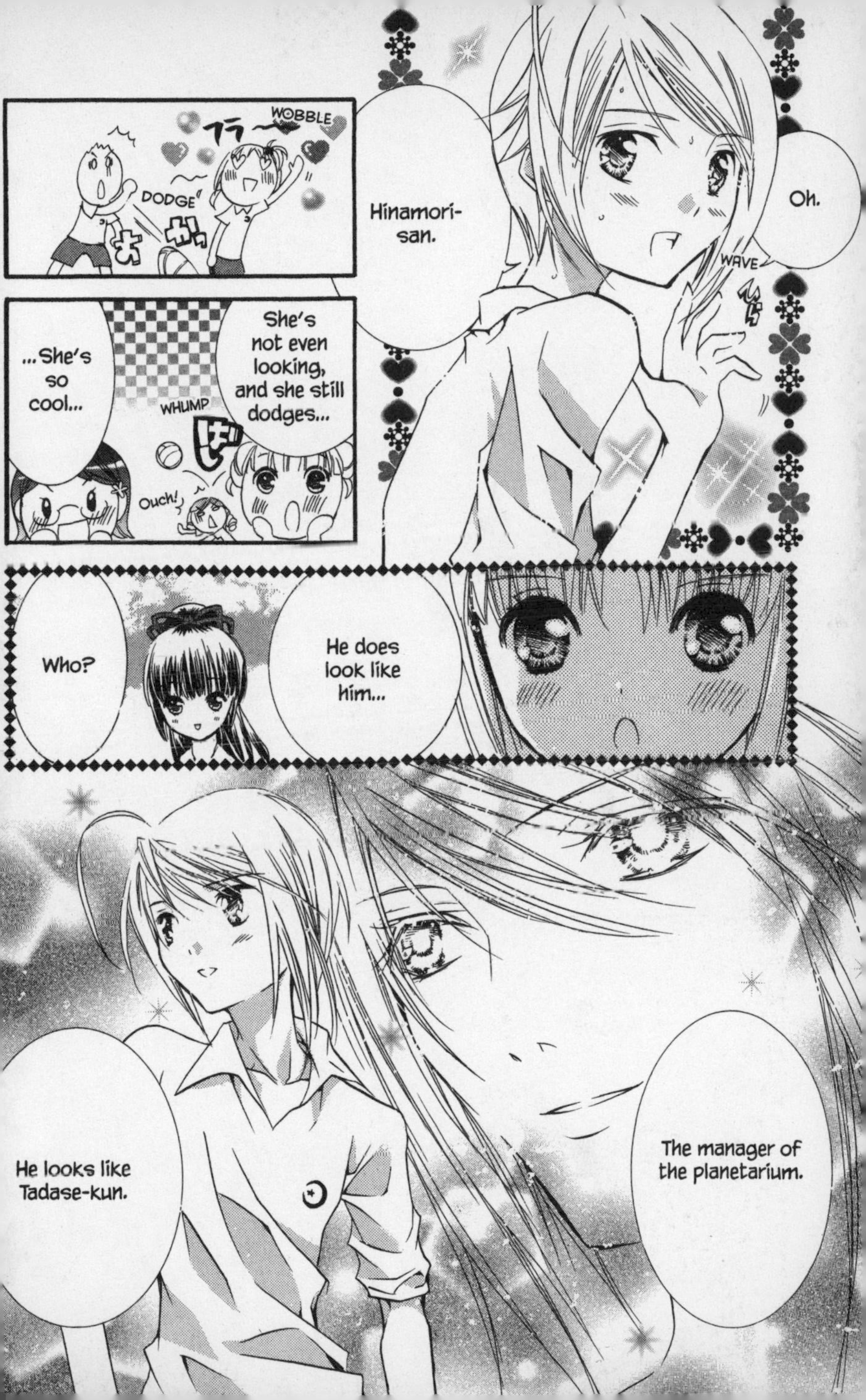
Hinamori-san.
Oh.
WAVE
WOBBLE
DODGE
She's not even looking, and she still dodges...
WHUMP
...She's so cool...
Ouch!
He does look like him...
Who?
The manager of the planetarium.
He looks like Tadase-kun.

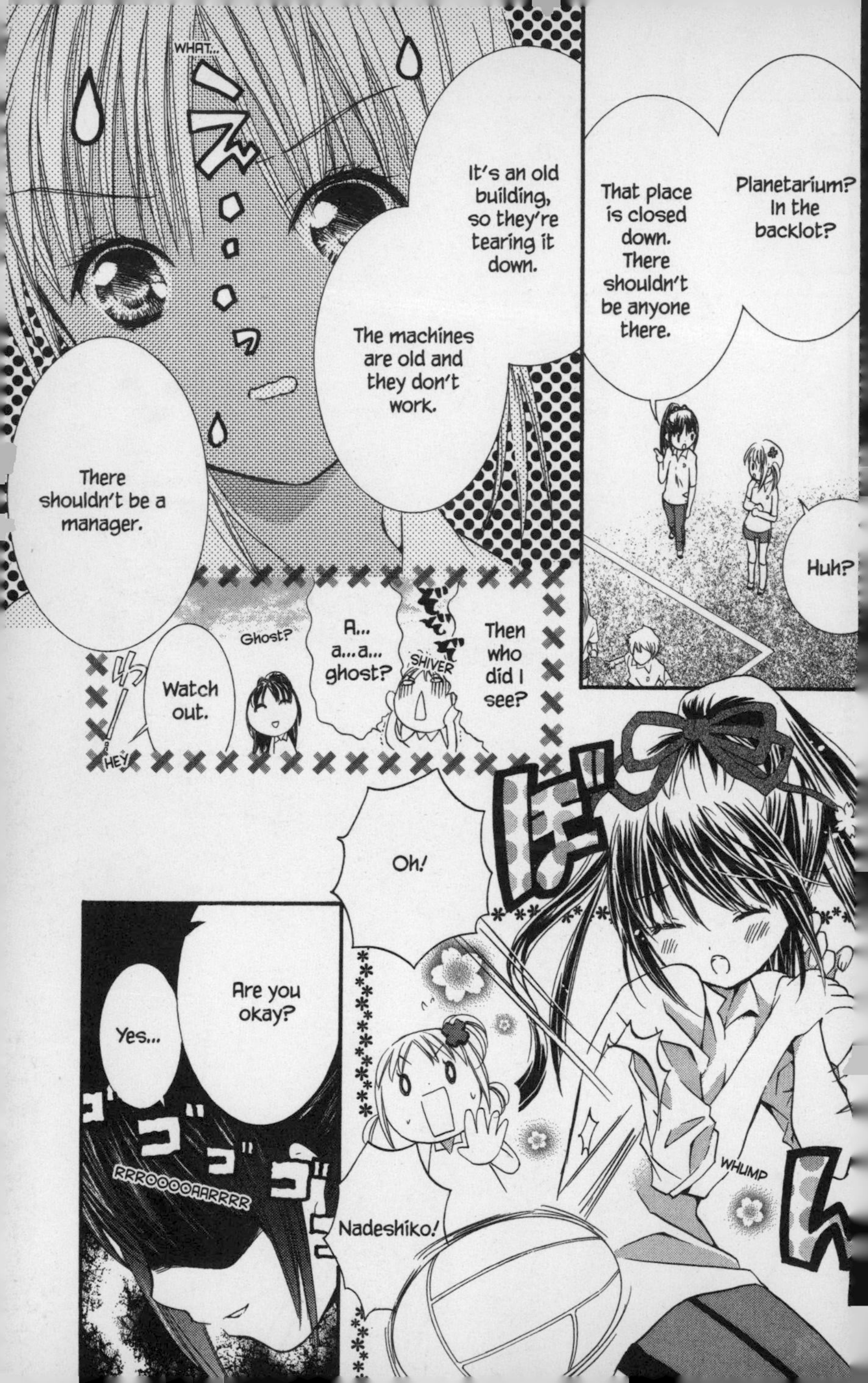
Planetarium? In the backlot?
That place is closed down. There shouldn't be anyone there.
Huh?
WHAT...
It's an old building, so they're tearing it down.
The machines are old and they don't work.
There shouldn't be a manager.
Then who did I see?
SHIVER
A... a...a... ghost?
Ghost?
Watch out.
HEY
Oh!
WHUMP
Nadeshiko!
Are you okay?
Yes...
RRROOOOAARRRR

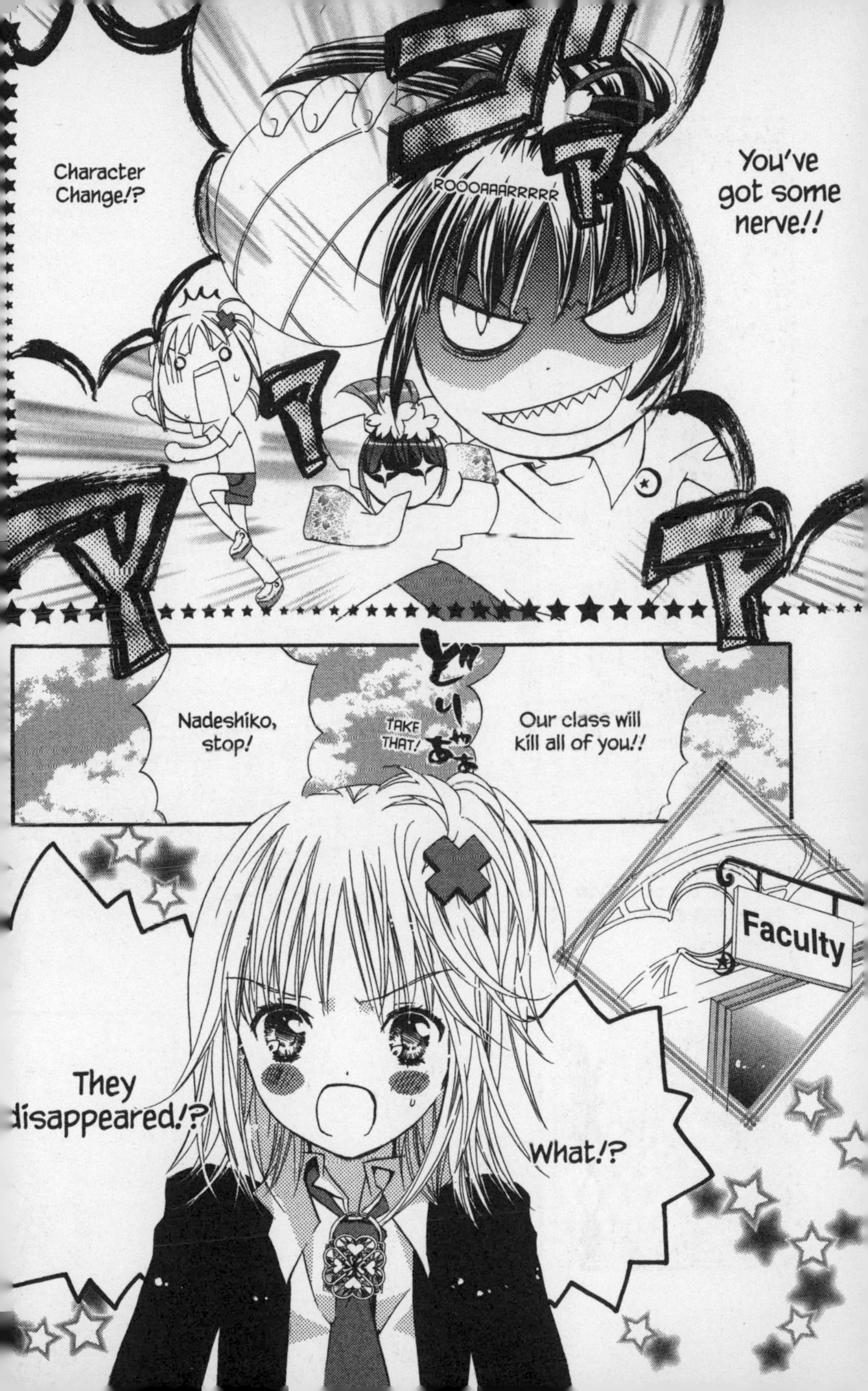
You've got some nerve!!
ROOOAAARRRRR
Character Change!?
Our class will kill all of you!!
TAKE THAT!
Nadeshiko, stop!
Faculty
What!?
They disappeared!?

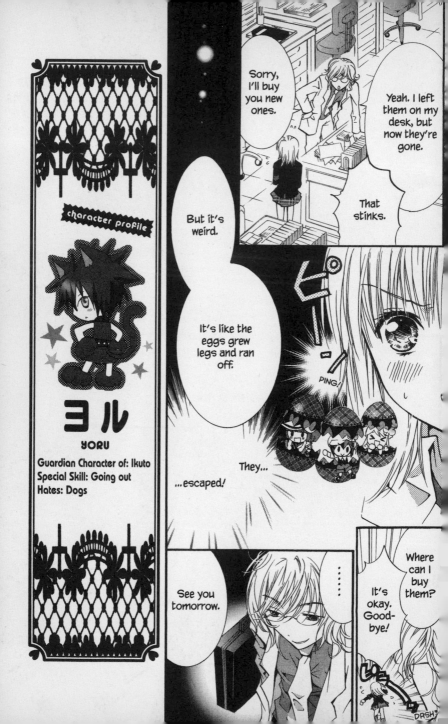

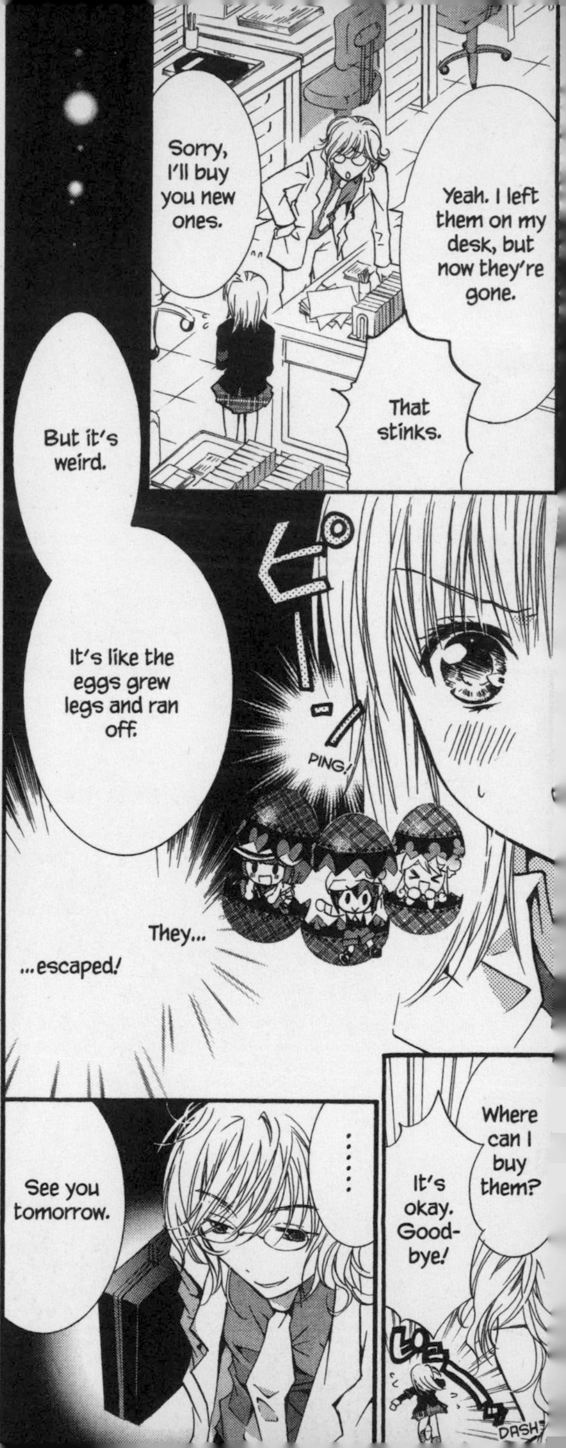
Yeah. I left them on my desk, but now they're gone.
That stinks.
Sorry, I'll buy you new ones.
But it's weird.
It's like the eggs grew legs and ran off.
ピーン
PING!
They...
...escaped!
Where can I buy them?
It's okay. Good-bye!
DASH
......
See you tomorrow.

character profile

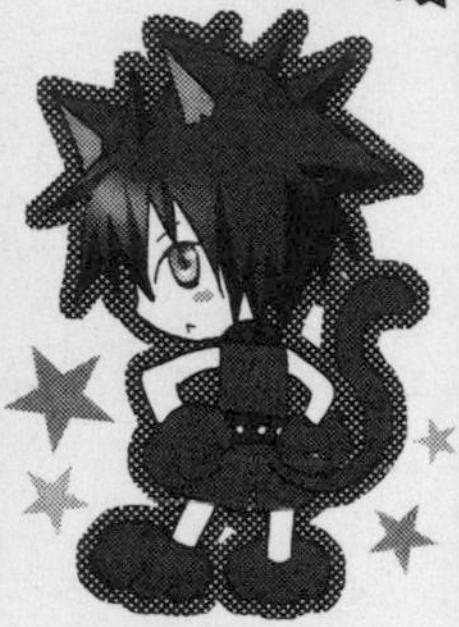

ヨル

YORU

Guardian Character of: Ikuto
Special Skill: Going out
Hates: Dogs

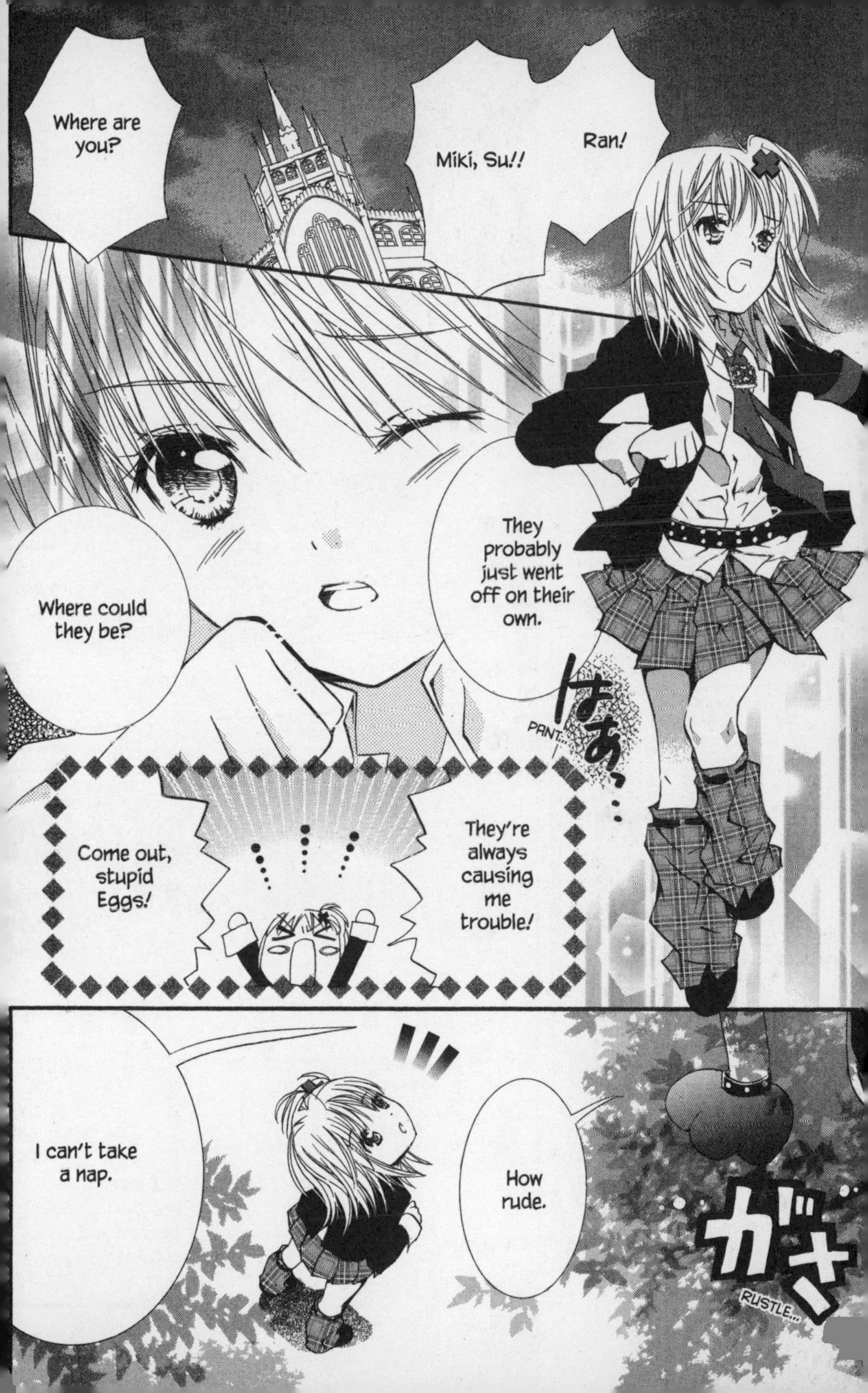
Ran!
Miki, Su!!
Where are you?
They probably just went off on their own.
PANT...
Where could they be?
They're always causing me trouble!
Come out, stupid Eggs!
RUSTLE...
How rude.
I can't take a nap.

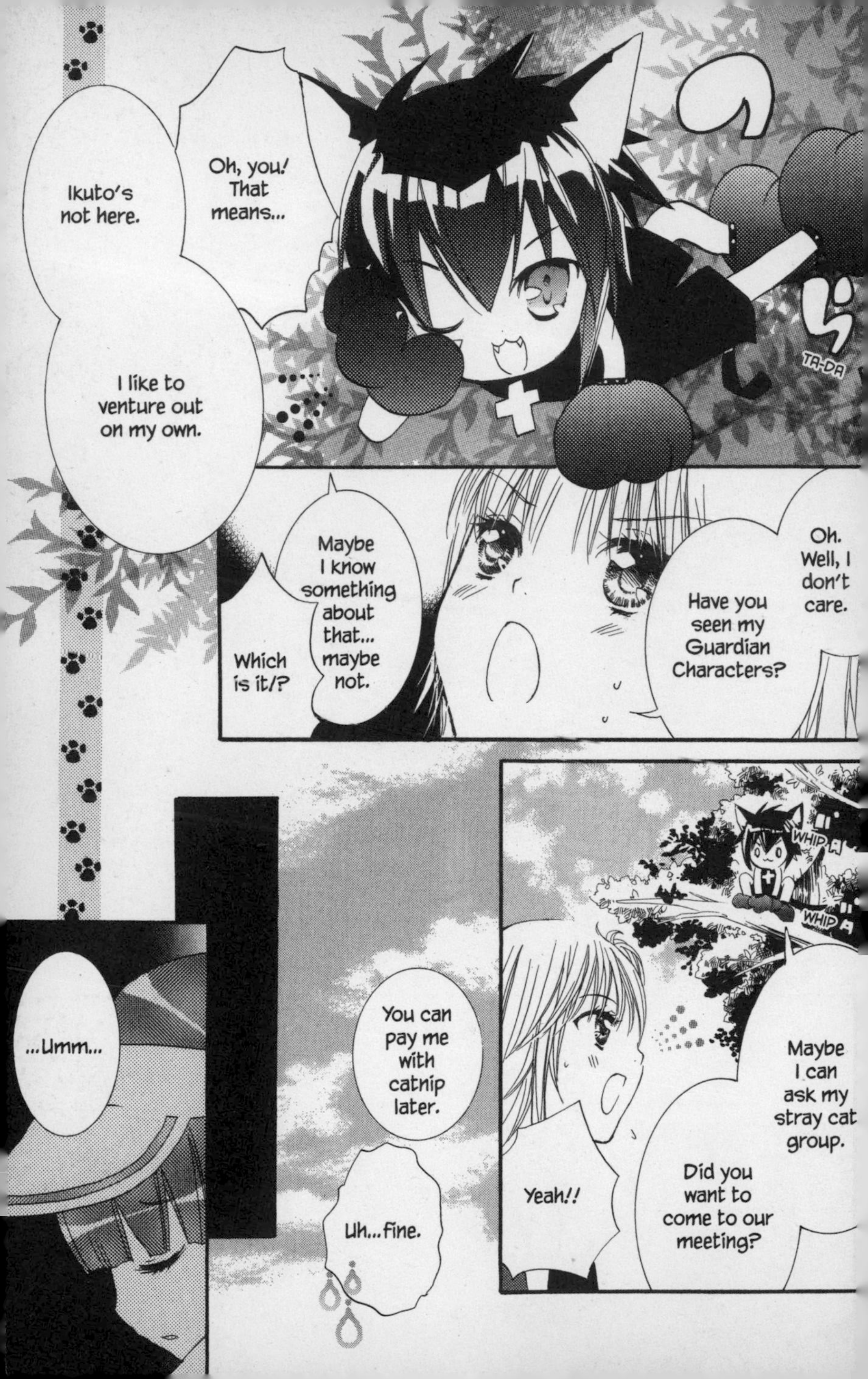
TA-DA
Oh, you! That means...
Ikuto's not here.
I like to venture out on my own.
Oh. Well, I don't care.
Have you seen my Guardian Characters?
Maybe I know something about that... maybe not.
Which is it!?
WHIP
WHIP
Maybe I can ask my stray cat group.
Did you want to come to our meeting?
Yeah!!
You can pay me with catnip later.
Uh...fine.
...Umm...

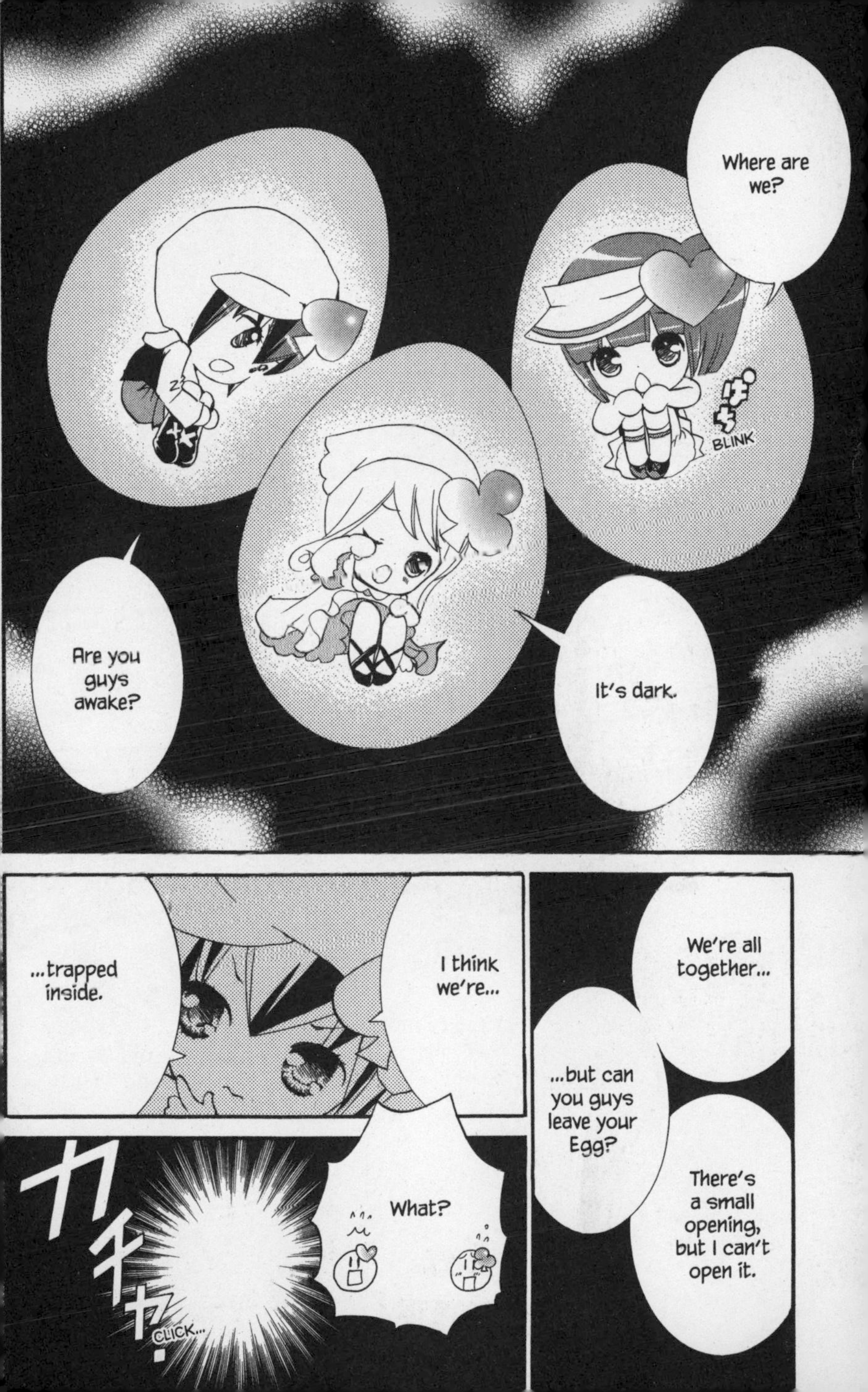
Where are we?
BLINK
It's dark.
Are you guys awake?
We're all together...
...but can you guys leave your Egg?
There's a small opening, but I can't open it.
I think we're...
...trapped inside.
What?
CLICK...

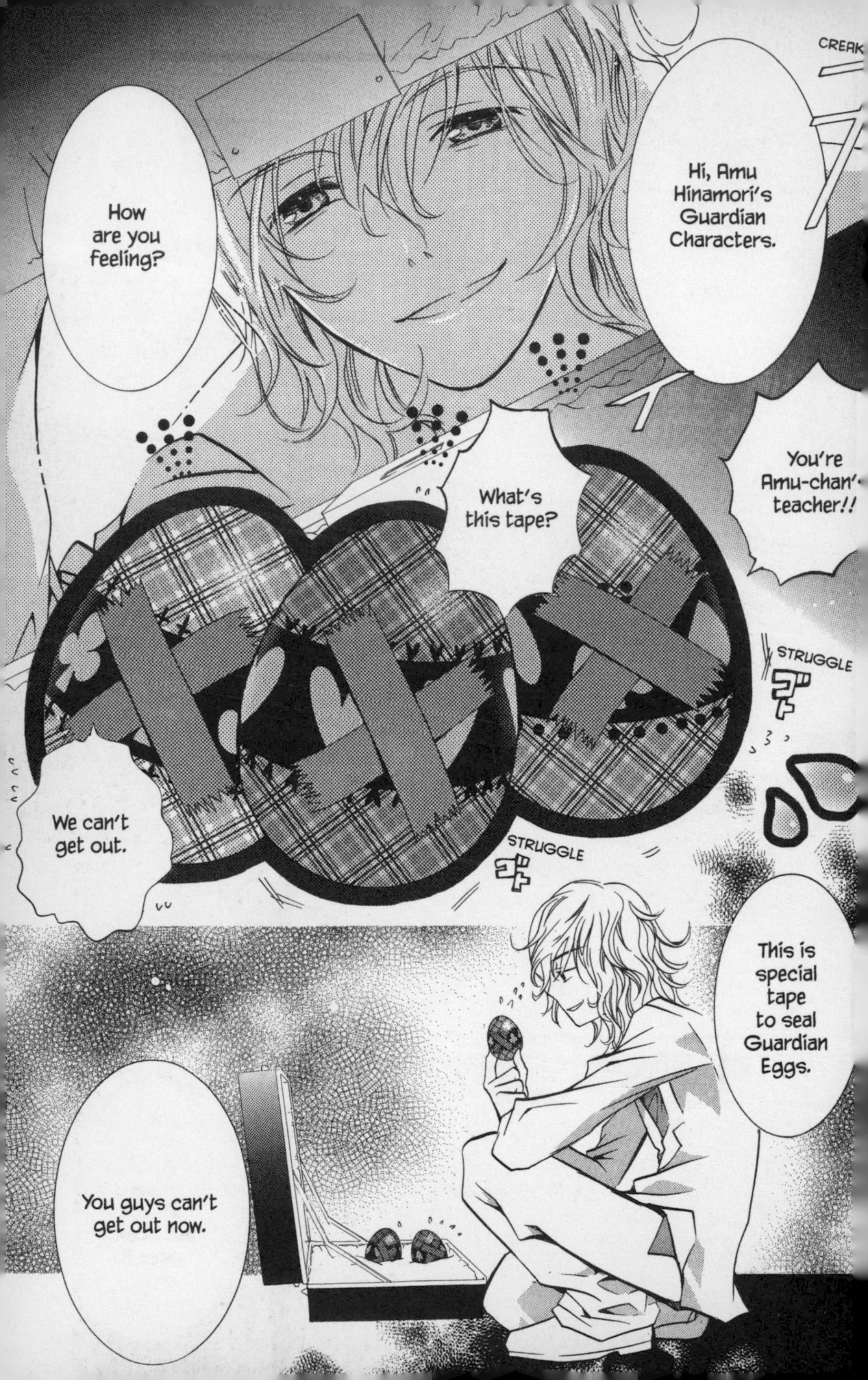
CREAK
Hi, Amu Hinamori's Guardian Characters.
How are you feeling?
You're Amu-chan' teacher!!
What's this tape?
STRUGGLE
We can't get out.
STRUGGLE
This is special tape to seal Guardian Eggs.
You guys can't get out now.

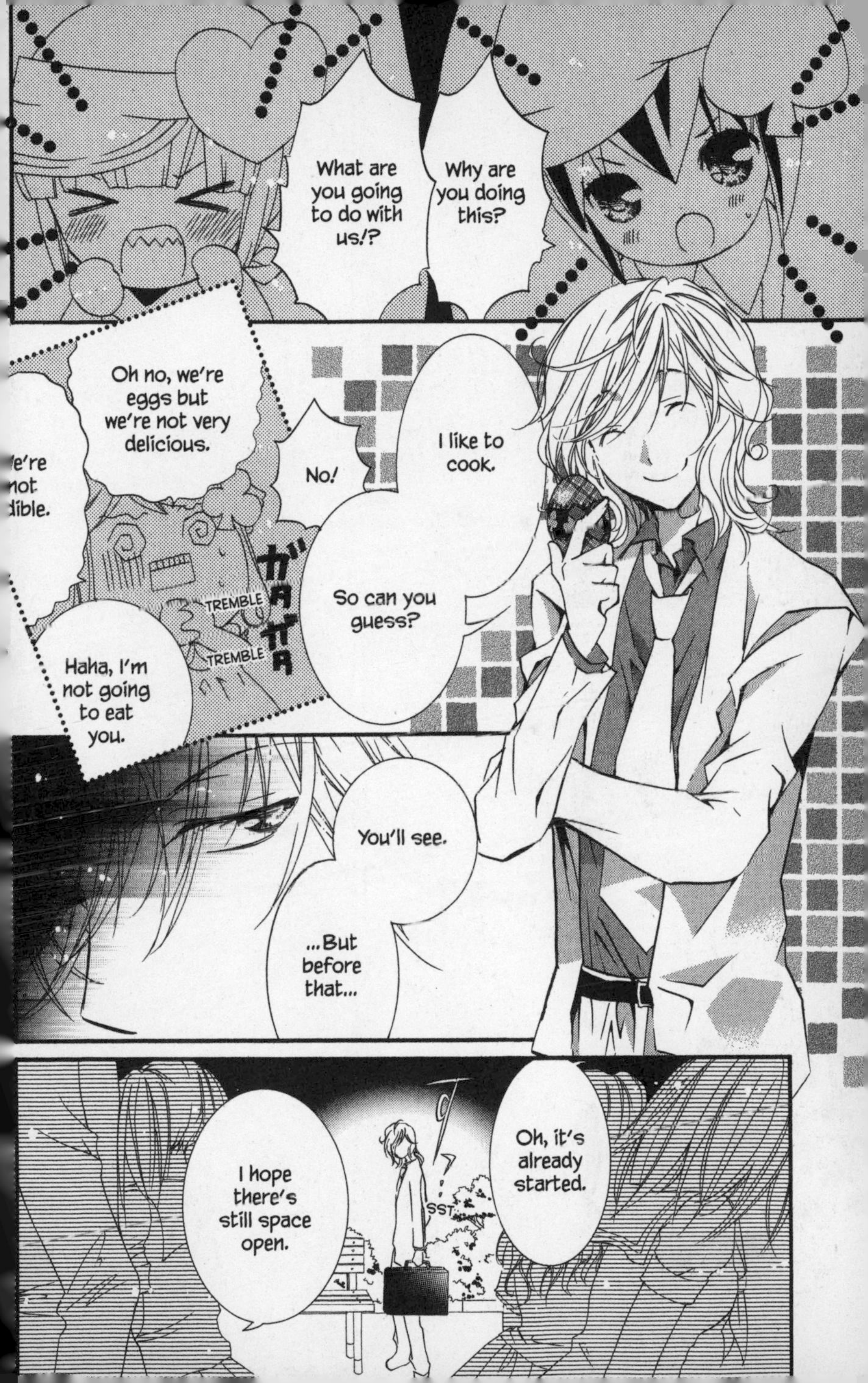
Why are you doing this?
What are you going to do with us!?
I like to cook.
No!
So can you guess?
Oh no, we're eggs but we're not very delicious.
e're not dible.
ガタガタ
TREMBLE
TREMBLE
Haha, I'm not going to eat you.
You'll see.
...But before that...
Oh, it's already started.
SST
I hope there's still space open.

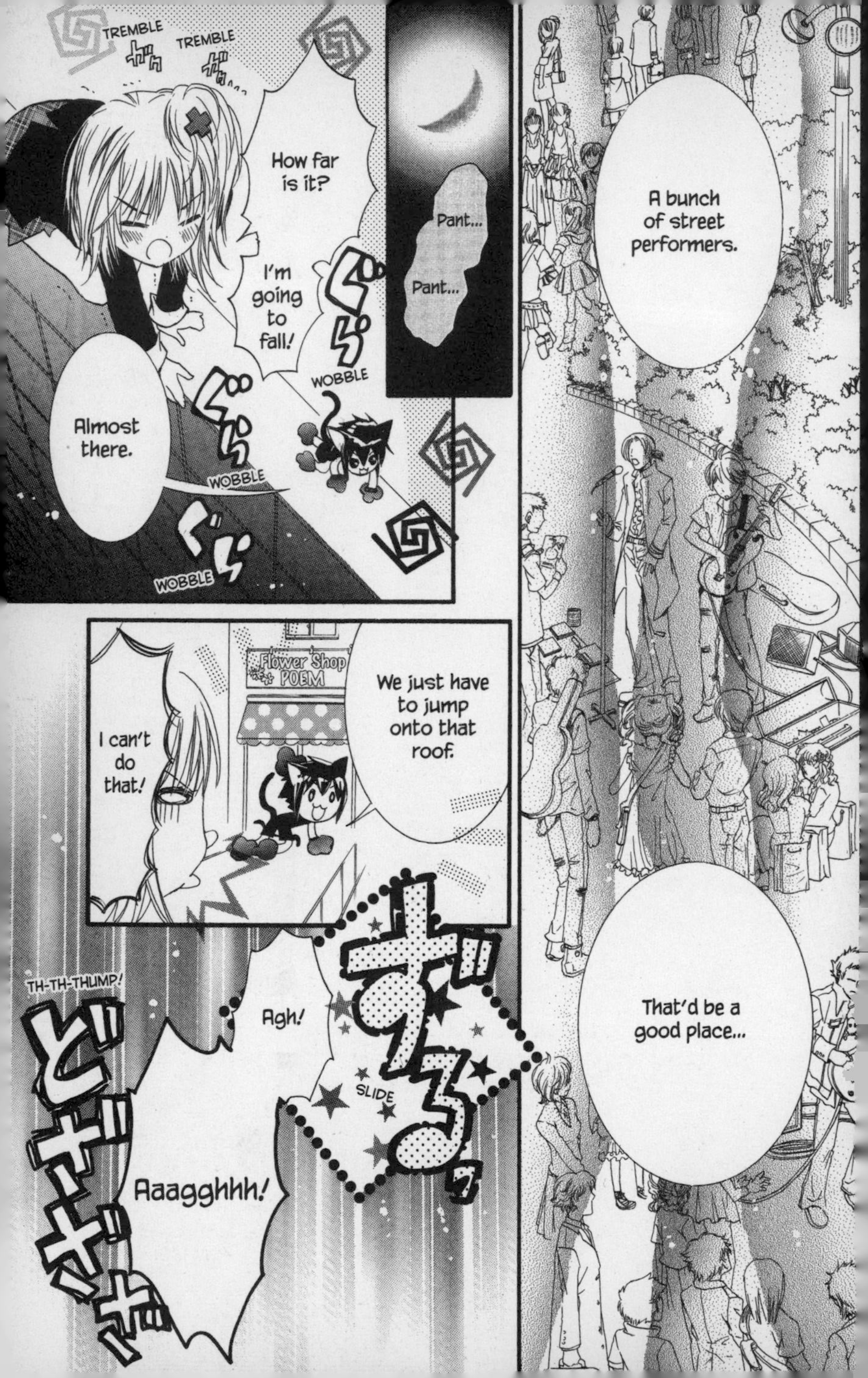
A bunch of street performers.
That'd be a good place...
Pant...
Pant...
TREMBLE
TREMBLE
How far is it?
I'm going to fall!
WOBBLE
Almost there.
WOBBLE
WOBBLE
Flower Shop POEM
We just have to jump onto that roof.
I can't do that!
SLIDE
Agh!
TH-TH-THUMP!
Aaagghhh!

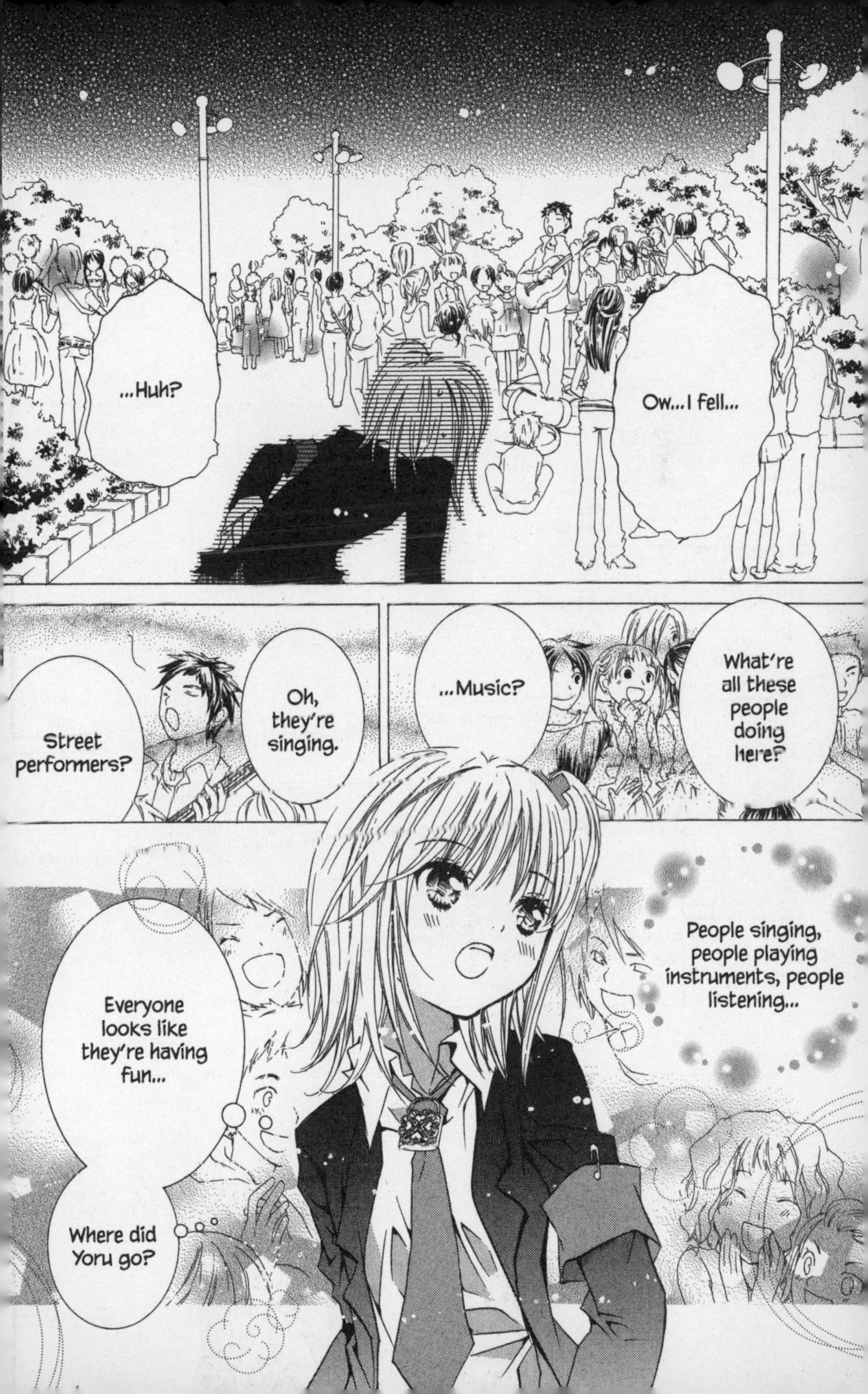
Ow...I fell...
...Huh?
What're all these people doing here?
...Music?
Oh, they're singing.
Street performers?
People singing, people playing instruments, people listening...
Everyone looks like they're having fun...
Where did Yoru go?

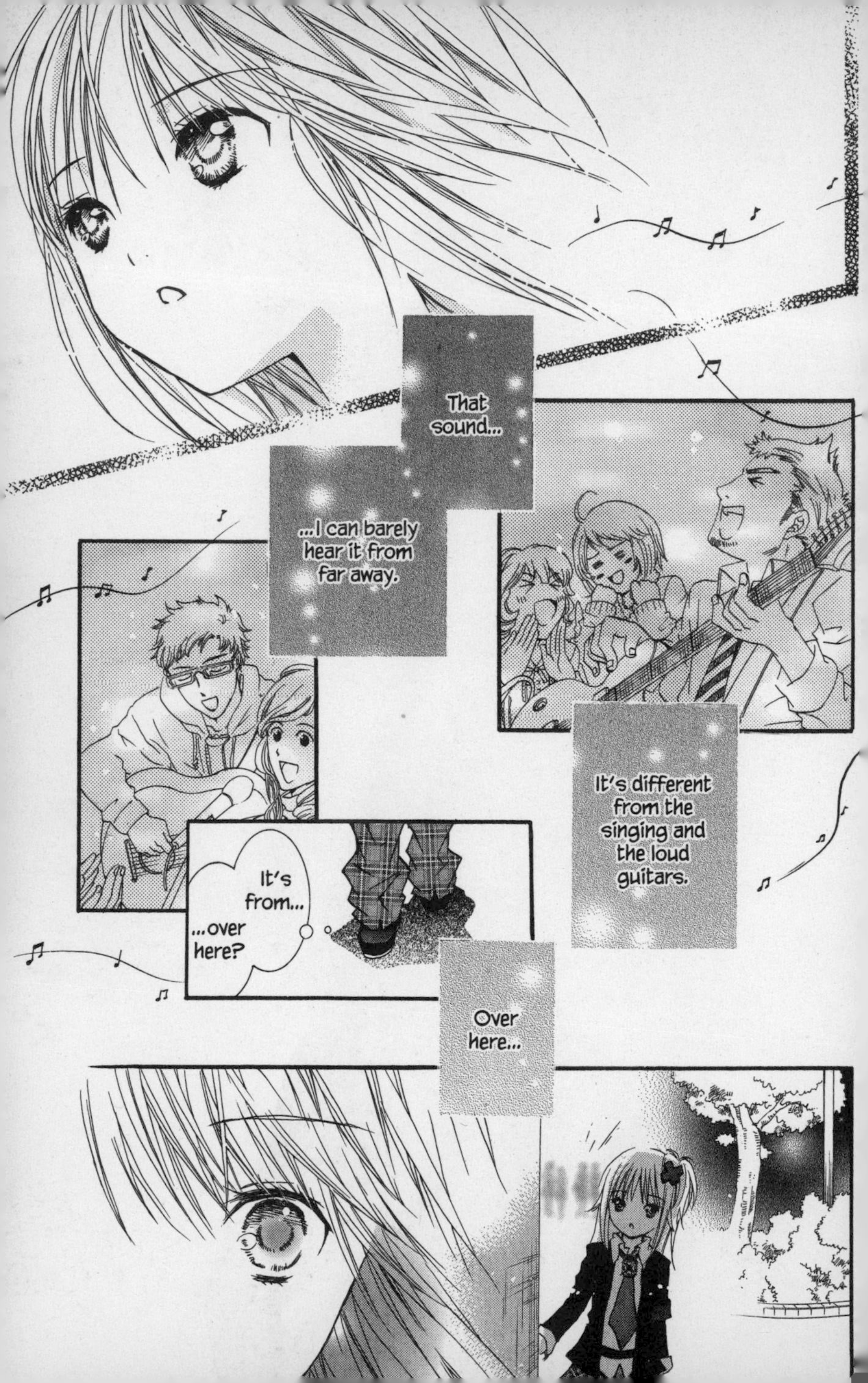
That sound...
...I can barely hear it from far away.
It's different from the singing and the loud guitars.
It's from...
...over here?
Over here...

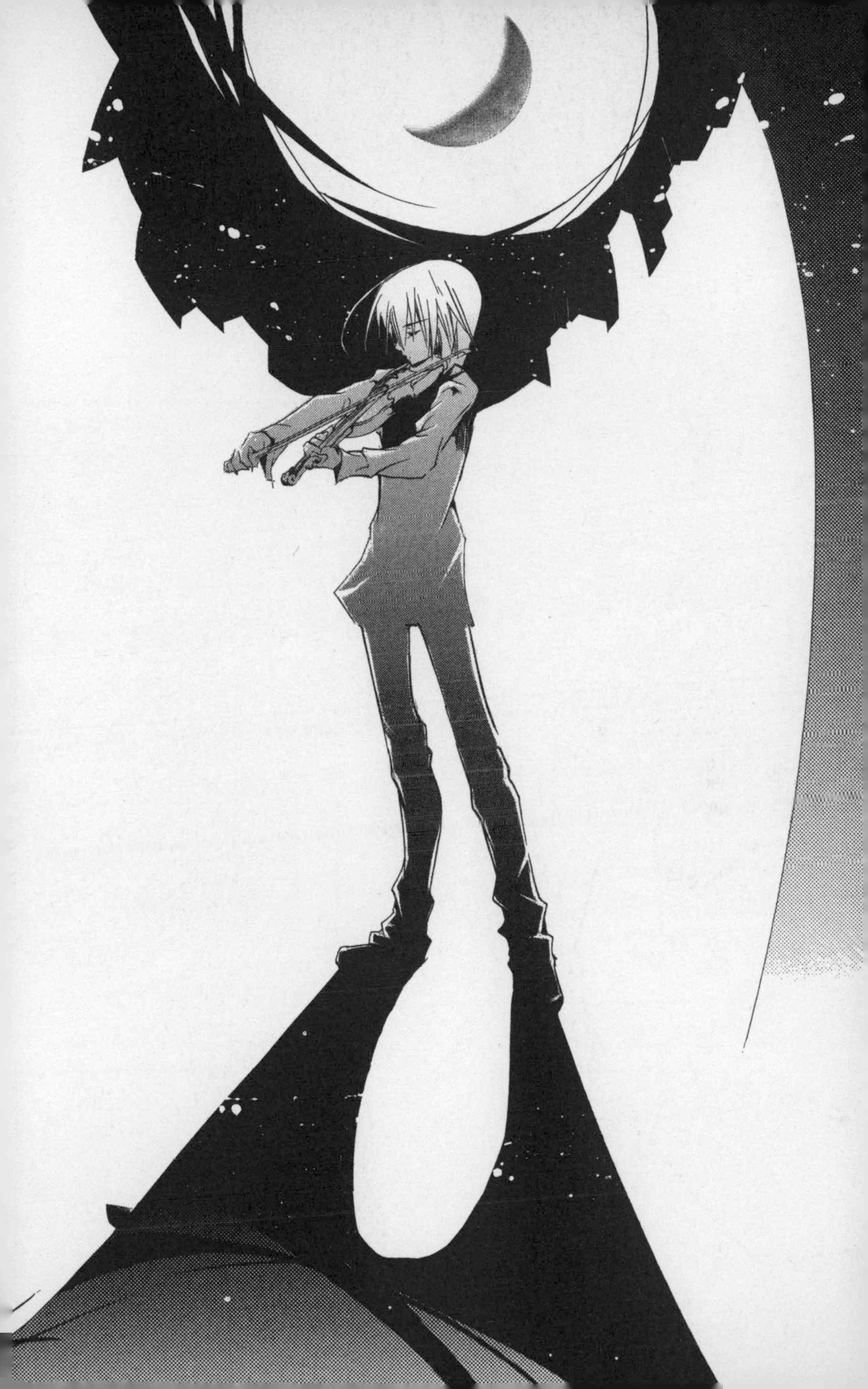

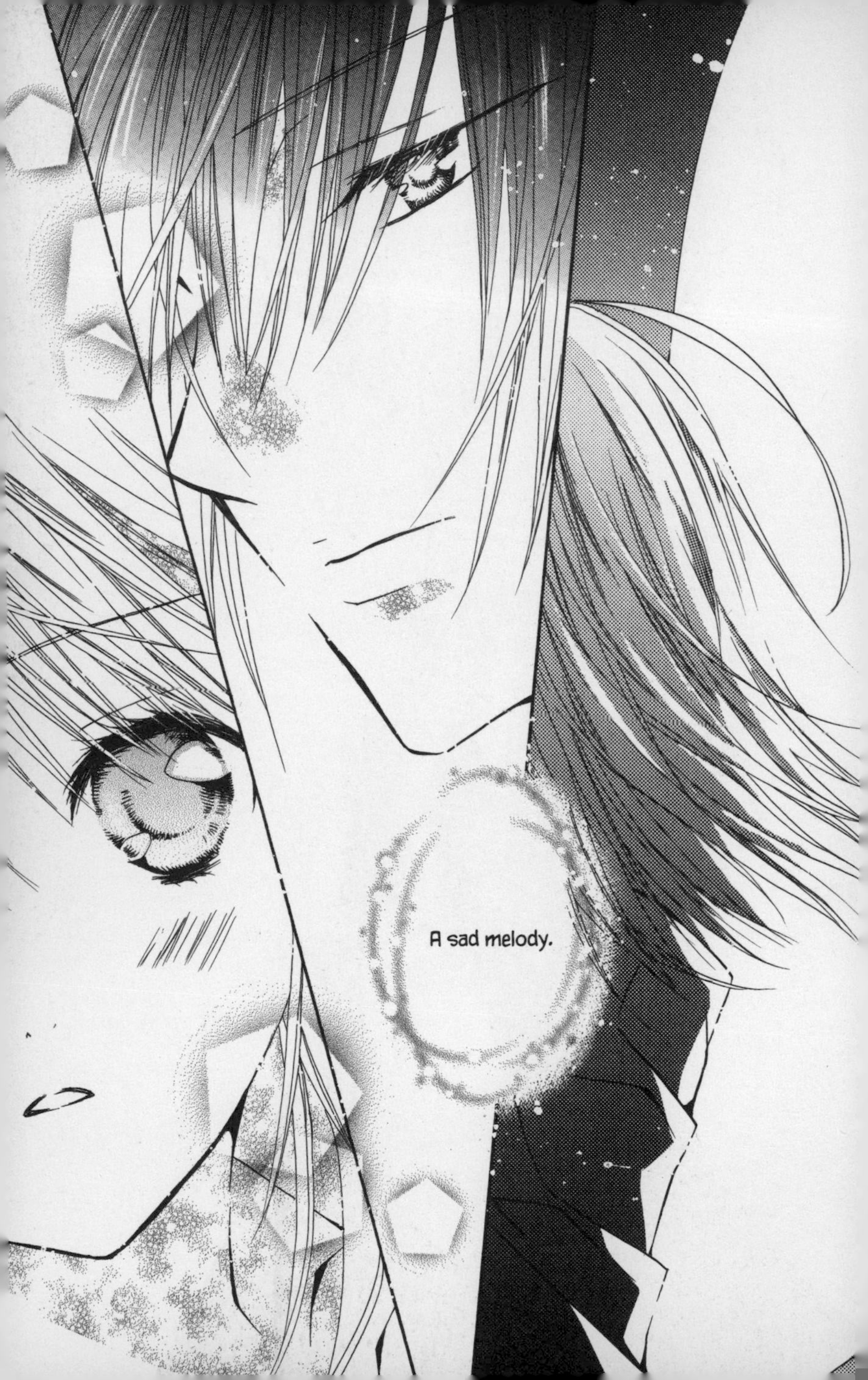
A sad melody.

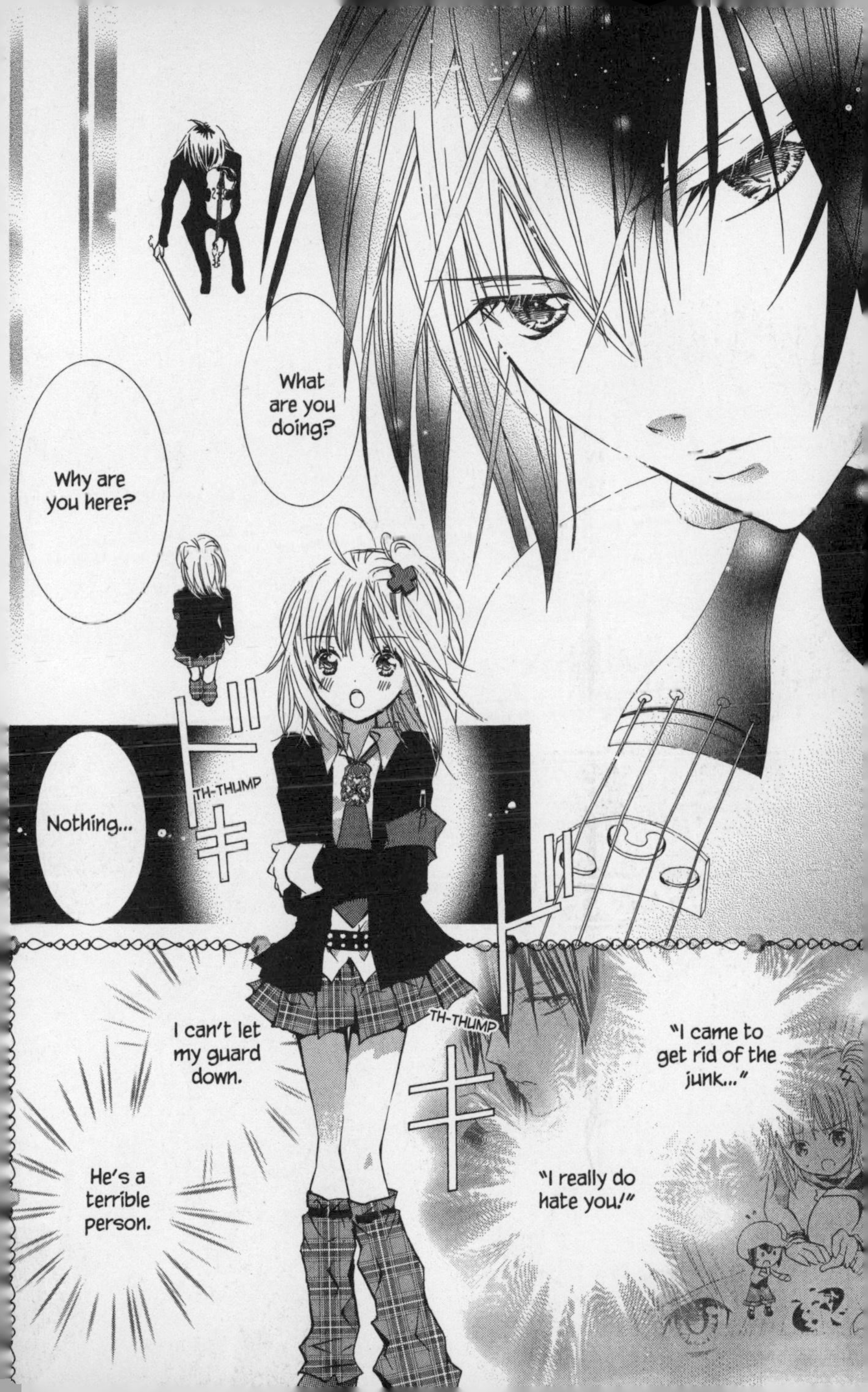
What are you doing?
Why are you here?
TH-THUMP
Nothing...
TH-THUMP
"I came to get rid of the junk..."
"I really do hate you!"
I can't let my guard down.
He's a terrible person.

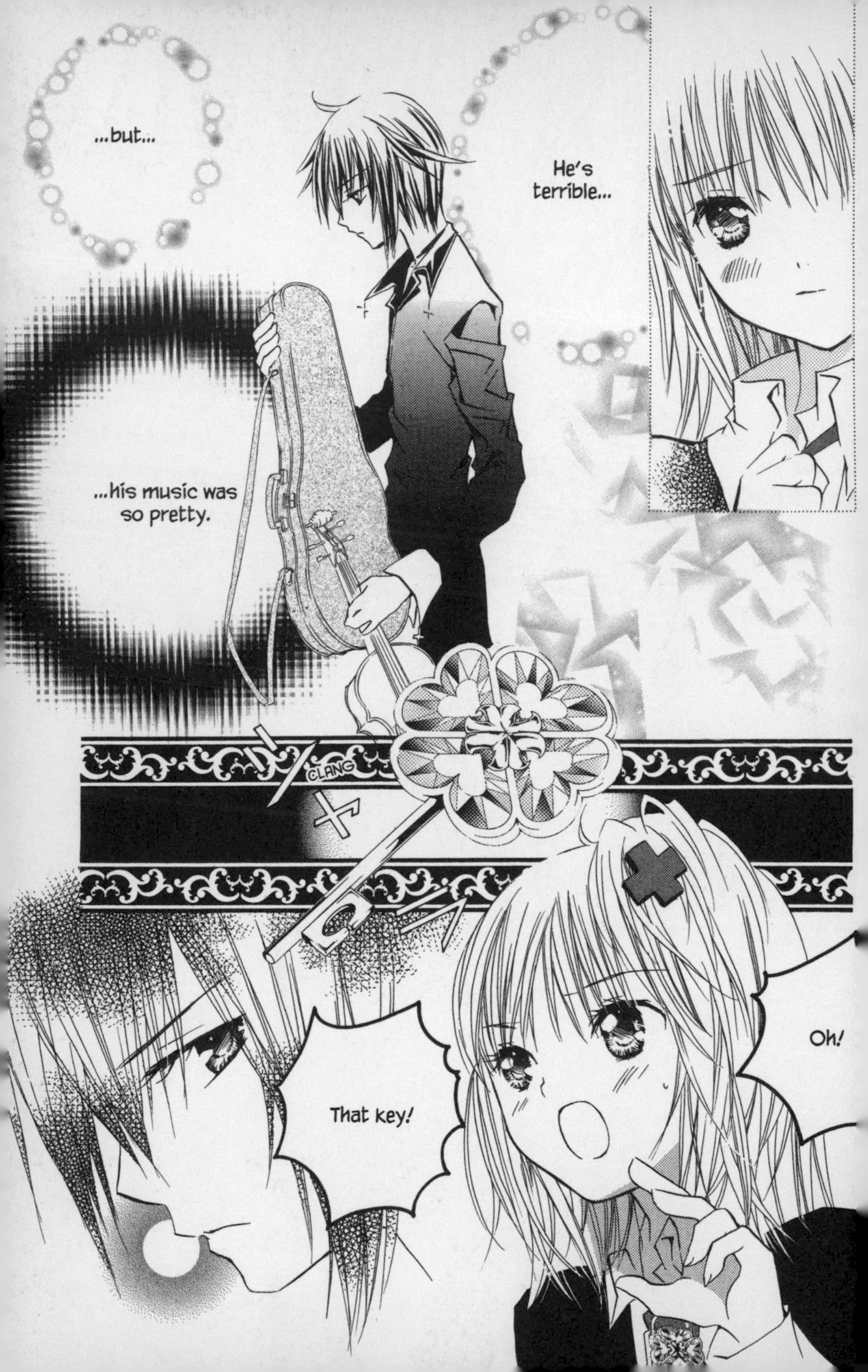
He's terrible...
...but...
...his music was so pretty.
CLANG
Oh!
That key!

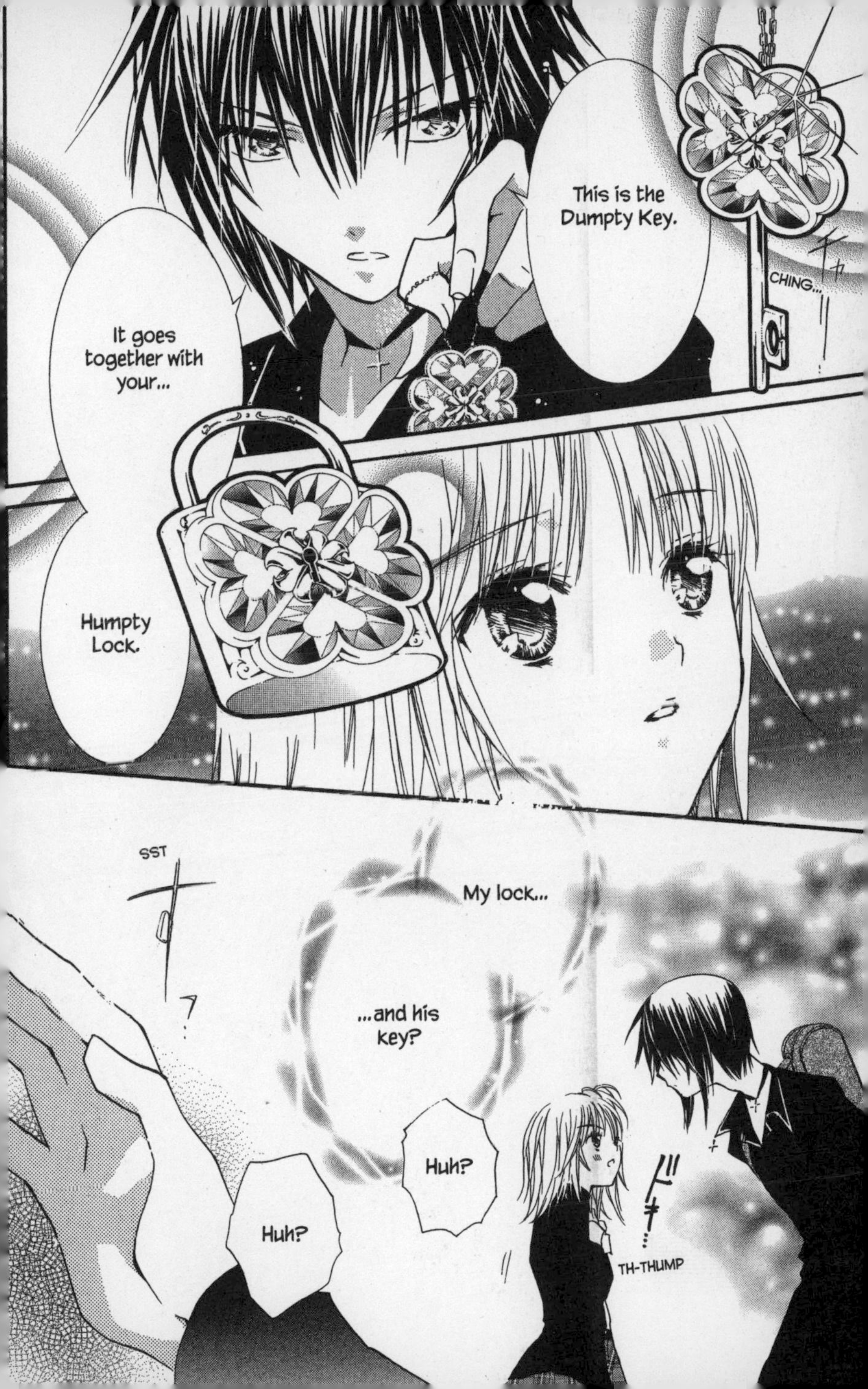
This is the Dumpty Key.
CHING...
It goes together with your...
Humpty Lock.
My lock...
...and his key?
SST
Huh?
TH-THUMP
Huh?

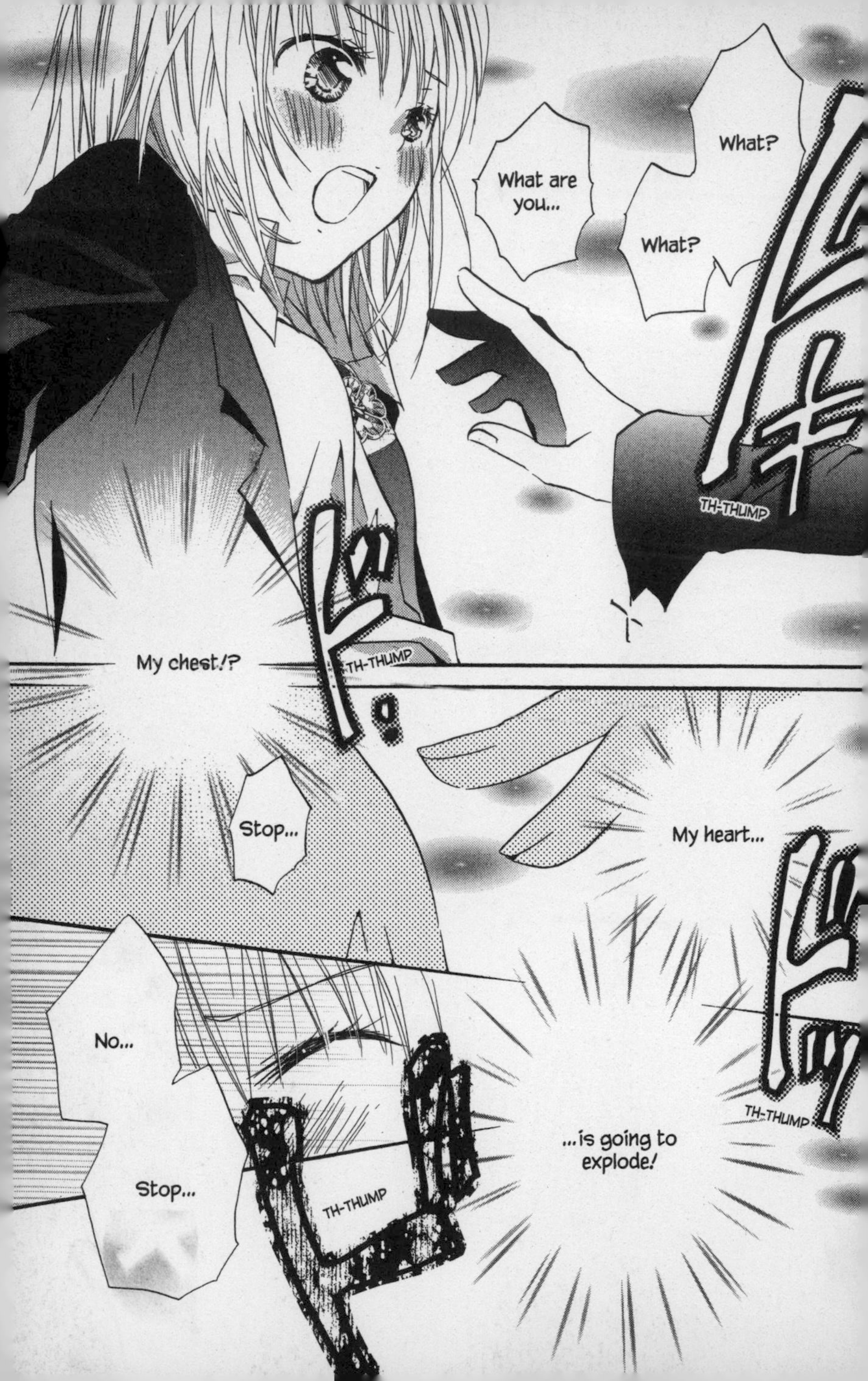
What?
What?
What are you...
TH-THUMP
TH-THUMP
My chest!?
My heart...
Stop...
TH-THUMP
...is going to explode!
TH-THUMP
No...
Stop...

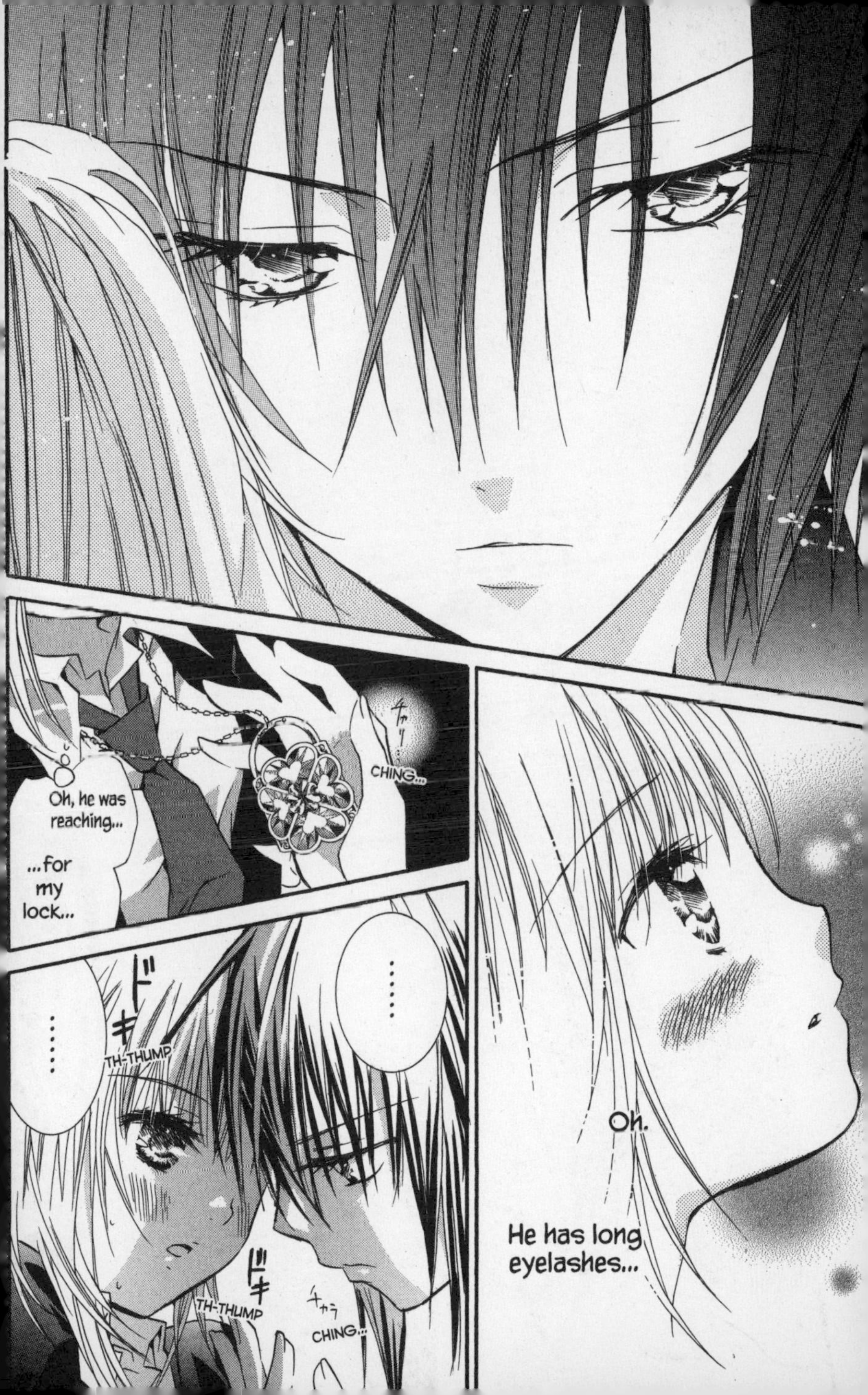
Oh.
He has long eyelashes...
チャリ…
CHING...
Oh, he was reaching...
...for my lock...
......
ドキ
TH-THUMP
......
ドキ
TH-THUMP
チャラ
CHING...

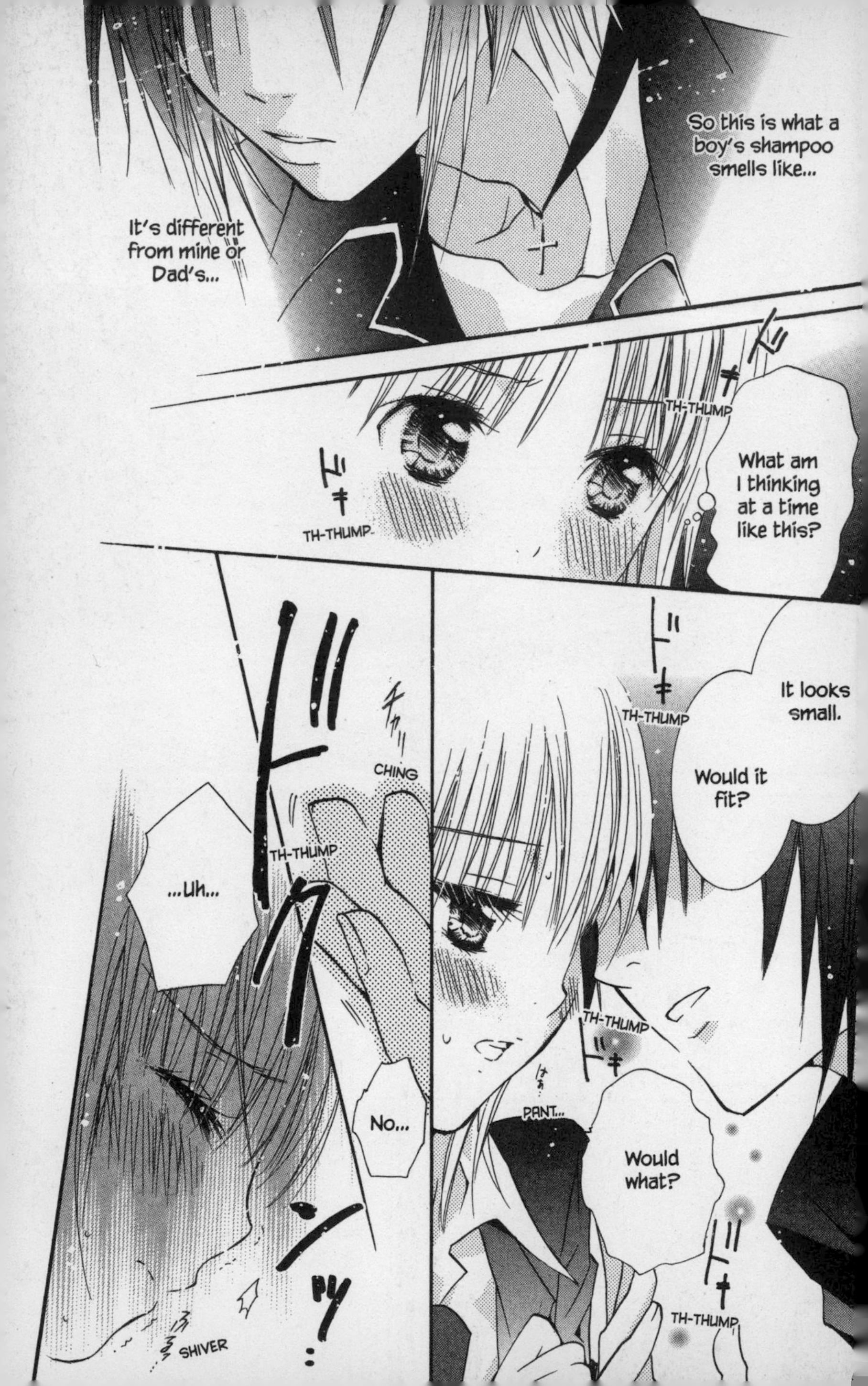

So this is what a boy's shampoo smells like...
It's different from mine or Dad's...
TH-THUMP
What am I thinking at a time like this?
TH-THUMP
TH-THUMP
It looks small.
Would it fit?
TH-THUMP
PANT...
Would what?
TH-THUMP
CHING
TH-THUMP
...uh...
No...
SHIVER

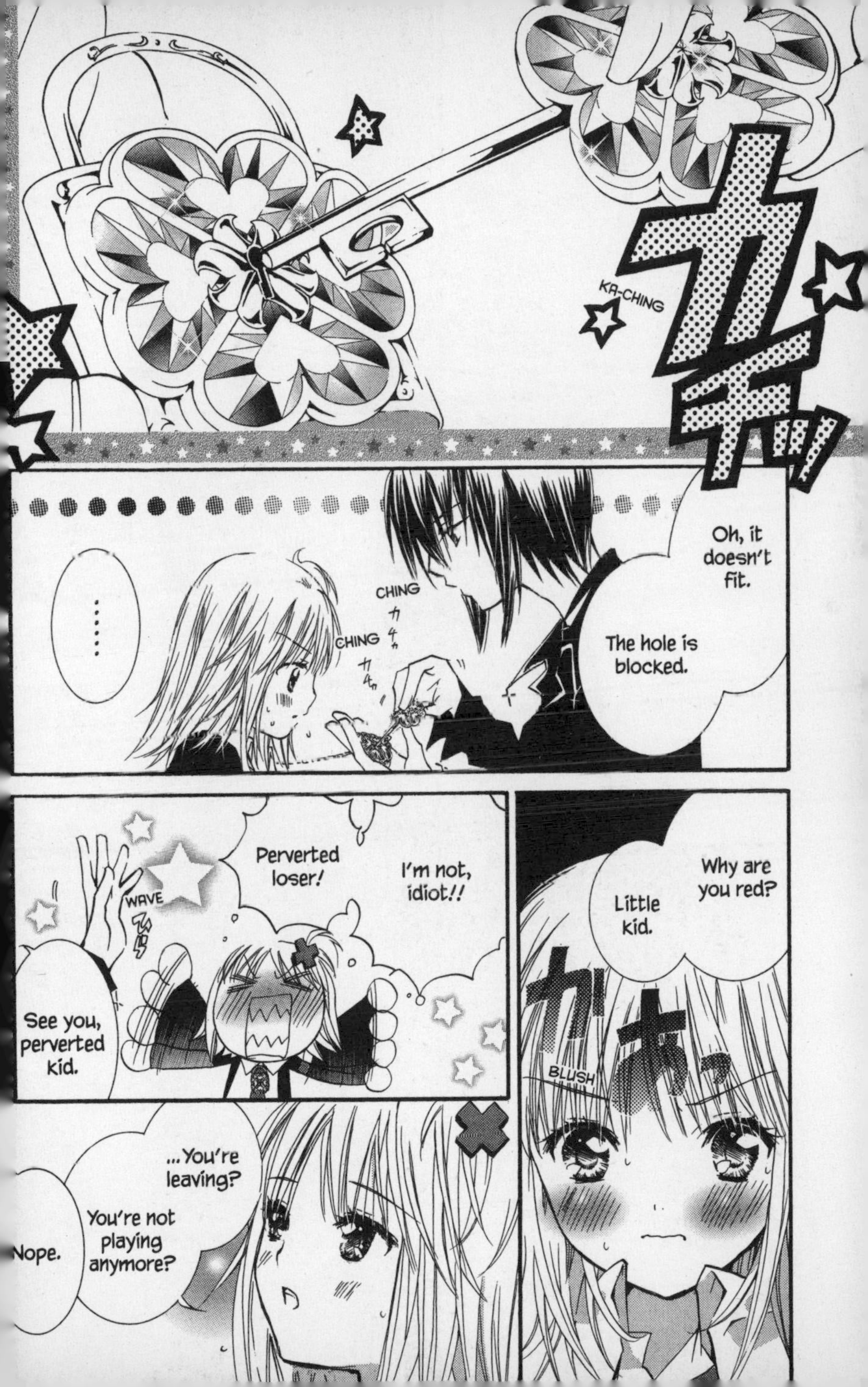
KA-CHING
Oh, it doesn't fit.
The hole is blocked.
CHING
CHING
......
Why are you red?
Little kid.
BLUSH
I'm not, idiot!!
Perverted loser!
WAVE
See you, perverted kid.
...You're leaving?
You're not playing anymore?
Nope.

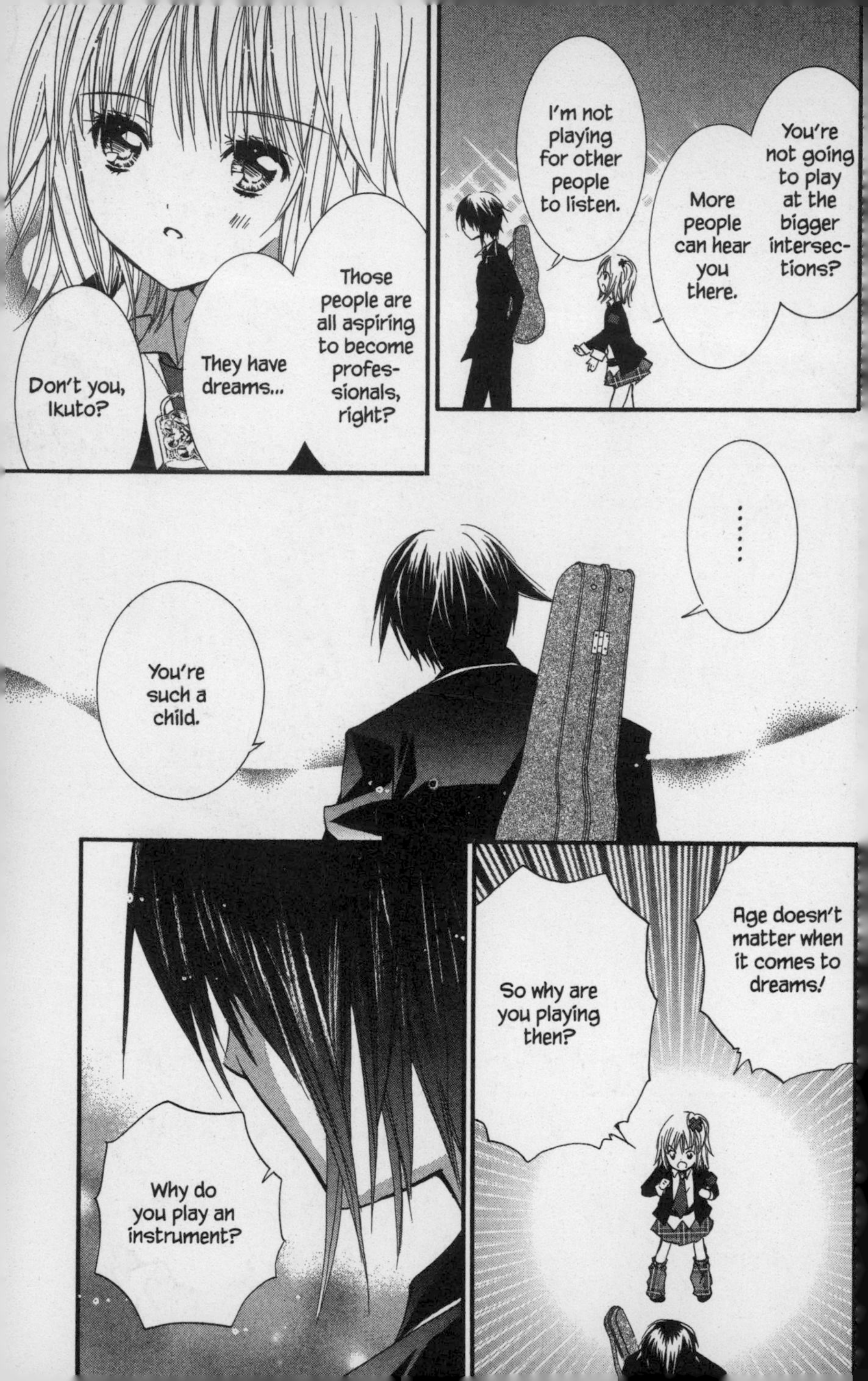
You're not going to play at the bigger intersections?
More people can hear you there.
I'm not playing for other people to listen.
Those people are all aspiring to become professionals, right?
They have dreams...
Don't you, Ikuto?
......
You're such a child.
Age doesn't matter when it comes to dreams!
So why are you playing then?
Why do you play an instrument?

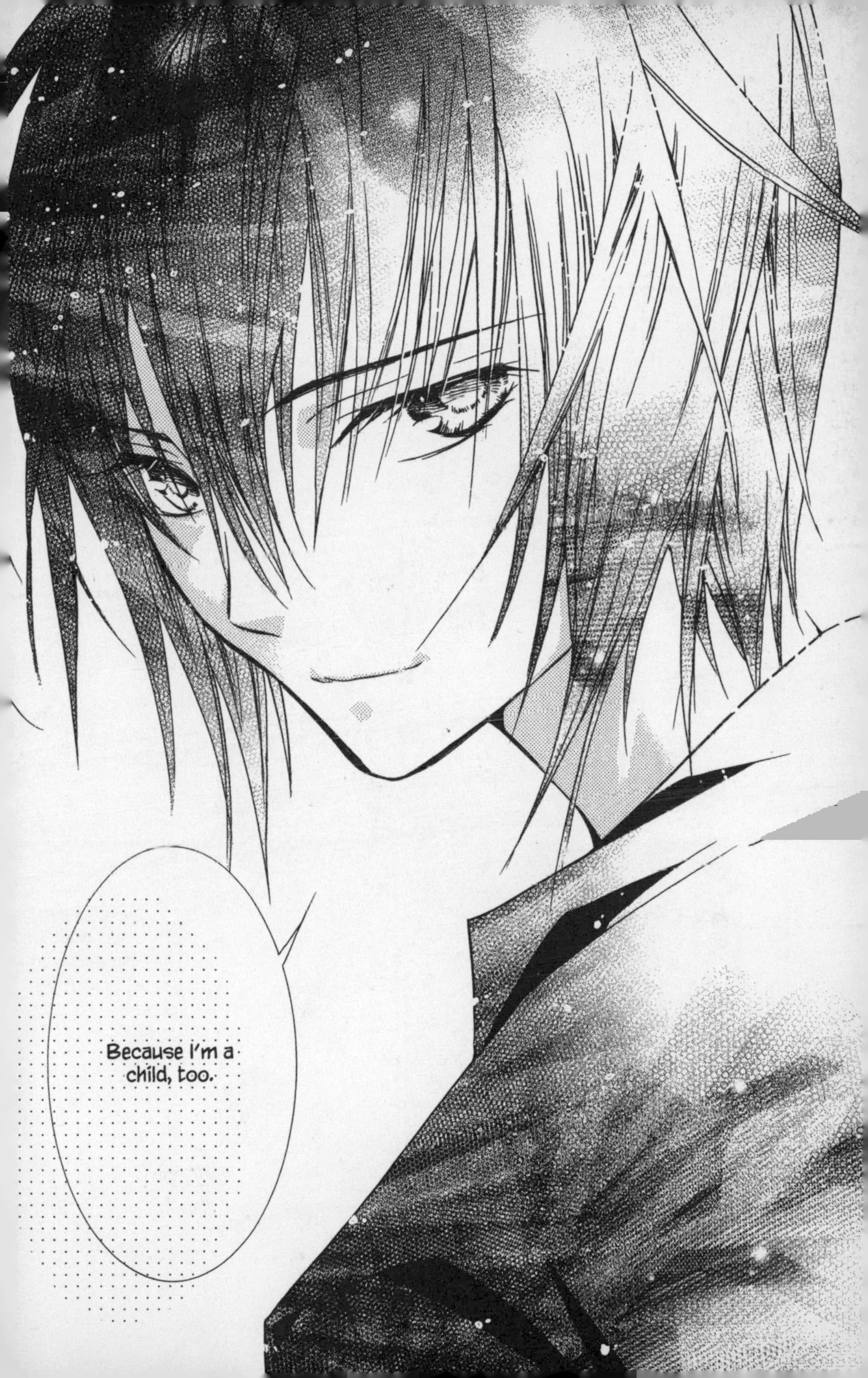
Because I'm a child, too.

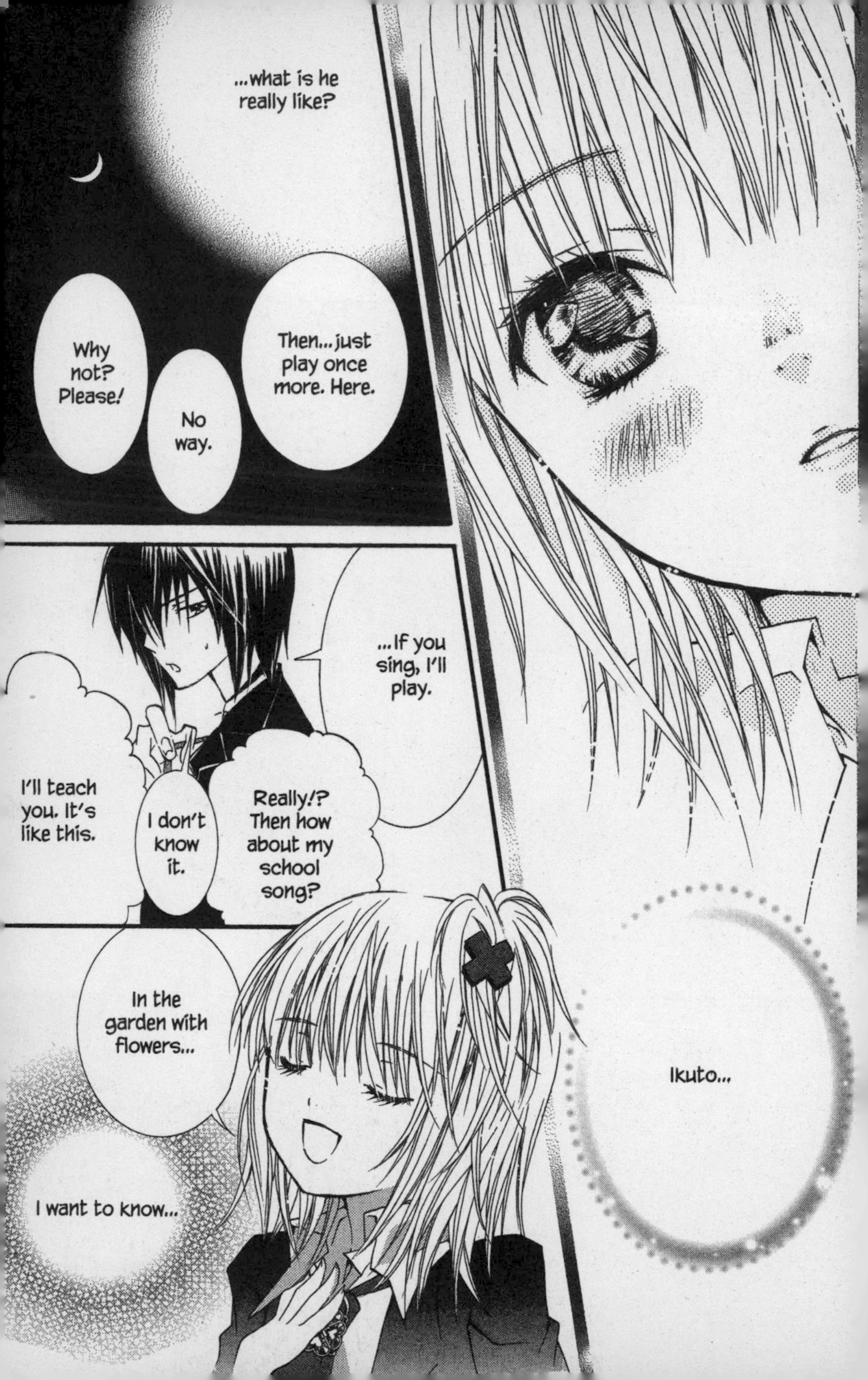
...what is he really like?
Then...just play once more. Here.
No way.
Why not? Please!
...If you sing, I'll play.
Really!? Then how about my school song?
I don't know it.
I'll teach you. It's like this.
Ikuto...
In the garden with flowers...
I want to know...

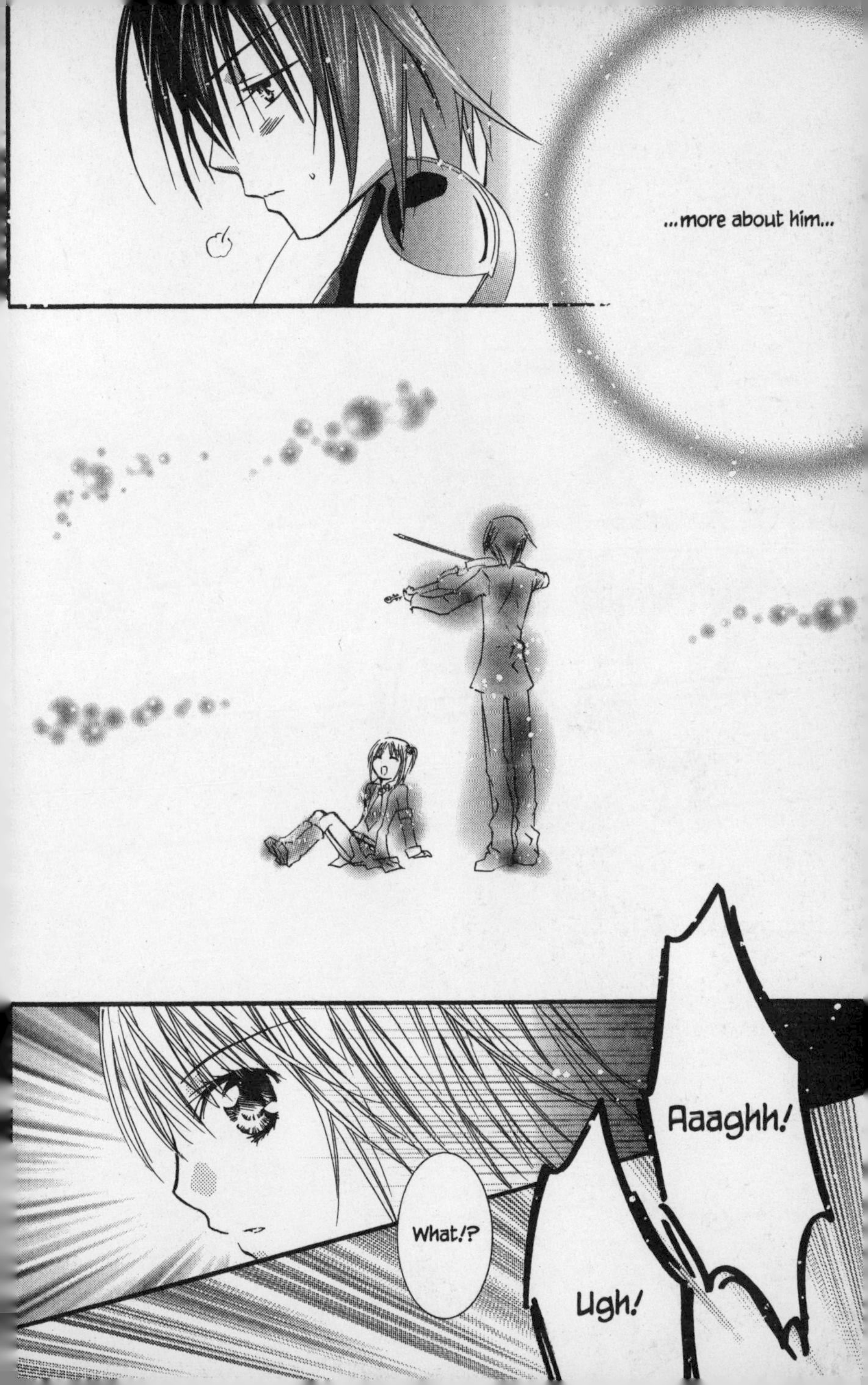
...more about him...
Aaaghh!
Ugh!
What!?

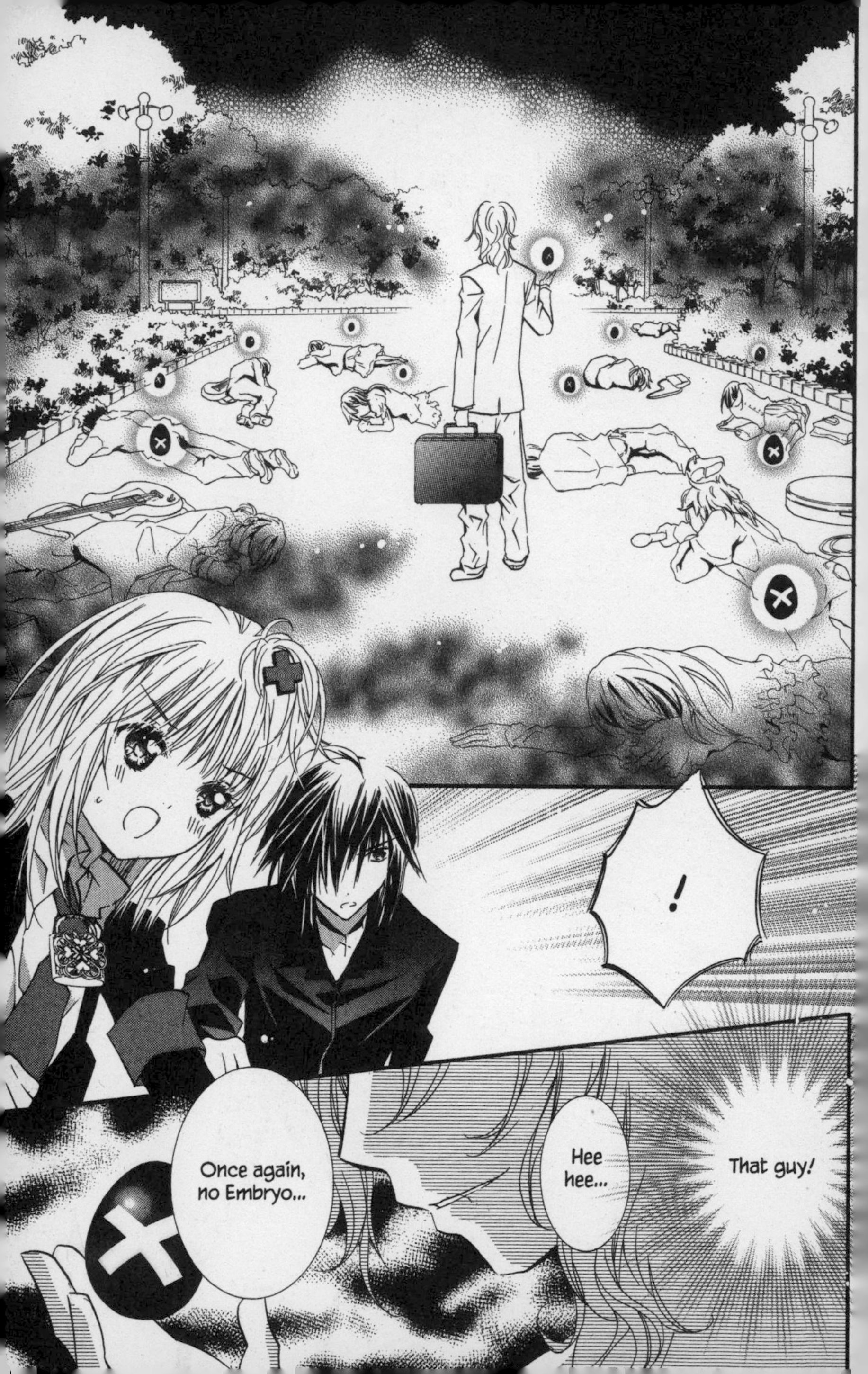
!
That guy!
Hee hee...
Once again, no Embryo...

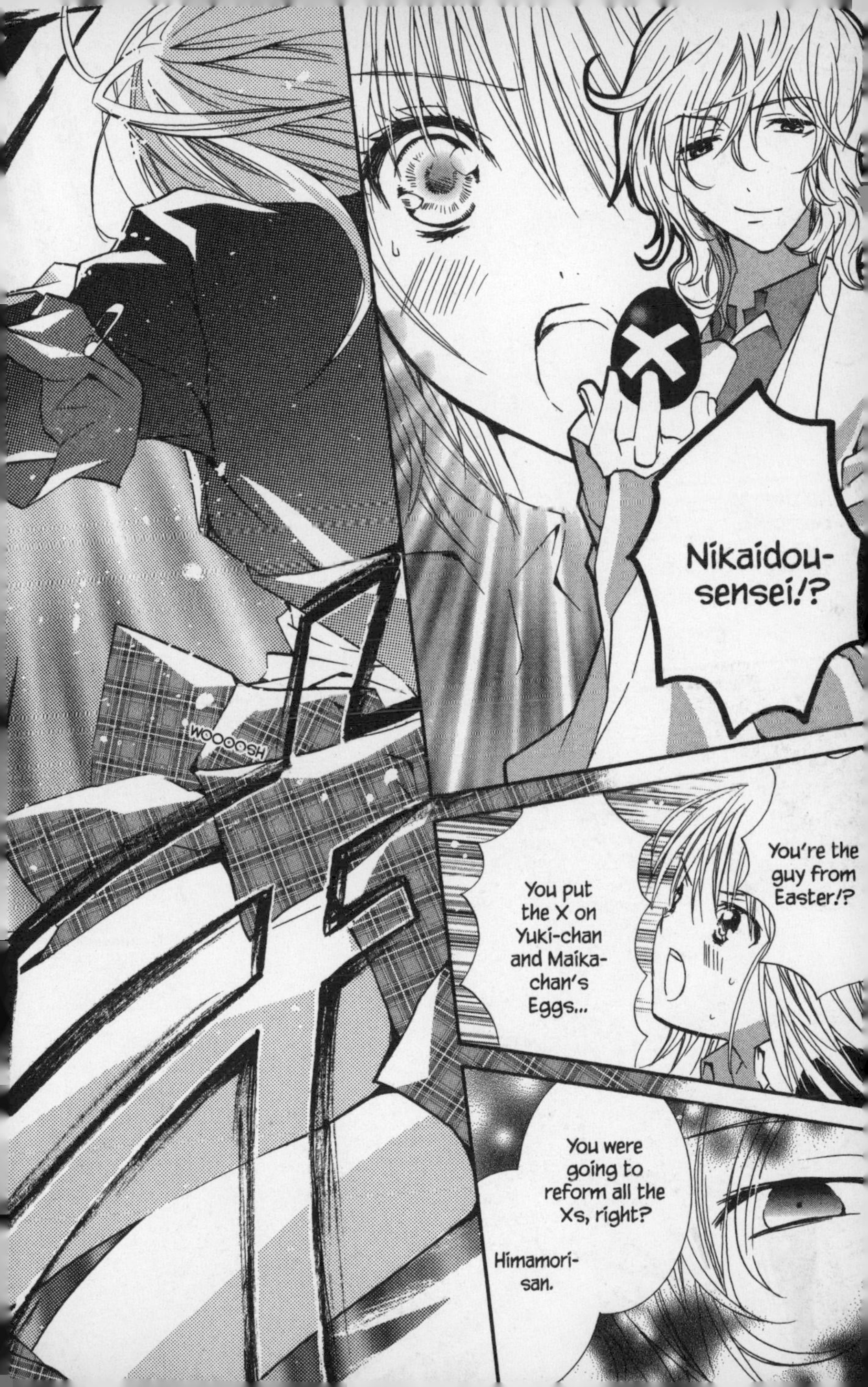
Nikaidou-sensei!?
You're the guy from Easter!?
You put the X on Yuki-chan and Maika-chan's Eggs...
You were going to reform all the Xs, right?
Himamori-san.
WOOOOSH

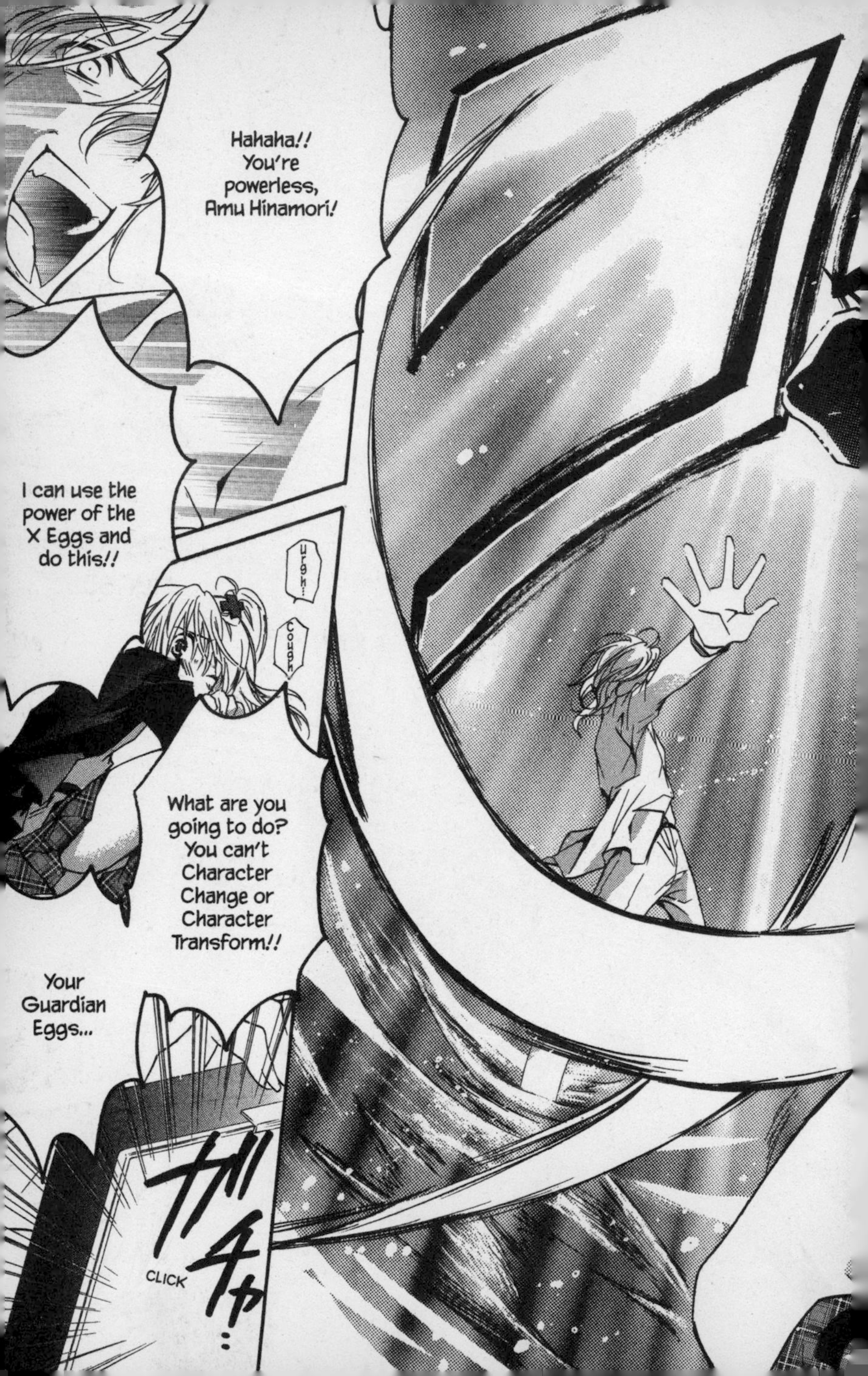
Hahaha!! You're powerless, Amu Hinamori!
I can use the power of the X Eggs and do this!!
Urgh...
Cough
What are you going to do? You can't Character Change or Character Transform!!
Your Guardian Eggs...
CLICK

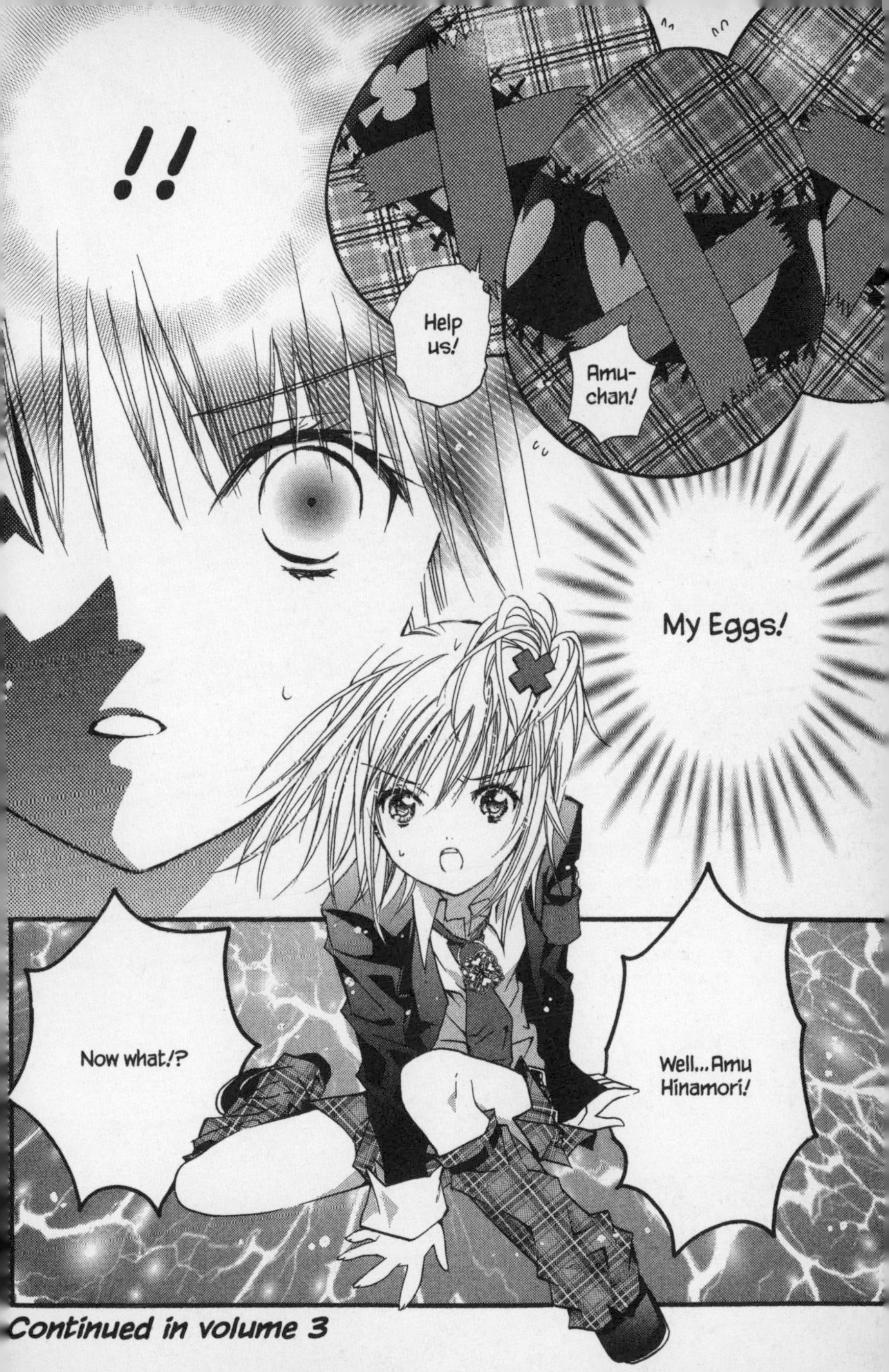
Amu-chan!
Help us!
!!
My Eggs!
Well...Amu Hinamori!
Now what!?

Continued in volume 3

Shugo Chara!

About the Creators

PEACH-PIT is:

Banri Sendo, born on June 7th

Shibuko Ebara, born on June 21st

We both are Gemini. We're a pair of manga
artists. Sendo enjoys sweets, but Ebara prefers spicy food. Our
favorite animals are cats and rabbits, and our recent hobbies are
making the ultimate *ajitama* and doing fingernail art.

Translation Notes

Japanese is a tricky language for most Westerners, and translation is often more art than science. For your edification and reading pleasure, here are notes on some of the places where we could have gone in a different direction in our translation of the work, or where a Japanese cultural reference is used.

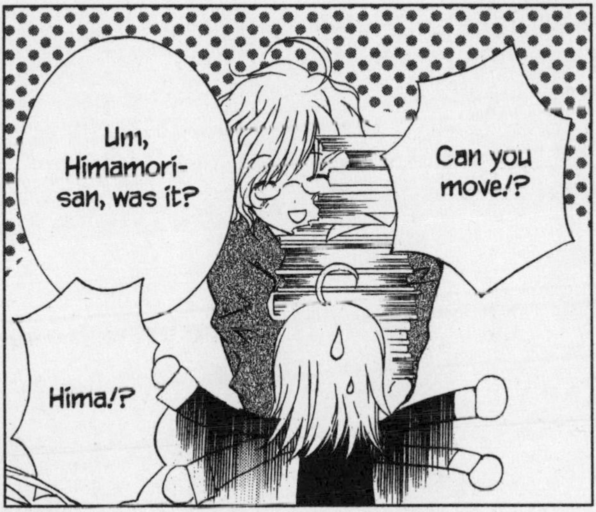
Can you move!?
Um, Himamori-san, was it?
Hima!?

Hima, page 24

This is a pun. *Hima* means "having spare time." *Hima* sounds like "Hina," the first two syllables of Amu's surname, and Yuu will continue calling her "Himamori-san" to belittle her.

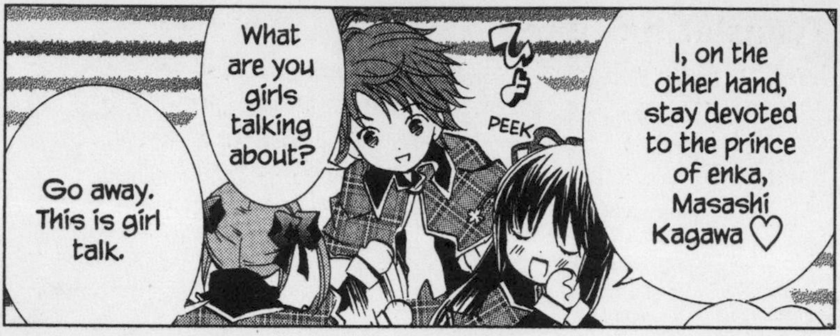
I, on the other hand, stay devoted to the prince of enka, Masashi Kagawa ♡
PEEK
What are you girls talking about?
Go away. This is girl talk.

Enka, page 46

Enka is a form of Japanese music that is similar to country music in the United States. It grew out of the democratic rights movement. When political speeches were punished in late nineteenth century Japan, political criticisms were voiced instead in the form of song. In present day, *enka* just refers to songs about certain themes such as the ocean, women, sake, tears, and goodbyes. In order to keep the Japanese style, most *enka* singers wear traditional clothing when performing.

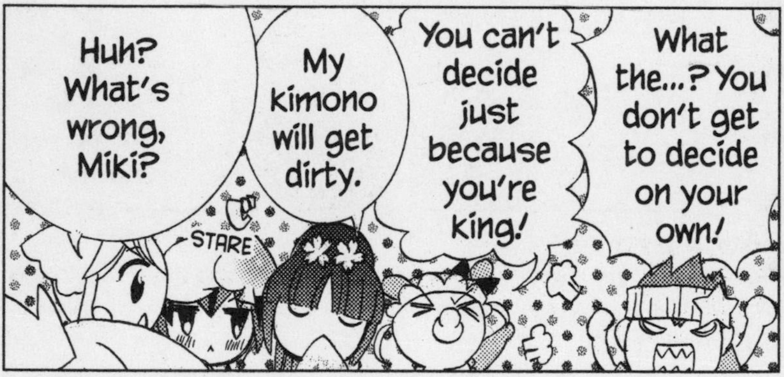
What the...? You don't get to decide on your own!
You can't decide just because you're king!
My kimono will get dirty.
STARE
Huh? What's wrong, Miki?

Kimono, page 51

A *kimono* is a piece of traditional Japanese clothing that looks like a robe. You wrap it around your body and tie a belt-like, long piece of cloth around it to keep it in place.

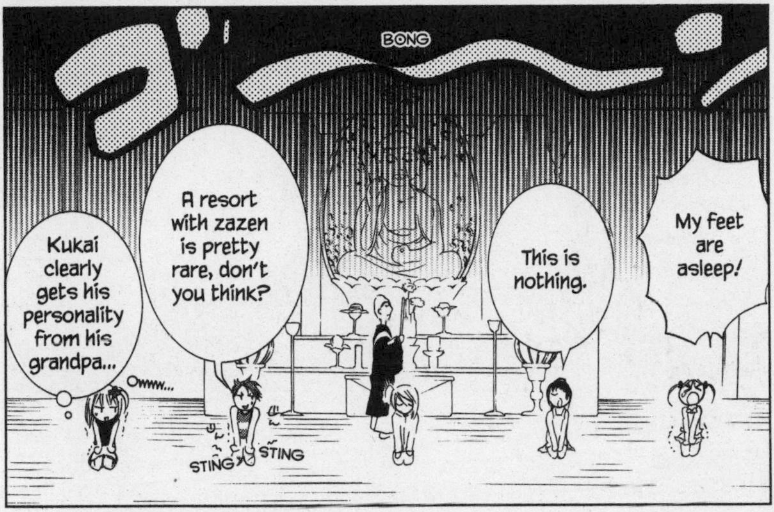
BONG
My feet are asleep!
This is nothing.
A resort with zazen is pretty rare, don't you think?
Kukai clearly gets his personality from his grandpa...
Owww...
STING
STING

Zazen, page 90

Zazen is the act of sitting and opening the hand of thought. It is a Zen Buddhist practice. The term *zazen* literally means "seated meditation." It calms the body and mind to lead the meditator to enlightenment.

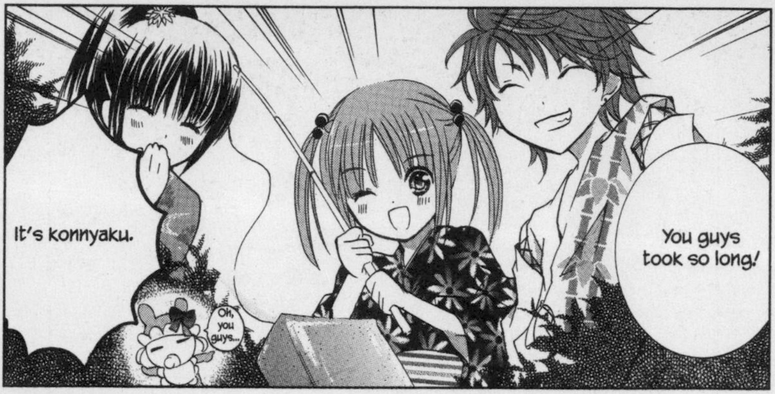
You guys took so long!
Oh, you guys...
It's konnyaku.

***Konnyaku,* page 112**

Konnyaku is a type of food in Japan made out of yams. It's like gelatin but much firmer, and it tastes a little like seaweed. Since it has no calories but is high in fiber, it's often eaten as diet food. Like *yaya,* many use it to scare others because in the dark a chilled *konnyaku* feels slippery and pretty gross.

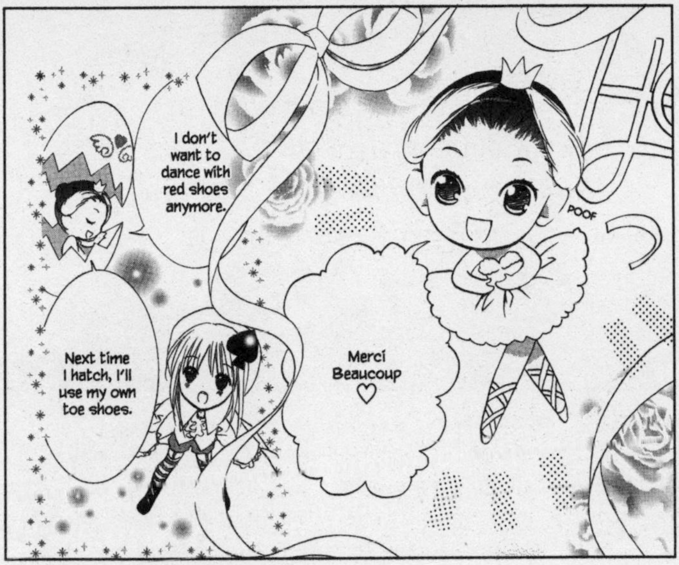
I don't want to dance with red shoes anymore.
Next time I hatch, I'll use my own toe shoes.
POOF
Merci Beaucoup ♡

Red shoes, page 154

The Character is making an allusion to *The Red Shoes* by Hans Christian Andersen. It is a story about a vain girl who was forced to dance in her red shoes until she couldn't bear it anymore and had to chop off her feet. The moral of the story is to not be so vain.

Please check our website (www.delreymanga.com) to see when *Shugo Chara!* volume 3 will be available in English. Don't miss it!

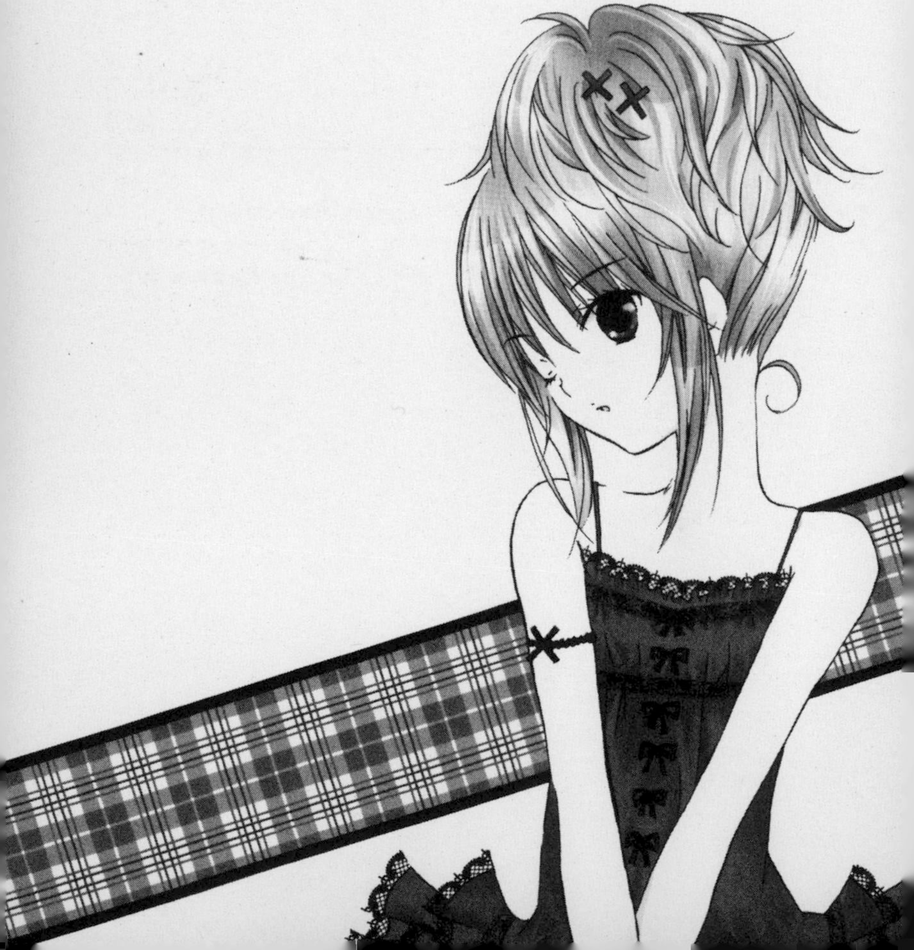

SHIKI TSUKAI

MANGA BY TORU ZEKU
ART BY YUNA TAKANAGI

DEFENDING THE NATURAL ORDER OF THE UNIVERSE!

The *shiki tsukai* are "Keepers of the Seasons"—magical warriors pledged to defend the planet's natural order against those who would threaten it.

When 14-year-old Akira Kizuki joins the *shiki tsukai,* he knows that it'll be a difficult life. But with his new friends and mentors, he's up to the challenge!

Special extras in each volume! Read them all!

VISIT WWW.DELREYMANGA.COM TO:
• Read sample pages
• View release date calendars for upcoming volumes
• Sign up for Del Rey's free manga e-newsletter
• Find out the latest about new Del Rey Manga series

RATING T AGES 13+

DEL REY MANGA

The Otaku's Choice.™

MICHIYO KIKUTA

BOY CRAZY

Junior high schooler Nina is ready to fall in love. She's looking for a boy who's cute and sweet—and strong enough to support her when the chips are down. But what happens when Nina's dream comes true . . . twice? One day, two cute boys literally fall from the sky. They're both wizards who've come to the Human World to take the Magic Exam. The boys' success on this test depends on protecting Nina from evil, so now Nina has a pair of cute magical boys chasing her everywhere! One of these wizards just might be the boy of her dreams . . . but which one?

Special extras in each volume! Read them all!

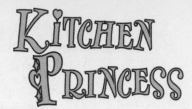

KITCHEN PRINCESS

STORY BY MIYUKI KOBAYASHI
MANGA BY NATSUMI ANDO
CREATOR OF ZODIAC P.I.

HUNGRY HEART

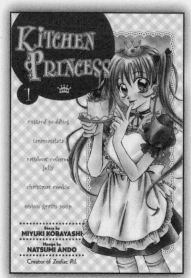

Najika is a great cook and likes to make meals for the people she loves. But something is missing from her life. When she was a child, she met a boy who touched her heart—and now Najika is determined to find him. The only clue she has is a silver spoon that leads her to the prestigious Seika Academy.

Attending Seika will be a challenge. Every kid at the school has a special talent, and the girls in Najika's class think she doesn't deserve to be there. But Sora and Daichi, two popular brothers who barely speak to each other, recognize Najika's cooking for what it is—magical. Could one of the boys be Najika's mysterious prince?

Kitchen Princess
1
custard pudding
taramasalata
rainbow colored jelly
christmas cookie
onion gratin soup
Story by
MIYUKI KOBAYASHI
Manga by
NATSUMI ANDO
Creator of Zodiac P.I.

Special extras in each volume! Read them all!

VISIT WWW.DELREYMANGA.COM TO:
- Read sample pages
- View release date calendars for upcoming volumes
- Sign up for Del Rey's free manga e-newsletter
- Find out the latest about new Del Rey Manga series

RATING T AGES 13+

DEL REY MANGA デルレイ

The Otaku's Choice

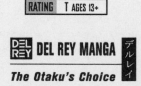

Sugar Sugar Rune

BY MOYOCO ANNO

QUEEN OF HEARTS

Chocolat and Vanilla are young witch princesses from a magical land. They've come to Earth to compete in a contest—whichever girl captures the most hearts will become queen! While living in a boarding school, they must make as many boys fall in love with them as possible if they want to achieve their goal. Standing against them are a pair of rival princes looking to capture their hearts because they want to be king!

There's danger for the witch-girls, though: If they give their hearts to a human, they may never return to the Magical World....

Ages: 10 +

Special extras in each volume! Read them all!

MY HEAVENLY HOCKEY CLUB

BY AI MORINAGA

WHERE THE BOYS ARE!

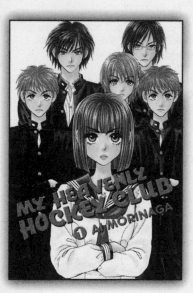

Hana Suzuki loves only two things in life: eating and sleeping. So when handsome classmate Izumi Oda asks Hana—his major crush—to join the school hockey club, convincing her proves to be a difficult task. True, the Grand Hockey Club is full of boys—and all the boys are super-cute—but, given a choice, Hana prefers a sizzling steak to a hot date. Then Izumi mentions the field trips to fancy resorts. Now Hana can't wait for the first away game, with its promise of delicious food and luxurious linens. Of course there's the getting up early, working hard, and playing well with others. How will Hana survive?

MY HEAVENLY HOCKEY CLUB
1 AI MORINAGA

Special extras in each volume! Read them all!

VISIT WWW.DELREYMANGA.COM TO:

- Read sample pages
- View release date calendars for upcoming volumes
- Sign up for Del Rey's free manga e-newsletter
- Find out the latest about new Del Rey Manga series

RATING | AGES T 13+

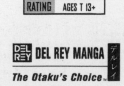

DEL REY MANGA デルレイ

The Otaku's Choice™

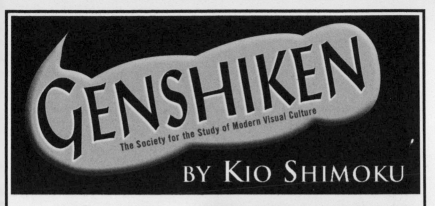

TOMA

D0485166

[STOP!]

You're going the wrong way!

Manga is a completely different type of reading experience.

To start at the *beginning*, go to the *end*!

That's right! Authentic manga is read the traditional Japanese way—from right to left. Exactly the opposite of how American books are read. It's easy to follow: Just go to the other end of the book, and read each page—and each panel—from right side to left side, starting at the top right. Now you're experiencing manga as it was meant to be!